Metele

Andrej L. Malchukov

Johannes Gutenberg University, Mainz and Institute for Linguistic Studies, Russian Academy of Sciences, Saint Petersburg

Altaic Languages Series 09

Metele

An Ewen Epic Tale by Darja Mixajlovna Osenina

Seoul National University Press
1 Gwanak-ro, Gwanak-gu, Seoul 08826, Republic of Korea

Homepage: www.snupress.com
Facebook: @snupress1947
Instagram: @snupress

First Printing: November 10, 2020
ISBN 978-89-521-2902-4 94790
978-89-521-2995-6 (set)

This work was supported by the National Research Foundation of Korea Grant funded by the Korean Government. (AKS-2016-LAB-2250004)

Metele

An Ewen Epic Tale by Darja Mixajlovna Osenina

edited by

Andrej L. Malchukov

Seoul National University Press

Contents

Figures

Figure 1. Darja Mixajlovna Osenina

Figure 2. Village Topolinoe (in 1980s)

Figure 3. Ewen folklore group "Maranga" from Topolinoe performing

Figure 4. Darja Mixajlovna Osenina performing with the folklore group Maranga

Figure 5. A. L. Malchukov with Xristina Mixajlovna Osenina (Darja Mixajlovna's sister)

Introduction

The volume presents a remarkable piece of Tungusic folklore, an Ewen epic tale "Metele". The text was recorded from Darja Mixajlovna Osenina (depicted on Figure 1), one of the last great storytellers, full in command of the Ewen epic tradition. The text was recorded by me in 1991 from D. M. Osenina, the speaker of the Oxotsk dialect, now resident in Topolinoje. Topolinoje is a community in the Tompo region of Yakutia, which is one of largest concentration of Ewen speakers (see Figure 2). This is the first publication of a Tungusic epic tale in English, which is intended for international readership interested in the culture and language of Ewens. The linguistic audience is not confined to experts in Tungusic languages, but also caters for typologists and general linguists interested in Siberian languages: for this reason the text is provided with glosses in accordance with typological practice.

Ewen (alongside with Ewenki, Negidal and Solon) belongs to the Northern Branch of Tungusic languages (see Doerfer 1978 for classification). Currently there are about 22,400 ethnic Ewens of which 33% still speak their mother tongue (according to the 2010 census of population). In fact, the percentage of native speakers may have been exaggerated: Ewen like a majority of Tungusic languages is severely endangered. The language is majorly spoken by elderly people, except for special settings where Ewen is a means of communications (like in reindeer herd brigades) or in a few settlements in Yakutia and Magadan region where Ewens constitute a majority of population. Topolinoe, which I visited on field trips in 1986-1992, belongs to a few such settlements in Yakutia (Republic of Sakha). At the time of my field research, also ethnic Ewens of a younger generation were in command of their language. Ewen was (and still is) also taught in primary school, although the success of school education is hampered by the fact that teaching materials in "standard Ewen" introduced in the campaigns against analphabetism in 1930s represents the norms of another, Eastern, dialect. The majority of Ewens speak the Western dialect, showing similarity to those language varieties of Yakutia (Republic of Sakha), like the Moma dialect described in Lebedev (1978). A few families, including Osenina's family are relative newcomers to the region, which means that they speak an Eastern dialect with an admixture of the western Tompo dialect (see also below).

Ewens are traditionally nomadic and practice reindeer-breeding. Most of them became sedentary in 1930s and especially in 1950s, as a result of reorganization of reindeer-breeding into reindeer state farms (*sovxozy*), followed by a "settlement enlargement" campaign in 1950s. Topolinoe is one of the few villages where settlement enlargement has not resulted in Ewens becoming a minority of a population, quickly losing their language. The economy is still dominated by traditional reindeer breeding, with state run reindeer herds nomadizing in the vicinity of the village. The traditional occupation in conjunction with a large percentage of Ewens in the overall population of Topolinoe (765 of ethnic Ewens in the overall population of 1170,[1] according to the 1993 local census) resulted in Ewen being relatively well preserved among the ethnic Ewens.

Ewen (also spelled as Even or Ėven, previously also known as Lamut) belongs to the northern branch of the Tungus-Manchu language family. Morphologically, it is an agglutinating language (using suffixes as the only means of word formation). Syntactically, it is a SOV language of nominative typology. It shows other typical traits of Altaic languages, including the use of head-marking in a possessive construction (cf. *bej ǯuu-n* [man house-his] 'The man's house'). Another syntactic feature which Ewen shares with many Altaic languages is "converb-prominence": use of non-finite converbial forms for clause chaining. The information on other linguistic features of Ewen can be obtained from the grammatical sketch in Malchukov (1995) or from Kim (2011), especially accessible for the readers of this series. Other standard sources on Ewen grammar include Cincius 1947, Novikova 1960, 1980, Robbek 1989; these studies are written in Russian and deal primarily with morphology; for syntax see Malchukov (2008), also in Russian. In addition to Russian sources there is an early German grammar by Benzing (1955) with a historical-comparative outlook, and more recent description in Kazama (2003). For most purposes, consultation with shorter descriptions in Malchukov (1995) and Kim (2011) should be sufficient; in particular, Malchukov (1995) includes a shorter text recorded from D.M. Osenina, introduced by

1 Currently 891 according to wikipedia.

the notes on the dialect of the speaker, which will also be relevant in this context. I will summarize below some of the prominent features of the Oxotsk dialect spoken by the Osenina family.

The Oxotsk dialect, spoken in the North of the Xabarovsk region, belongs to Eastern dialects of Ewen (Lebedev 1982), sometimes treated as a separate branch, or an intermediate Central dialect, sharing features with both eastern and western dialects (Burykin 2004). It has developed some peculiar features, partly due to the influence of the genealogically closely related Ewenki. In phonetics, these features include loss of distinctions between "hard" and "soft" high vowels belonging to different vowel harmony series (/ɪ/ vs. /i/, /ů/ vs. /u/[2]) occasional neutralization of [u] and [ö] (absent in Ewenki), specific patterns of consonant assimilation emulating the Ewenki pattern (cf. *ŋen-niǯi* < *ŋen-riǯi* 'going'). In morphology, the dialect reveals such traces of Ewenki influence as use of the imperative in *-galla* (cf. Ewk *-kalla*), proliferation of the durative forms in *-ǯaan-* (note that *-d*-progressive is more grammaticalized in Ewenki), use of non-reduced forms of aorist (Ew. standard *maa-n*, Ox. *maa-ra-n*, Ewk. *waa-re-n* 'he killed'). In syntax, it shares with the Western dialects loss of the simple possessive form of the pronouns, using personal pronouns instead (cf. Ox. *bii hut-če-mu* [I child-1SG.POS] 'my child' instead of *min hut-če-mu* [my child-1SG.POS] 'my child'). Most of these features can be explained by influence from Ewenki, which exerted adstratic influence on the Oxotsk Ewen. In lexicon, there is also cer-

2 For this reason these distinctions are not represented in the transcribed glossed text.

tain evidence for the lexical influence from Ewenki (on which I comment in the notes to the glossed text), but also from Yakut. The latter influence can be partially traced to the features of Oxotsk dialect, but may be also due to idiolectal peculiarities of the speech of Darja Mixajlovna Osenina. Darja Mixajlovna spent most of her life in the village of Topolinoe on the territory of Yakutia (Republic of Sakha); correspondingly, her speech shows more pronounced influence from Yakut characteristic of Western Ewen dialects. Among the varieties of Oxotsk dialect ("subdialects") described in the literature (Lebedev 1982, Burykin 2004), the variety of Darja Mixajlovna Osenina is closest to the Arka variety, not surprisingly as her parents stem from Arka (a village in the Oxotsk region).

Darja Mixajlovna belongs to the last outstanding Ewen storytellers in command of the epic tradition of the Ewen (Tungus) population. This tradition is better preserved among Ewenkis, for which it has been documented by G. M. Vasilevich and A. N. Myreeva among others (Vasilevich 1966, Myreeva & Trofimov 1990). The Tungusic epic tales are reminiscent of the Olonxo-songs of the Yakutia (Sakha), which may be due to areal influence (Vasilevich 1966). In particular, the texts of the Tungusic epic tales, like Olonxos, is a mixture of the narrated fragments with songs, introducing monologues and dialogues of the protagonists. The songs are introduced by special refrain words (Rus. *zapevki*), which serve to identify a protagonist; these are unique for each character and often derived from his/her name, or the name of the clan (cf. Myreeva 1980 for Ewenki). The language of the song fragments show further peculiarities, in that they frequently feature "filler syllables", apparently, for prosodic/metrical reasons (cf. the frequent use of *-kan/-ken* and *-gu/-ku* syllables in the text). Similar use of "filler syllables" (Germ. *Füllsilben*) has been documented for Ewenki, including language of epic tales (Vasilevich 1969), but also language of shamanic songs (Menges & Ryčkov 1993).

The epic tradition of the Ewens is arguably less well documented as compared to Ewenki. Most Ewen folklore texts appearing in text collections such as (Novikova 1958, Kazama 2009) belong to other genres (mostly, fairy tales and myths). In both Ewenki and Ewen epic tales are restricted to Eastern dialects, which is suggestive of influence of the Yakut Olonxo tradition; other dialects show reduced or modified forms of this genre. The only major publication of the Oxotsk epic tales until recently is a collection of three epic tales, recorded by N. P. Tkachik, and edited by V. D. Lebedev and Zh. K. Lebedeva (Lebedeva & Lebedev 1986). The texts are in the Cyrillic transcription with a free translation in Russian. The publication of the texts has done a great service to preservation of the Ewen folklore tradition, yet its use for linguistic purposes is somewhat diminished due to errors in re-transcribing the Ewen texts according to conventions of the modified Yakut-style orthography advocated by its compilers V. D. Lebedev and Zh. K. Lebedeva (cf. Burykin 2004). Until very recently, this was the only publication of the Ewen heroic epos; in 2013 there appeared a shorter collection of texts recorded from Darja Mixajlovna Osenina by A. Lavrillier and transcribed by D. Matić (Matić & Lavrillier, eds. 2013). This collection presents the text in the conventional Cyrillic alphabet with a Russian translation, and is intended for the use in the Ewen community and possibly as an aid in school education. Apart from its obvious social value, within the context of the present volume it has an additional value in that it contains some ethnographic commentary, as well as biographical notes about the storyteller, Darja Mixajlovna Osenina. The present publication is intended to open the treasures of the Ewen historical epos to a wider international community interested in the culture of North Tungus people, as well as to linguists interested in Ewen grammar.

Darja Mixajlovna Osenina, is one of the last great representatives of Ewen storytellers (Rus. *skazitelj*), which is comparable to masters of Olonxo (Olonxosuns). Darja Mixajlovna was born in 1947 in Arka, later attended primary school in Allax-Junj, before settling in Topolinoe, where she worked as a nurse but also as a reindeer herder. Darja Mixajlovna is a uniquely talented person and a goldmine for researchers of Tungusic culture. I was privileged to work with Darja Mixajlovna in late 1980s early 1990s and recorded a number of epic tales from her (transcribed only in part). The present text was prepared for publication in 1995 and intended as a part of a larger folklore collection, but its implementation was delayed because other projects and commitments interfered with this more ambitious plan. For this reason the publication of this text has been delayed for 20 years: Дарья Михайловна, простите меня. Therefore, I decided to take on the opportunity kindly suggested by Prof. KIM Juwon to publish the English form of the text with glosses and English translation. At a later stage of editing, I added the original Ewen text in the standard orthography and a Russian translation meant for the use of the Ewen community.

A number of people helped me at different points in preparation of this text for publication. Obviously, I am indebted to Darja Mixajlovna for sharing her cultural heritage with me. In addition, I would like to acknowledge a generous help by her sister Xristina Mixajlovna Osenina, in the help of transcribing the text. Xristina Mixajlovna, is another talented representative of the Osenina-family; professionally a nurse, she is also a poet, publishing poems in Ewen in the local press. Back in 1990s, Vanessa Locke kindly checked the English free translations, while I was staying at the department of Oriental Studies at The University of Mainz in 1994-1995: I am grateful to Vanessa, and to my host professor Lars Johanson for help. Shifting to now, I would like to thank Prof. KIM Juwon for the invitation to contribute to his series, as well as for his help and the help of his students in the editorial work. Finally, I am indebted to Prof. PARK Jinho for inviting me to Seoul, which ultimately made this publication possible. At the last stages of editing, my student assistant Iris Rieder helped me with alignment of glosses, and my wife Larissa typed the Russian translation and helped with proofreading. During the last stages of preparation of the manuscript for submission editorial work was supported by the Laboratory Program for Korean Studies through the Ministry of Education of the Republic of Korea and the Korean Studies Promotion Service of the Academy of Korean Studies.

Abbreviations

ABL	ablative (case)
ACC	accusative (case)
AL	alienable (possession)
ANT	anterior (converb)
ASSOC	associative (plural)
AUGM	augmentative
CAUS	causative (suffix)
CLIT	clitic
COMIT	comitative (case)
CONAT	conative (aspect)
COND	conditional (converb)
CONJ	conjunctional (coordinating) clitic
CONT	contrastive suffix
CONV	converb
DAT	dative (case)
DIM	diminutive (suffix)
DELIM	delimitative (suffix)
DES	designative (case)
DIR	directive (case)
DIRECT	directional (aspect)
DIST(R)	distributive (aspect)
DS(CONV)	different subject (converb)
DUR	durative aspect
ELAT	elative (case)
EPENTH	epenthetic (vowel/segment)
EQUAT	equative (case)

FUT	future
HABIT	habitual (aspect)
IMIT	imitative (modal marker)
IMP	imperative
INCL	inclusive (pronoun)
INCH	inchoative aspect
INDEF	indefinite (clitic)
INST	instrumental (case)
INT	interrogative
INTENS	intensity (adjectival marker)
ITER	iterative
LOC	locative (case)
MED	medio-passive
MOM	momentative (aspect)
NEC	necessitative (converb)
NEG	negative
NLOC	locative nominalizer
NMZR	nominalizer
NONFUT	nonfuture (tense)
PART	participle
PASS	(adversative) passive
PAST	past
PERF	perfect
PL	plural
POL	polite (imperative)
POS	possessive (suffix)
PRE	preceding (converb)
PREV	preventive (admonitive) mood
PROG(R)	progressive
PROL	prolative (case)
PROP(R)	proprietive ('having') suffix
PURP	purposive (converb)
REC	reciprocal (suffix)

REF	reflexive (ending)
RES	resultative (aspect)
REST	restrictive (clitic)
RETR	retroactive aspect
SG	singular
SIM	simultaneous (converb)
SIMIL	simulative (nominal form)
SPEC	specification marker (suffix, particle)
STAT	stative-resultative aspect
SUBJ	subjunctive (mood)
TOP	topic (marker)
VOC(AT)	vocative (form)
VOL	volitive (desiderative) aspect

1. Metele: Glossed text

(1)

Metele	*uñača-kan*	*ǯuu-lkan*
Metele	tiny-DIM	house-PROP

'Metele had a tiny jurta.'

(2)

Erek	*noŋan*	*koobak-u*[1]	*hialaki-w*	*bejči-niken*
this	(s)he	hare-ACC	partridge-ACC	hunt-SIM.CONV

tara-ŋ-i	*ǯep-niken,*	*bi-weeč-te-n*
that-AL.POS-REF.POS.SG	eat-SIM.CONV	be-HABIT-NONFUT-3SG

'He lived from hunting hares and partridges.'

(3)

Noŋan	*ojo-n*	*bököč-čö-n*	*koobak*	*nanna-duku-n*
(s)he	cloth-3SG	all-ACC-3SG	hare	skin-ABL-3SG

oo-p-ča
make-MED-PERF.PART

'All his clothes were made of hare-skin.'

(4)

Teeden-ni	*hulla-n-da*	*koobak*	*nanna-duku-n*
mat-3SG	blanket-3SG-CONJ.CLIT	hare	skin-ABL-3SG

oo-p-ča
make-MED-PERF.PART

'The floor covering and the blanket were made of hare-skin too.'

(5)

Erek	*bej*	*bi-mi*	*nööki-čen-ni*	*koobak*
this	man	be-COND.CONV	arrow-DIM-3SG	hare

ewetle-duku-n	*nöökič-te-n*
rib-ABL-3SG	shoot-NONFUT-3SG

1 < Jak. *куобах* 'hare'.

'His bow was made of a rib of a hare.'

(6) *Tara-ŋa-n* *koobak* *hum-ǯi-n* *tomko-tla*
that-AL.POS-3SG hare sinew-INSTR-3SG twist-RES.PART

ilte-lken *koobak* *časamna-ǯi-n*
bow-string-PROPR hare skin_bone-INSTR-3SG

ñurat-ta-n
have.as.an.arrow-NONFUT-3SG

'His bow was strung with the twisted hare's sinew, his arrows were made of a hare's skin-bone.'

(7) *Erek* *bej-čen* *tačin* *bi-weeč-te-n*
this man-DIM so be-HABIT-NONFUT-3SG
'So he lived.'

(8) *tara-ŋ-čan-ǯi-i* *koobak*
that-AL.POS-DIM-INSTR-REF.POS.SG hare

dikeŋ-či-d-di-wu *nemke-riǯi*
hide-STAT-PROG-NONFUT.PART-ACC shoot-ANT.CONV.SG

maa-waač-ta-n *hialaki*
kill-HABIT-NONFUT-3SG partridge

bukceng-ci-d-di-wu *tara-ŋ-ǯi*
huddle.up-STAT-PROG-NONFUT.PART-ACC that-AL.POS-INSTR

nemke-t-niken *maa-waač-ta-n*
shoot-STAT-SIM.CONV kill-HABIT-NONFUT-3SG

'Hunting with his bow he shot hares, hiding, and huddled up partridges.'

(9) *ičin* *hoo-kan* *goru* *bi-s-ni*
like.this very-DIM for_a_long_time be-NONFUT-3SG
'Well, so he lived for a long time.'

(10) *hoo-kan* *goru* *bi-t-če-le-n*
very-DIM for_a_long_time be-STAT-PERF.PART-LOC-3SG

okata-ŋ-ma-n *hol-gič* *araj*[2] *iaak-kal*
river-AL.POS-ACC-3SG upstream-ELAT suddenly what-NONREF.CLIT

em-ne-n *noŋan*
come-NONFUT-3SG (s)he

e-s-ni *haa-r* *iaa-wa-n-da*
not_do-NONFUT-3SG know-NEG.CONV what-ACC-3SG-CONJ.CLIT

'One day somebody came downstream along the river, who was coming, - he didn't know.'

(11) *kiŋgelen-boralan* *ii-s-ni* *bukatyn*[3]
jingle-jungle sound-NONFUT-3SG all_the_time
'Only the jingling of the bells was heard.'

(12) *urke-j* *ǯapka-li-n* *eŋen-eke-n*
door-REF.POS.SG between-PROL-3SG peep-COND.DS.CONV-3SG

hol-giǯi-n *noŋan* *ureči-n* *bi-niken* *ŋonom*
upstream-ELAT-3SG (s)he similar-3SG be-SIM.CONV long

ñuurite-lken *ŋonom* *ojo-lkan* *hoo-kan* *nooda-č*
hair-PROPR long cloth-PROP very-DIM beautiful-INSTR

ojo-lkan *asi* *em-ne-n*
cloth-PROP woman come-NONFUT-3SG

'He peeped out through the doorway - downstream along the river somebody was wandering, who looked like him, but had long hair and long clothes.'

(13) *asi* *em-niǯii* *diejdee-du-n* *kirgin-du*
woman come-ANT.CONV above-DAT-3SG hill-side-DAT

2 < Jak. *арай* 'suddenly, just'.
3 < Jak. *букатын* 'quite, wholly, completely'.

ineg-riǯii	*ǯuuŋ-na-n*
unpack-ANT.CONV	pitch a jurta-NONFUT-3SG

kaltu-ča-kkan	*ǯuu-(w)*	*ǯuuŋ-na-n*
half-conic-PERF.PART-DIM	house-ACC	pitch a jurta-NONFUT-3SG

'The woman came nearer, unpacked her reindeer, pitched a jurta on the hillside, half-conic jurta.'

(14)

erek	*Metele*	*bi-mi*	*erek*	*asi*
this	Metele	be-COND.CONV	this	woman

oro-r-ǯi-n	*ŋeele-l-liǯii*
reindeer-NEG.CONV-INSTR-3SG	be_afraid-INCH-ANT.CONV

dikeŋ-či-weeč-te-n
hide-STAT-HABIT-NONFUT-3SG

'Metele, being afraid of the reindeer of this woman hid himself.'

(15)

ora-r-ni	*bi-mi*	*ǯuu-ča-ma-n*	*ereli*
reindeer-PL-3SG	be-COND.CONV	house-DIM-ACC-3SG	around

uǯmi-l-liǯur	*ǯuu-wa-n-da*
lick_urine-INCH-ANT.CONV.PL	house-ACC-3SG-CONJ.CL

čapči-waač-ta
tread-HABIT-NONFUT:3PL

'Her reindeer grazed around his little jurta, licked his frozen urine, trod on his jurta.'

(16)

erek	*ineŋ*	*bi-mi*	*Metele*	*e-ti*
this	day	be-COND.CONV	Metele	not_do-NONFUT.PART

ñöö-r	*oo-d-ni*	*e-ti*
go_out-NEG.CONV	become-NONFUT-3SG	not_do-NONFUT.PART

ñöö-r	*oo-d-ni*
go_out-NEG.CONV	become-NONFUT-3SG

‘From this day on Metele didn’t go outside any more.’

(17)

ora-r	*hör-reke-ten*	*ñöö-weeč-te-n*
reindeer-PL	go-COND.DS.CONV-3PL	go_out-HABIT-NONFUT-3SG

ora-r	*hör-če-le-ten*	*hurka-i*
reindeer-PL	go-PERF.PART-LOC-3PL	loop-REF.POS.SG

naŋ-i	*it-ne-weeč-te-n*
trap-REF.POS.SG	see-DIRECT-HABIT-NONFUT-3SG

‘Only when the reindeer go away, he goes outside to check the loops and traps that he had set.’

(18)

hurka-j	*naŋ-i*
loop-REF.POS.SG	trap-REF.POS.SG

it-ne-se-ssi-mi	*bi-mi oro-m*	*oro-m*
see-DIRECT-ITER-CONAT-COND.CONV	be-COND.CONV	reindeer-ACC

it-tiʒi	*dikeŋ-ket-niken*	*ič-weeč-te-n*
see-ANT.CONV	hide-DISTR-SIM.CONV	see-HABIT-NONFUT-3SG

‘While inspecting them, if he saw the reindeer, he hid himself.’

(19)

hurka-wa-n-da	*iaa-wa-n-da*	*ora-r*
loop-ACC-3SG-CONJ.CLIT	what-ACC-3SG-CONJ.CLIT	reindeer-PL

čapči-ča-l
tread-PERF.PART-PL

‘It turned out that his loops and all are trodden down by the reindeer.’

(20)

erek	*koobaka-ŋa-n-da*	*hialaki-ŋa-n-da*
this	hare-AL.POS-3SG-CONJ.CLIT	partridge-AL.POS-3SG-CONJ.CLIT

hiŋa-sn-a-n	*ureči-n*	*erek*	*asi*
flee-MOM-NONFUT-3SG	similar-3SG	this	woman

em-če-le-n	*adiku-l-la-n*
come-PERF.PART-LOC-3SG	decrease-INCH-NONFUT-3SG

'It seemed as if hares and partridges dispersed, decreased in number, since the woman appeared.'

(21)

tarič	*tačin*	*bi-d-niken*	*araj*	*asi-ŋa-n*
then	so	be-PROG-SIM.CONV	suddenly	woman-AL.POS-3SG

noŋan-taki-n	*girka-n-ni*	*ii-s-ni*
(s)he-DIR-3SG	walk-NMZR-3SG	sound-NONFUT-3SG

'Once he heard the steps, - the woman approached him.'

(22)

erek	*dikeŋ-de-i-de*	*ñeke-ssi-n*
this	hide-PURP.CONV-REF.POS.SG-PURP.CONV	do-CONAT-3SG

ñoon-da-i-da	*ñeke-ssi-n*
run-PURP.CONV-REF.POS.SG-CONJ.CLIT	do-CONAT-3SG

ŋeele-l-liǯii	*tarič*	*e-s-ni*	*ñoon*
be afraid-INCH-ANT.CONV	then	not_do-NONFUT-3SG	run.NEG.CONV

'Metele was scared. He didn't know what to do – either to hide himself or run away. Finally, he decided to stay.'

(23)

iaa-ǯi-n-ka	*em-niǯii*	*göön-ni*
what_do-FUT-3SG-CLIT	come-ANT.CONV	say-NONFUT.3SG

'"What will she do when she comes?" he wondered.'

(24)

tarak	*asi*	*em-niǯii*	*ii-riǯii*
that	woman	come-ANT.CONV	enter-ANT.CONV

tööre-ǯe-l-le-n	*erek*	*Metele-tki*
talk-PROG-INCH-NONFUT-3SG	this	Metele-DIR

'And that woman approached his jurta and said.'

(25)

Deñee-gu	*Metele-ken*
Den'ee-INT.CLIT	Metele-DIM

Deñee-gu	*hii-ŋen*	*iaaka*
Den'ee-INT.CLIT	you-CLIT	what

Deñee-gu	*ñari-kan-a*
Den'ee-INT.CLIT	man-DIM-EPENTH

Deñee-gu	*gerbe-lken-e*
Den'ee-INT.CLIT	name-PROPR-EPENTH

'-*Deñee-gu*, Metele, and yet they call you a man!'

(26)

Deñee-gu	*iaami*	*e-se-nni*
Den'ee-INT.CLIT	why	not_do-NONFUT-NONFUT.2SG

Deñee-gu	*ǯuumi-ǯ-waač-ta*
Den'ee-INT.CLIT	visit-PROG-HABIT-NEG.CONV

'Why don't you come to visit me!'

(27)

Deñee-gu	*hii-ken*	*iaak-a*
Den'ee-INT.CLIT	you-DIM	what-EPENTH

Deñee-gu	*ǯuuma-ri-wa-s*
Den'ee-INT.CLIT	visit-NONFUT.PART-ACC-NONFUT

Deñee-gu	*alat-tiǯi*
Den'ee-INT.CLIT	wait-ANT.CONV

Deñee-gu	*udal-liǯii*
Den'ee-INT.CLIT	get.bored-ANT.CONV

Deñee-gu	*tarpač-kan-da*
Den'ee-INT.CLIT	anyway-DIM-CONJ.CLIT

Deñee-gu	*meen-ke-ken*
Den'ee-INT.CLIT	self's-DIM-DIM

Deñee-gu	*ǯuuma-ǯaañ-na-m*
Den'ee-INT.CLIT	visit-DUR-NONFUT-ACC

'I waited and waited, hoping that you would come, became bored waiting and so have come myself.'

(28) *Deñee-gu* *ötel-titel*
Den'ee-INT.CLIT long_ago

Deñee-gu *ulgu-r*
Den'ee-INT.CLIT tale-PL

Deñee-gu *bi-ǯ-gere-re-n*
Den'ee-INT.CLIT be-PROG-PAST.ITER-NONFUT-3SG

'-*Deñee-gu*, there are old tales.'

(29) *Deñee-gu* *asi* *gerbe-lken*
Den'ee-INT.CLIT woman name-PROPR

Deñee-gu *ǯuu-la-n-a*
Den'ee-INT.CLIT house-LOC-3SG-EPENTH

Deñee-gu *ñari-kan-da*
Den'ee-INT.CLIT man-DIM-CONJ.CLIT

Deñee-gu *ǯuuma-ri-wa-n*
Den'ee-INT.CLIT visit-NONFUT.PART-ACC-3SG

Deñee-gu *ulgu-r* *bi-gre-n*
Den'ee-INT.CLIT be-PAST.ITER-3SG

Deñee-gu *göön-ni*
Den'ee-INT.CLIT say-NONFUT.3SG

'The old tales relate that a man should first go to visit a woman.'

(30) *erek* *Metele* *oon-da* *göö-nne-j*
this Metele how-CONJ.CLIT say-NEC.PART-REF.POS.SG

ŋeele-l-li-n *eme*[4] *ñaan*
be afraid-INCH-PAST-3SG so again

'At first Metele was afraid to say anything.'

---

4 < Jak. *эмиэ* 'again, still, so.'

(31)

ičin-gel	*e-se-m*	*ǯuumi-waač-ta*
like.this-INDEF.CLIT	not_do-NONFUT-1SG	visit-HABIT-NEG.CONV

kiptu-waač-ta-m-da
be_shy-HABIT-NONFUT-1SG-CONJ.CLIT

iaa-waač-ta-m-da	*ǯöör*
what_do-HABIT-NONFUT-1SG-CONJ.CLIT	two

böödele-lken	*er*	*elekes*	*er*	*hin-u*
feet-PROPR	now	for_the_first_time	now	you-ACC

it-te-m	*Metele*	*bi-mi*
see-NONFUT-ACC	Metele	be-COND.CONV

'Then Metele said: "I was scared that's why I didn't come to see you. I see a human being (lit. two-legged), like you for the first time".'

(32)

tarak	*erek*	*iaa-ǯi-n*	*koobaka-ŋ-i*
that	this	what_do-FUT-3SG	hare-AL.POS-REF.POS.SG

gajsa-ča-ma-n	*öle-riǯi*
pad-DIM-ACC-3SG	cook-ANT.CONV.SG

asi-ŋ-di	*töj-re-n*
woman-AL.POS-DAT:REF.POS.SG	serve-NONFUT-3SG

'So what could he do? He cooked a hare's pad, and treated the woman.'

(33)

ǯööriǯur	*ǯebe-ǯ-de*
two_of_them	eat-PROG-NONFUT.3PL

'They ate together.'

(34)

tarič	*ǯebe-ǯ-diǯii*	*od-diǯii*	*alik-ča-ma-n*
then	eat-PROG-ANT.CONV	finish-ANT.CONV	dish-DIM-ACC-3SG

hiru-mken-iǯii	*tööre-ǯe-l-le-n*
move-CAUS-ANT.CONV	talk-PROG-INCH-NONFUT-3SG

'When they finished eating the woman pushed the dishes away and said.'

(35) *Deñee-gu* *Metele-ke-en*
Den'ee-INT.CLIT Metele-DIM-EPENTH

Deñee-gu *bi* *hin-dule*
Den'ee-INT.CLIT I you-LOC

Deñee-gu *ǯuumi-ǯaañ-na-m*
Den'ee-INT.CLIT visit-DUR-NONFUT-1SG

Deñee-gu *ñan-a* *hi-ken*
Den'ee-INT.CLIT again-EPENTH you-DIM

Deñee-gu *min-dule*
Den'ee-INT.CLIT I-LOC

Deñee-gu *ǯuuma-ǯ-li-la*
Den'ee-INT.CLIT visit-PROG-IMP.2SG-CLIT

Deñee-gu *göön-ni*
Den'ee-INT.CLIT say-NONFUT.3SG

'-*Deñee-gu*, Metele, I've payed a visit to you, now come to see me.'

(36) *Iŋe-e* *iaa-ǯi-m-da-si*
OK-EPENTH what_do-FUT-1SG-CONJ.CLIT-CLIT

ǯuuma-da-ku-ta *göön-ni*
visit-PURP.CONV-1SG.IRR-CONJ.CLIT say-NONFUT.3SG

'"All right, I'll come, why not", Metele said.'

(37) *tačin* *göö-niken* *bod-da-n* *erek*
so say-SIM.CONV follow-NONFUT-3SG this

asi-ŋ-i *ǯuu-la-n*
woman-AL.POS-REF.POS.SG house-LOC-3SG

'He accompanied the woman to her jurta.'

(38) *erek* *asi* *ǯuu-la-n* *ŋen-neken* *erek*
this woman house-LOC-3SG go-COND.DS.CONV this

ǯuu-n *emŋe-n* *noŋan* *ǯuu-du-n*
house-3SG spacy-3SG (s)he house-DAT-3SG

göö-mi *aja-n* *hoo*
say-COND.CONV good-3SG very

'He enters her jurta and sees that the jurta is very spacious and much better than his own.'

(39) *hoo* *aji-č* *čaku-č-ta-n* *čakuti-n-da* *hoo*
very good-INSTR tidy-STAT-NONFUT-3SG tidy-3SG-CONJ.CLIT very
'A very cosy jurta.'

(40) *oja-n-da* *ǯuu-n-da* *ñama*
cloth-3SG-CONJ.CLIT house-3SG-CONJ.CLIT warm
'Both the jurta and the clothes are warm.'

(41) *ǯe-e* *erek* *asi* *bi-mi* *erek* *Metele*
Well-EPENTH this woman be-COND.CONV this Metele

ǯep-te-n *öle-n*
eat-PURP.CONV-3SG cook-NONFUT.3SG

'Well, the woman cooked.'

(42) *ǯep-te-n* *öle-riǯii* *ulič-ta-n*
eat-PURP.CONV-3SG cook-ANT.CONV feed-NONFUT-3SG
'She invited Metele to the meal.'

(43) *ǯeple-ŋe-n-de* *dalla-n* *hoo*
food-AL.POS-3SG-CONJ.CLIT sweet-3SG very
'The food was delicious.'

(44) *erek* *Metele* *bi-mi* *ere-w* *hiisečin* *bi-mi*
this Metele be-COND.CONV this-ACC evening be-COND.CONV

ǯuu-la-j *e-s-ni* *muču-r*
house-LOC-REF.POS.SG not_do-NONFUT-3SG return-NEG.CONV

'Well, Metele didn't come back home that evening.'

(45)

erek	*e-du*	*bi-ǯe-l-le-n*
this	this-DAT	be-PROG-INCH-NONFUT-3SG

‘(He) stayed in the woman’s jurta.’

(46)

erek	*asi*	*ukčeneke-n-de*	*hooja*	*bi-weeč-te-n*
this	woman	story-3SG-CONJ.CLIT	many	be-HABIT-NONFUT-3SG

ečin	*awaŋ-či-ra*	*bukatyn*
this_way	entertain-STAT-NONFUT.3PL	all the time

‘The woman entertained him with stories for a long time.’

(47)

tačin	*hiisel-leke-n*	*tege-č-te-n*
so	get dark-COND.DS.CONV-3SG	sit_down-STAT-NONFUT-3SG

‘So they conversed till the evening.’

(48)

erek	*asi-ŋa-n*	*bi-mi*	*Metele*
this	woman-AL.POS-3SG	be-COND.CONV	Metele

hara-ŋa-n	*ǯiejde-li-n*	*oo-n*
bed-AL.POS-3SG	other_side-PROL-3SG	make-NONFUT.3SG

‘Then the woman made up a bed for him.’

(49)

Deñee-gu	*Metele-ke-en*
Den’ee-INT.CLIT	Metele-DIM-EPENTH

Deñee-gu	*hi-ke-en-gu*
Den’ee-INT.CLIT	you-DIM-EPENTH-INT.CLIT

Deñee-gu	*e-ǯi-de*
Den’ee-INT.CLIT	not_do-NEG.IMP.2SG-PURP.CONV

Deñee-gu	*ǯuu-la-ji*
Den’ee-INT.CLIT	house-LOC-REF.POS.SG

Deñee-gu	*höre-ǯeeñ-ne*
Den’ee-INT.CLIT	go-DUR-NEG.CONV

Deñee-gu	*gööñ-ni*
Den’ee-INT.CLIT	say-NONFUT.3SG

'-*Deñee-gu,* Metele, don't go home.'

(50) *erek* *Metele* *tarapač* *asi-ŋ-i*
this Metele then woman-AL.POS-REF.POS.SG

ǯuu-la-n *bi-ǯe-l-le-n*
house-LOC-3SG be-PROG-INCH-NONFUT-3SG

'So Metele stayed in that woman's jurta.'

(51) *hoo-ka-m* *goru* *bi-se*
very-DIM-ACC for_a_long_time be-NONFUT.3PL
'So they lived for a long time.'

(52) *erek* *oro-l-tan* *gorol-či-l-la*
this reindeer-PL-3PL move_away-STAT-INCH-NONFUT.3PL
'Their reindeer wandered off.'

(53) *oro-ñ-da* *e-ǯi* *ŋeel-le*
reindeer-INSTR-CONJ.CLIT not_do-NEG.IMP.2SG be afraid-NEG CONV

göö-niken *ere-w* *bej-u* *hupku-č-weeč-te-n*
say-SIM.CONV this-ACC man-ACC teach-STAT-HABIT-NONFUT-3SG

'"Don't be afraid of the reindeer", the woman taught.'

(54) *erek* *bej* *sin* *oro-l-ǯi-n* *elem-ne-n*
this man meanwhile reindeer-PL-INSTR-3SG get_used_to-NONFUT-3SG
'Meanwhile he got used to the reindeer.'

(55) *oro-ñ-da* *e-ti*
reindeer-INSTR-CONJ.CLIT not_do-NONFUT.PART

ŋeel-li *oo-d-ni* *iintu-t-ti*
be afraid-NONFUT.PART become-PROG-3SG gather-STAT-NONFUT.PART

iaa-ri *oo-d-ni*
what_do-NONFUT.PART become-NONFUT-3SG

'He learned how to graze the reindeer and the like.'

(56) *tarič* *ömneken* *asi-ŋa-n* *tööre-ǯe-l-le-n*
then once woman-AL.POS-3SG talk-PROG-INCH-LOC-3SG

Deñee-gu *Metele-ke-en*
Den'ee-INT.CLIT Metele-DIM-EPENTH

Deñee-gu *edin-ke-mu*
Den'ee-INT.CLIT husband-DIM-1SG.POS

Deñee-gu *oro-l-ti-da*
Den'ee-INT.CLIT reindeer-PL-1PL.INC.POS-CONJ.CLIT

Deñee-gu *gorol-či-l-la*
Den'ee-INT.CLIT move_away-STAT-INCH-NONFUT.3PL

Deñee-gu *oŋko-kan-ti*
Den'ee-INT.CLIT pasture-DIM-1PL.INC.POS

Deñee-gu *emŋel-le*
Den'ee-INT.CLIT widen-NONFUT.3PL

Deñee-gu *oro-l-ti-da*
Den'ee-INT.CLIT reindeer-PL-1PL.INC.POS-CONJ.CLIT

Deñee-gu *beri-b-ne-l-le*
Den'ee-INT.CLIT lose-MED-DIRECT-INCH-NONFUT.3PL

Deñee-gu *mut-ŋen* *iaak-a*
Den'ee-INT.CLIT we-CLIT what-EPENTH

Deñee-gu *nulge-ǯ-ger-e*
Den'ee-INT.CLIT nomadize-PROG-ITER.PAST-EPENTH

örikič-ur
nomadic_camp-REF.POS.PL

Deñee-gu *hönteru-ger*
Den'ee-INT.CLIT change-IMP.1PL

Deñee-gu *göön-ni*
Den'ee-INT.CLIT say-NONFUT.3SG

Metele

‘Once the woman said: “*Deñee-gu*, Metele, my dear husband, our reindeer are wandering off, the pasture is far away, the reindeer are getting lost. Let us change the pasture”, she said.’

(57)

tačin	*göön-če-le-n*	*erek*	*Metele*	*bi-mi*
so	say-PERF.PART-LOC-3SG	this	Metele	be-COND.CONV

baa-l-la-n
not want-INCH-NONFUT-3SG

‘Although she said that, Metele didn’t want to move.’

(58)

Gerijen-gerijen	*asi-jan*	*Ömček-ken*
Gerijen-gerijen	woman-CLIT	Omchek-DIM

Gerijen-gerijen	*bi-kene*	*oon-a*
Gerijen-gerijen	I-DIM	how-EPENTH

Gerijen-gerijen	*uñačan-duk-i*	*höre-ǯeen-ǯi-m*
Gerijen-gerijen	tiny_house-ABL-REF.POS.SG	go-DUR-FUT-1SG

Gerijen-gerijen	*uñača-mi*	*mulaan-a-m*
Gerijen-gerijen	tiny_house- REF.POS.SG	pity-NONFUT.1SG

Gerijen-gerijen	*tunŋana*	*naŋ-ka-mu*
Gerijen-gerijen	five	trap-DIM-1SG.POS

Gerijen-gerijen	*tunŋana*	*hurka-wu*
Gerijen-gerijen	five	loop-1SG

Gerijen-gerijen	*bi-kene-gu*	*hör-rek-u*
Gerijen-gerijen	I-DIM-INT.CLIT	go-COND.CONV-1SG

Gerijen-gerijen	*ača*	*hunŋi-la-č*
Gerijen-gerijen	without	owner-NEG.PROP-INSTR

Gerijen-gerijen	*eme-be-ǯeen-ǯi-n*
Gerijen-gerijen	come-MED-DUR-INSTR-3SG

Gerijen-gerijen	*nulge-m-mi-ken*	*hii-gu*
Gerijen-gerijen	nomadize-VOL-COND.CONV-DIM	you-INT.CLIT

Gerijen-gerijen *meenken* *nulge-t-so-li*
Gerijen-gerijen (one)self nomadize-STAT-ATTEN-IMP.2SG

Gerijen-gerijen *göön-ni*
Gerijen-gerijen say-NONFUT.3SG

‘-*Gerijen-gerijen*, my dear wife, Omchek, it would be a pity to abondon my little jurta. If I move away, my five loops and five traps will be left without their owner. If you want to move away, do it alone.’

(59) *erek* *asi* *“Emeb-li* *eme-b-li-de!”*
this woman leave-MED -IMP.2SG leave-MED-IMP.2SG-CONJ.CLIT

göön-ni
say-NONFUT.3SG

‘The woman said: “All right, stay (alone), stay.”’

(60) *erek* *or-mi* *iaa-ji* *iintu-rižii*
this reindeer-REF.POS.SG what-REF.POS.SG gather-ANT.CONV

abdu-i *čak-rižii* *asi-ŋa-n*
belonging-REF.POS.SG gather-ANT.CONV woman-AL.POS-3SG

okata-ŋ-i *ejeki* *nulge-n*
river-AL.POS-REF.POS.SG downstream nomadize-NONFUT.3SG

‘She packed her things, harnessed the reindeer and moved away downstream.’

(61) *erek* *Metele* *öme-kke-ken* *e-du* *eme-p-te-n*
this Metele one-DIM-DIM this-DAT leave-MED-NONFUT-3SG
‘And Metele stayed alone.’

(62) *erek* *hoo-ka-m* *goru* *bi-s-ni*
this very-DIM-ACC for_a_long_time be-NONFUT-3SG
‘So he lived for some time.’

(63) *erek* *Metele* *hurka-j* *naŋ-i* *oo-d-nikan*
this Metele loop-REF.POS.SG trap-REF.POS.SG make-PROG-SIM.CONV

hurka-j-da	*tulu-če-ssi-n*
loop-REF.POS.SG-CONJ.CLIT	set-STAT-CONAT-3SG

naŋ-i-da	*tulu-če-ssi-n*
trap-REF.POS.SG-CONJ.CLIT	set-PERF.PART-CONAT-3SG

'Metele set the traps and loops as he had done before.'

(64)

koobaka-ŋa-n-da	*uǯa-n*	*ačča*	*oo-ča*
hare-AL.POS-3SG-CONJ.CLIT	track-3SG	not_exist	make-PERF.PART

hialaki-ŋa-n-da	*ačča*
partridge-AL.POS-3SG-CONJ.CLIT	not_exist

'But the footprints(tracks) of hares and partridges disappeared.'

(65)

erek	*adi-da*	*ineŋi-w*	*bi-s-ni*
this	how many-CONJ.CLIT	day-ACC	be-NONFUT-3SG

'The days passed.'

(66)

ǯuu-n	*bi-mi*	*iŋeni-n-de*	*hoo*
house-3SG	be-COND.CONV	frost-3SG-CONJ.CLIT	very

oo-ča
become-PERF.PART

'It became very cold in his jurta.'

(67)

tarič	*imanna-č*	*iaa-č-ta*
then	snow-INSTR	what-INSTR-CONJ.CLIT

ima-ssi-waač-ta-n	*sinbir*[5]	*iŋeñ-meč-te-n*
snow-CONAT-HABIT-NONFUT-3SG	anyway	freeze-HABIT-NONFUT-3SG

erek	*ora-r*	*ejdu*	*gudek-če-l*
this	reindeer-PL	all	tear-PERF.PART-PL

'Although the snow covered the jurta, Metele froze inside, because the reindeer had torn his tiny jurta.'

---

5 < Jak. *син биир* 'anyway'.

(68) *erek* *Metele* *tarpač-ta* *ñömu-n-da*
this Metele anyway-CONJ.CLIT starvation-NONFUT.3SG-CONJ.CLIT

köke-nne-n *oo-di-mdas*
die-NEC.PART-3SG become-NONFUT.PART-sort of

'And he almost starves to death.'

(69) *tarič* *ömnekeñ* *ǯe* *tööre-ǯe-l-le-n*
then once Well talk-PROG-INCH-NONFUT-3SG
'And once he said to himself.'

(70) *Gerijen-gerijen* *eči-ke-ken* *ogla-mi*
Gerijen-gerijen so-DIM-DIM become-COND.CONV

Gerijen-gerijen *Ömček* *asi-duk*
Gerijen-gerijen Omchek woman-ABL

Gerijen-gerijen *bodu-t-ti-kla-n*
Gerijen-gerijen follow-STAT-NONFUT.PART-DIR.LOC-3SG

eme-be-ǯeeñ-ni-w *göön-ni*
leave-MED-DUR-PAST-1SG say-NONFUT.3SG

'-*Gerijen-gerijen*, what a miserable life! Although my dear wife Omchek wanted me to go with her, I stayed here.'

(71) *Gerijen-gerijen* *oon-kan* *bi-ǯi-n-e*
Gerijen-gerijen how-DIM be-FUT-3SG-EPENTH

Gerijen-gerijen *uñačan* *bi-mi*
Gerijen-gerijen tiny_house be-COND.CONV

Gerijen-gerijen *uñačan-da*
Gerijen-gerijen tiny_house-CONJ.CLIT

bi-č-sö-de-n-e
be-STAT-ATTEN-PURP.CONV-3SG-EPENTH

Gerijen-gerijen *tunŋana* *naŋa* *bi-mi*
Gerijen-gerijen five trap.EPENTH be-COND.CONV

Gerijen-gerijen	*tunŋana*	*naŋa*
Gerijen-gerijen	five	trap.EPENTH

bi-č-sö-de-n-e
be-STAT-ATTEN-PURP.CONV-3SG-EPENTH

Gerijen-gerijen	*tunŋana*	*hurka-wu*	*bi-mi*
Gerijen-gerijen	five	loop-1SG	be-COND.CONV

Gerijen-gerijen	*tunŋana*	*hurka-da*
Gerijen-gerijen	five	loop-CONJ.CLIT

bi-č-sö-de-n-e
be-STAT-ATTEN-PURP.CONV-3SG-EPENTH

'-*Gerijen-gerijen*, Let my jurta stay here, let my five traps, let my five loops stay here.'

(72)

Gerijen-gerijen	*koobaka-ŋ-u-da*	*hinŋa-san-ča-kan*
Gerijen-gerijen	hare-AL.POS-1SG-CONJ.CLIT	flee-MOM-PERF.PART-DIM

Gerijen-gerijen	*Ömček*	*asi-kan*	*eŋeje-n-ǯi*
Gerijen-gerijen	Omchek	woman-DIM	rich-NMZR-INSTR

Gerijen-gerijen	*hialaki-ka-m-da*	*e-knen-ten*
Gerijen-gerijen	partridge-DIM-1SG-CONJ.CLIT	not_do-DELIMIT.CONV-3PL

Gerijen-gerijen	*emnewu*	*doo-ma-l-la*
Gerijen-gerijen	not_do-PROB-1SG	settle-MOM-INCH-NEG.CONV

'My hare scattered, the reindeer herds of Omchek scared my partridges away, so they do not even dare to settle down. If I stay here, I starve to death for sure.'

(73)

goö-niken	*meen*	*doo-li*	*tööre-ǯ-de-n*
say-SIM.CONV	self's	inside-PROL	talk-PROG-NONFUT-3SG

erek	*Metele*	*ǯe*	*ŋerile-wči-n*
this	Metele	Well	dawn-wait_for-NONFUT.3SG

ere-w	*hiiseči-m*	*tege-či-mnin*
this-ACC	evening-ACC	sit_down-STAT-CONSEC.CONV

aanŋa-č-ta-n	*ŋerile-d-dike-m*
stay_overnight-STAT-NONFUT-3SG	dawn-PROG-SIM.CONV-ACC

okata-ŋ-i	*ejeki*	*asi-ŋ-i*
river-AL.POS-REF.POS.SG	downstream	woman-AL.POS-REF.POS.SG

hooč-ta-n	*höč-te-n*
track-NONFUT-3SG	chase-NONFUT-3SG

'So Metele talked to himself. Well, he spent the night, waiting till dawn, and at dawn followed the tracks of his wife.'

(74)

ŋene-ǯeeñ-ne-n	*hoo-kan*	*goru*	*ŋen-ne-n*
go-DUR-NONFUT-3SG	very-DIM	for_a_long_time	go-NONFUT-3SG

ŋen-če-ken	*ŋen-ne-n*
go-PERF.PART-DIM	go-NONFUT-3SG

'So he went and went ahead.'

(75)

tarpač-ta	*hatara-l-la-n*	*adi-da*
anyway-CONJ.CLIT	get dark-INCH-NONFUT-3SG	how many-CONJ.CLIT

ineŋi-w	*dolbani-ŋ-i*	*ineŋi-ŋ-i*
day-ACC	night-AL.POS-REF.POS.SG	day-AL.POS-REF.POS.SG

ŋen-ne-n	*ömneken*	*tačin*
go-NONFUT-3SG	once	so

ŋene-d-deke-n	*ǯulde-le-n*	*tog*
go-PROG-COND.DS.CONV-3SG	ahead-LOC-3SG	fire

hutapki-t-ta-n
sparkle-STAT-NONFUT-3SG

'It became dark but he kept going ahead many days and nights, without any rest. Once he saw far ahead flashes of fire.'

(76)

ta-la	*ŋene-ǯeeñ-ne-n*	*erek*	*Metele*
this-LOC	go-DUR-NONFUT-3SG	this	Metele

ñöme-ri-de *ureči-n* *heč-te-n*
starve-NONFUT.PART-CONJ.CLIT similar-3SG get tired-NONFUT-3SG

'Exhausted and starving, Metele made his way towards the fire.'

(77) *ǯebe-me-n-de* *hoo* *iŋeñe-n-de* *hoo*
eat-VOL-NMZR-CONJ.CLIT very freeze-NMZR-CONJ.CLIT very

ojo-n *butun-ni* *gudeku*
cloth-3SG all-3SG torn

'He suffered from hunger and cold, his clothes were torn to pieces.'

(78) *ta-la* *ǯuu-la* *ŋen-če-le-n* *asi-ŋa-n*
this-LOC house-LOC go-PERF.PART-LOC-3SG woman-AL.POS-3SG

bi-mi *deepki* *tijun-ǯi-i* *togta-n*
be-COND.CONV meeting staff-INSTR-REF.POS.SG batter-NONFUT.3SG

'As he approached the jurta his wife came out and began to batter him with her crook.'

(79) *uñačan-ǯi-i* *eme-p-li*
tiny_house-INSTR-REF.POS.SG leave-MED-IMP.2SG
'"Stay in your little jurta!"'

(80) *tunŋan* *hurka-wu* *tunŋan* *naŋ-u* *mula-a* *göön-i-s*
five loop-1SG five trap-1SG alas-EPENTH say-PAST-2SG

iaa-w *gelne-nni* *mulan-daŋ-ǯi-i*
what-ACC look for-NONFUT.2SG pity-PAST.PART-INSTR-REF.POS.SG

bi-d-deke-s *iaak-a* *göö-niken*
be-PROG-COND.DS.CONV-2SG what-EPENTH say-SIM.CONV

'"How can I leave my five loops without the owner?" didn't you say so, why have you then come here?'

(81) *erek* *barda-li-n* *em-uken-ni*
this opposite side-PROL-3SG come-CAUS-NONFUT.3SG
'"Stay with the things you are so fond of", she said.'

(82)

Gerijen-gerijen	*asi-jan*	*Ömček-ken,*
Gerijen-gerijen	woman-EPENTH	Omchek-DIM

Gerijen-gerijen	*e-duku-n*	*ǯuleski*	*iaa-ka-m-da*
Gerijen-gerijen	this-ABL-3SG	ahead	what-DIM-ACC-CONJ.CLIT

göön-eke-s
say-COND.DS.CONV-2SG

Gerijen-gerijen	*e-te-m-ele*	*hieŋke-le*
Gerijen-gerijen	not.do-FUT-1SG-CLIT	ground-LOC

tikkön-či-ǯeeñ-ne
drop-STAT-DUR-NEG.CONV

Gerijen-gerijen	*e-ǯi*	*min-u*	*ilbe-ǯeeñ-ne*
Gerijen-gerijen	not_do-IMP.2SG	I-ACC	chase-DUR-NEG.CONV

‘-*Gerijen-gerijen*, my dear wife Omchek, from now on I shall do, whatever you tell me. Don’t turn me out of doors!’

(83)

Gerijen-gerijen	*ooti-gda-ǯii*
Gerijen-gerijen	suffer-DELIM-INSTR.SG.REF.POS

eme-ǯ-de-m
come-PROG-NONFUT-3SG

Gerijen-gerijen	*ǯem-du-de*	*köke-nne-wu*
Gerijen-gerijen	hunger-DAT-CONJ.CLIT	die-NEC.PART-1SG

oo-ǯaañ-na-n
become-DUR-NONFUT-3SG

Gerijen-gerijen	*iŋeñ-si-du-de*
Gerijen-gerijen	freeze-NONFUT.PART-DAT-CONJ.CLIT

hinŋe-riǯii
freeze-ANT.CONV

Gerijen-gerijen	*köke-mne-wu*	*oo-ǯaañ-na-n*
Gerijen-gerijen	die-PROB-1SG	become-DUR-NONFUT-3SG

Gerijen-gerijen	*göön-ni*
Gerijen-gerijen	say-NONFUT.3SG

e-ǯi	*ilbe-re*	*göön-ni,*
not_do-NEG.IMP.2SG	chase-NEG.CONV	say-NONFUT.3SG

bi-wke-li	*göö-niken*
be-CAUS-IMP.2SG	say-SIM.CONV

'-*Gerijen-gerijen*, I'm so exhausted, nearly dying of hunger, I've nearly frozen to death. Don't drive me away, - he said. "Let me in".'

(84)

ejlini-w-riǯii	*ejlini-w-riǯii-ǯe,*
plead-PASS-ANT.CONV	plead-PASS-ANT.CONV-CONJ.CLIT

ii.w-re-n	*erek*	*asi*
enter.CAUS-NONFUT-3SG	this	woman

'So he begged for a long time. Then, finally, she let him in.'

(85)

erek	*Metele*	*asatkan*	*hute-lken*	*oo-ča*
this	Metele	girl	child-PROPR	become-PERF

'Meanwhile Metele's wife gave birth to a daughter.'

(86)

ečin	*hoo-ka-m*	*goru*	*bi-s-ni*
like.this	very-DIM-ACC	long	be-NONFUT-3SG

'So they lived for a long time.'

(87)

erek	*Metele*	*e-ti-de*
this	Metele	not_do-NONFUT.PART-CONJ.CLIT

buju-s-se	*iaa-r-da*
go hunt-ITER-NEG.CONV	what_do-NEG.CONV-CONJ.CLIT

ǯuu-di	*bi-ǯ-weeč-te-n*
house-DAT:REF.POS	be-PROG-HABIT-NONFUT-3SG

'Metele didn't hunt, spent all his time sitting in the jurta.'

(88)

ömneken	*asi-kan*	*tööre-ǯe-l-le-n*
once	woman-DIM	say-PROG-INCH-NONFUT-3SG

'Once his wife said to him:'

(89)

Deñee-gu	*Metele-ke-en*	
Den'ee-INT.CLIT	M.-DIM	
Deñee-gu	*edi(n)-ke-mu*	
Den'ee-INT.CLIT	husband-DIM-1SG	
Deñee-gu	*ere*	*oona*
Den'ee-INT.CLIT	this	how
Deñee-gu	*mut-ŋeni*	
Den'ee-INT.CLIT	we-CLIT	
Deñee-gu	*or-mar-ñun-da*	
Den'ee-INT.CLIT	reindeer-REF.POS.PL-CLIT-CLIT	
Deñee-gu	*ǯeb-niken*	
Den'ee-INT.CLIT	eat-SIM.CONV	
Deñee-gu	*bi-ǯeen-ǯi-p*	
Den'ee-INT.CLIT	be-DUR-FUT-1PL	
Deñee-gu	*hi-ŋen*	*iaak-a*
Den'ee-INT.CLIT	you(SG)	what
Deñee-gu	*bejŋe-w-de*	
Den'ee-INT.CLIT	pray-ACC-CONJ.CLIT	
Deñee-gu	*gele-t-kere-li*	
Den'ee-INT.CLIT	look.for-STAT-ITER.PAST-IMP.2SG	
Deñee-gu	*buju-s-kere-li*	
Den'ee-INT.CLIT	go.hunt-ITER-ITER.PAST-IMP.2SG	

'-*Deñee-gu*, Metele, my dear husband, why do we live eating the meat of our tame reindeer all the time? Why don't you go hunting wild reindeer?'

(90)

Deñee-gu	*töör*	*oj-li-n*
Den'ee-INT.CLIT	earth	on-PROL-3SG

Deñee-gu *giaki* *bejŋe*
Den'ee-INT.CLIT different pray

Deñee-gu *i-le* *ŋen-ǯi-n?*
Den'ee-INT.CLIT which-LOC go-FUT-3SG

'After all, aren't there (enough) different game in this country?'

(91) *Deñee-gu* *oon* *ora-gda-w*
Den'ee-INT.CLIT how reindeer-DELIM-ACC

Deñee-gu *ǯebe-d-ǯi-p*
Den'ee-INT.CLIT eat-PROG-FUT-1PL

Deñee-gu *göön-ni*
Den'ee-INT.CLIT say-NONFUT.3SG

'Why should we eat all the time our tame reindeer?'

(92) *Deñee-gu* *göön-ni*
Den'ee-INT.CLIT say-NONFUT.3SG

Deñee-gu *hii-ken* *iaak-a*
Den'ee-INT.CLIT you(SG)-DIM what

Deñee-gu *tieke-le*
Den'ee-INT.CLIT now-CLIT

Deñee-gu *e-duk* *nulge-riǯur*
Den'ee-INT.CLIT this-ABL nomadize-ANT.CONV.PL

Deñee-gu *neeji* *töör-du*
Den'ee-INT.CLIT fresh earth-DAT

Deñee-gu *örin-iǯur*
Den'ee-INT.CLIT make a camp-ANT.CONV.PL

Deñee-gu *buju-s-ŋe-nni*
Den'ee-INT.CLIT go hunt-ITER-POL.IMP-2SG

'Why don't we move and you go hunting in a new country?'

(93)	*Deñee-gu*	*tiek-neñe*	
	Den'ee-INT.CLIT	now-CLIT	
	Deñee-gu	*nulge-ǯ-gere*	
	Den'ee-INT.CLIT	nomadize-PROG-IMP.1PL	
	Deñee-gu	*mut-ŋen*	*iaak-a*
	Den'ee-INT.CLIT	we-CLIT	what
	Deñee-gu	*göön-ni*	
	Den'ee-INT.CLIT	say-NONFUT.3SG	

'Let's move further to new lands.'

(94)	*eǯe*	*nulge-gelle*
	OK	nomadize-IMP.2PL

'All right, let's get going'

(95)	*orar-ba*	*iintu-li*	*göön-ni*	*erek*	*asi*
	reindeer-ACC	gather-IMP.2SG	say-NONFUT.3SG	this	woman

'"Go gather our reindeer", she said.'

(96)	*Oj-i*	*haka-ǯa-l-la-n*		
	cloth-REF.POS.SG	pack-PROG-INCH-NONFUT-3SG		
	abdu-i,	*orar-ba*	*ǯaw-li*	
	belonging-REF.POS.SG	reindeer-ACC	catch-IMP.2SG	
	göön-ni,	*erek*	*Metele-i*	*oro-r-bi*
	say-NONFUT.3SG	this	M.-REF.POS.SG	reindeer-PL-REF.POS.SG
	iintu-na-wkan-ni			
	gather-DIRECT-CAUS-NONFUT.3SG			

'The wife packed the clothes and their belongings and sent Metele to gather the reindeer.'

(97)	*Oro-m*	*iintu-n*	*iaami*	*aj-ǯi-n*
	reindeer-ACC	gather-NONFUT.3SG	why	help-FUT-3SG

ör	*göön-ǯi-ǯek-i*	*hieŋke-le*	*tööre-m*
previously	say-PROG-Nloc-REF.POS.SG	ground-LOC	speech-ACC

e-de-j	*tikkön*
not_do-PURP.CONV-REF.POS.SG	drop.NEG.CONV

or-mi	*ǯaw-ra-n*	*iaa-n'*
reindeer-REF.POS.SG	catch-NONFUT.3SG	what_do-NONFUT.3SG

'So he herded in the reindeer. What else could he do, if he had promised to pay heed to her words.'

(98)

erek	*Metele*	*uučak-ka-n*	*karaw-amkar*
this	Metele	saddle reindeer-DES-3SG	skewbold-AUGM

atakiča-m	*böö-n*
old reindeer-ACC	give-NONFUT.3SG

'The wife saddled an old skewbald reindeer for him.'

(99)

erek	*Metele*	*asi-ŋ-i*	*amarda-du-n,*	*ǯe*
this	Metele	woman-AL.POS-REF.POS.SG	behind-DAT-3SG	Well

nulge-de-j	*ineŋi-nǯa-ka-m*
nomadize-PURP.CONV-REF.POS.SG	day-AUGM-DIM-ACC

koŋdas	*tike-tne-n*	*erek*	*uučak-tu*
throughout	fall-MULT-NONFUT.3SG	this	saddle reindeer-DAT

badu-ssi-mi	*turku-t-mi*
ride-CONAT-COND.CONV	not able-STAT-COND.CONV

'Metele riding after his wife kept falling down, he couldn't ride properly.'

(100)

asi-ŋa-n	*uučak-wa-n*	*ǯaw-riǯii*
woman-AL.POS-3SG	saddle reindeer-ACC-3SG	catch-ANT.CONV

uu-wkan-iǯii	*badu-ssi-raka-n*
mount-CAUS-ANT.CONV	ride-CONAT-COND.DS.CONV-3SG

ǯegen-teki *hetke-weeč-te-n*
side-DIR fall-HABIT-NONFUT-3SG

oonki-da *tik-weeč-te-n*
on the back-CONJ.CLIT fall-HABIT-NONFUT-3SG

'The wife helped him to get in the saddle again, he rode a little bit and then fell down on his back again.'

(101) *erek* *Metele* *asi-ŋ-i* *amarda-du-n-ǯe*
this Metele woman-AL.POS-REF.POS.SG behind-DAT-3SG-CL

nulge-de-j *ineŋi-nǯe-ke-m*
nomadize-PURP.CONV-REF.POS.SG day-AUGM-DIM-ACC

koŋdas *tike-tne-n*
throughout fall-MULT-NONFUT.3SG

'Metele riding behind his wife kept falling down.'

(102) *erek* *uučak-tu* *badu-ssi-mi*
this saddle reindeer-DAT ride-CONAT-COND.CONV

turku-t-mi *asi-ŋa-n*
not able-STAT-COND.CONV woman-AL.POS-3SG

uučak-wa-n *ǯaw-riǯi*
saddle reindeer-ACC-3SG catch-ANT.CONV.SG

uu-wkan-iǯii *badu-ssi-raka-n*
mount-CAUS-ANT.CONV ride-CONAT-COND.DS.CONV-3SG

ǯegen-teki *hetke-weeč-te-n*
left side-DIR fall-HABIT-NONFUT-3SG

oonki-da *tik-weeč-te-n*
on the back-CONJ.CLIT fall-HABIT-NONFUT-3SG

'Metele was unable to ride, when his wife helped him mount again, he still kept falling down, now to the left side, now backwards.'

(103) *Deñee-gu* *Metele-ken*
Den'ee-INT.CLIT Metele-DIM

Deñee-gu *olbañ-kan-si*
Den'ee-INT.CLIT unskillful-DIM-CLIT

Deñee-gu *oo-waač-ta-n*
Den'ee-INT.CLIT become-HABIT-NONFUT-3SG

Deñee-gu *ñoog-i*
Den'ee-INT.CLIT bridle-REF.POS.SG

Deñee-gu *aji-č*
Den'ee-INT.CLIT good-INSTR

Deñee-gu *ǯawu-t-li-la*
Den'ee-INT.CLIT catch-STAT-IMP.2SG-CLIT

'-*Deñee-gu*, Metele, how unskilful you are! Hold fast the bridle, how long are you going to fall down? - the wife said.'

(104) *Deñee-gu* *iaak-man-takan*
Den'ee-INT.CLIT what-CLIT-REST.CLIT

Deñee-gu *tike-tne-nni*
Den'ee-INT.CLIT fall-MULT-NONFUT.2SG

Deñee-gu *göö-niken*
Den'ee-INT.CLIT say-SIM.CONV

'How long are you going to fall down? - the wife said.'

(105) *erek* *ǯe* *Metele-ñǯe* *ineŋi-w* *kooŋdas*
this Well Metele-AUGM day-ACC throughout

hil-niken *ǯe* *nuulge-n*
suffer-SIM.CONV Well nomidize-NONFUT.3SG

'So Metele suffered all day long as they nomadized.'

(106) *ǯe* *örin-iǯur* *ǯe* *erek* *beji-l*
Well make a camp-ANT.CONV.PL.PL Well this man-PL

ǯuu-ga-wur *iaa-ga-wur*
house-DES-REF.POS.PL what-DES-REF.POS.PL

ǯuuŋ-niǯur *ǯe* *aanŋa-ra*
pitch a jurta-ANT.CONV.PL Well stay_overnight-NONFUT.3PL

'Once they stopped, built a nomad tent, overnighted there.'

(107) *Deñee-gu* *Metele-ken*
Den'ee-INT.CLIT Metele-DIM

Deñee-gu *hii-ŋene*
Den'ee-INT.CLIT you-CLIT

Deñee-gu *buju-m-de*
Den'ee-INT.CLIT wild reindeer-ACC-CONJ.CLIT

Deñee-gu *buju-ǯ-li-le*
Den'ee-INT.CLIT go hunt-PROG-IMP.2SG-CLIT

Deñee-gu *oron*
Den'ee-INT.CLIT reindeer

Deñee-gu *e-dle-n*
Den'ee-INT.CLIT not_do-NEG.FIN-3SG

Deñee-gu *hinŋa-sa-mkan*
Den'ee-INT.CLIT flee-MOM-CAUS.NEG.CONV

'-*Deñee-gu*, Metele, what if you go hunt wild reindeer till we scare them away.'

(108) *Deñee-gu* *oron-ni*
Den'ee-INT.CLIT reindeer-3SG

Deñee-gu *uret-ken-ni*
Den'ee-INT.CLIT similar-DIM-3SG

Deñee-gu *užа-lkan*
Den'ee-INT.CLIT track-PROP

'The tracks of wild reindeer are like the traces of tame reindeer.'

(109) *Deñee-gu* *mut* *oron-ti*
Den'ee-INT.CLIT we reindeer-1PL.INC.POS

Deñee-gu *uremeken*
Den'ee-INT.CLIT similar

Deñee-gu *bujun-de-gu*
Den'ee-INT.CLIT wild reindeer-CONJ.CLIT-INT.CLIT

Deñee-gu *gerbe-ken*
Den'ee-INT.CLIT name-DIM

Deñee-gu *bi-gre-re-n*
Den'ee-INT.CLIT be-PAST.ITER-NONFUT-3SG

Deñee-gu *oron-duku-n*
Den'ee-INT.CLIT reindeer-ABL-3SG

Deñee-gu *egže-dme-ken*
Den'ee-INT.CLIT big-COMP-DIM

'They look like traces of our tame reindeer, are just bigger.'

(110) *Deñee-gu* *oron-duku-n*
Den'ee-INT.CLIT reindeer-ABL-3SG

Deñee-gu *egže-dme-ken*
Den'ee-INT.CLIT big-COMP-DIM

Deñee-gu *buju-se-l-mi*
Den'ee-INT.CLIT go hunt-ITER-INCH-COND.CONV

Deñee-gu *iče-žeen-ni*
Den'ee-INT.CLIT see-DUR-3SG

Deñee-gu *Metele-ken* *göön-ni*
Den'ee-INT.CLIT Metele-DIM say-NONFUT.3SG

'When you go hunting, you'll see it yourself.'

(111) *erek* *tačin* *göön-če-le-n* *Metele*
this so say-PERF.PART-LOC-3SG Metele

uučaka-nǯa-j *karaw* *uučak-wa-n*
saddle reindeer-AUGM-REF.POS.SG gray saddle reindeer-ACC-3SG

tara-ŋ-i *asi-ŋa-n* *ǯaw-ra-n*
that-AL.POS-REF.POS.SG woman-AL.POS-3SG catch-NONFUT.3PL-3SG

asi-ŋa-n *nam-na-n* *emgu-me-n*
woman-AL.POS-3SG attach a saddle-NONFUT-3SG saddle-ACC-3SG

'When the wife said so, she caught his skewbald reindeer and saddled it for Metele.'

(112) *ñur-ga-n* *iaa-ga-n* *nöki-ten* *iaa-ga-n* *erek*
arrow-DES-3SG what-DES-3SG bow-3PL what-DES-3SG this

asi-ŋa-n *meen-duki-n* *böö-re-n*
woman-AL.POS-3SG self's-ABL-3SG give-NONFUT-3SG

eri-t *ǯoodan-ǯi* *hör-re*
this-INST thing-INSTR go-NONFUT.3PL

'She gave him the bow and arrows and he set out.'

(113) *ečin* *hoo-kan* *goru* *badu-riǯii* *gia* *okaat*
this_way very-DIM for_a_long_time ride-ANT.CONV other river

deren-gide-du-n *buju-r-be* *it-te-n*
river-head-LOCAT-DAT-3SG wild reindeer-PL-ACC see-NONFUT-3SG

'He rode for a long time until he saw wild reindeer near the upper waters of the river.'

(114)	*tara-ŋ-duk-i*	*ömen*	*buju-m*
	that-AL.POS-ABL-REF.POS.SG	one	wild reindeer-ACC

tikkön-ni	*nemke-riʒii*
let fall.NEG.CONV-NONFUT.3SG	shoot-ANT.CONV

'He shot one of them.'

(115)	*erek*	*Metele*	*bi-mi*	*ere-ŋ-i*
	this	Metele	be-COND.CONV	this-AL.POS-REF.POS.SG

higi-ʒe-l-le-n
skin-PROG-INCH-NONFUT-3SG

'Then Metele began to skin it in the way he had skinned a hare.'

(116)	*Metele*	*koobak-kačin*	*töke-hen-de-j*
	Metele	hare-EQUAT	turn over-MOM-PURP.CONV-REF.POS.SG

ñek-reke-n	*ani*[6]	*koobak-tuk*	*egʒen*
do-COND.DS.CONV-3SG	but	hare-ABL	big

oo-d-ni
become-NONFUT-3SG

'But the reindeer is much bigger.'

(117)	*hee-mke-t-tiʒii*	*turku-riʒii*
	try-CAUS-STAT-ANT.CONV	not able-ANT.CONV

hige-ʒe-l-le-n
skin-PROG-INCH-NONFUT-3SG

'Metele tried in vain to turn it over.'

(118)	*Metele*	*ilan*	*dolbani-lka-m*	*ineŋi-w*	*kooŋdas*
	Metele	three	night-PROP-ACC	day-ACC	throughout

6 < Jak. *аны* 'now, but'.

beri-p-te-n
lose-MED-NONFUT-3SG

erek	*haakač*	*hige-ssi-ǯ-weeč-te-n*
this	"as a whole"	skin-CONAT-PROG-HABIT-NONFUT-3SG

humeldi-nuke-niken
roll-INTENS-SIM.CONV

'So Metele is away for three days trying to skin the reindeer as a hare, turning the reindeer over, trying to remove its skin as a whole (without cutting).'

(119)	*tačin*	*bi-d-deke-n*	*erek*
	so	be-PROG-COND.DS.CONV-3SG	this

asi-ŋa-n	*em-ne-n*
woman-AL.POS-3SG	come-NONFUT-3SG

'Finally his wife came.'

(120)	*Deñee-gu*	*Metele-ken*
	Den'ee-INT.CLIT	Metele-DIM
	Deñee-gu	*edi-ñ-ke-mu*
	Den'ee-INT.CLIT	husband-DIM-1SG.POS
	Deñee-gu	*olbañ-kan-si*
	Den'ee-INT.CLIT	unskillful-DIM-2SG.POS

'-*Deñee-gu*, Metele, how unskilful you are!'

(121)	*Deñee-gu*	*irek*	*ösi*
	Den'ee-INT.CLIT	which	previously
	Deñee-gu	*buju-m-a*	
	Den'ee-INT.CLIT	wild reindeer-ACC-EPENTH	
	Deñee-gu	*tačimar-a*	
	Den'ee-INT.CLIT	this_way-EPENTH	

Deñee-gu	*higri-ke-me-n*
Den'ee-INT.CLIT	skin-DIM-ACC-3SG

Deñee-gu	*haa-ri-s-a*	*göön-ni*
Den'ee-INT.CLIT	know-PAST-2SG-EPENTH	say-NONFUT.3SG

'"Where have you seen that reindeer is skinned in such a way?" she said.'

(122)

tarak	*tačin*	*göö-niken*	*asi-ŋa-n*	*amar-gič*
that	so	say-SIM.CONV	woman-AL.POS-3SG	behind-ELAT

em-niǯii	*erek*	*buju-ŋ-če-me-n*
come-ANT.CONV	this	wild reindeer-AL.POS-PERF.PART-ACC-3SG

hinma-ja-č	*hige-sn-e-n*
quick-ASSOC-INSTR	skin-MOM-NONFUT-3SG

'She came, flayed the reindeer quickly cutting its skin.'

(123)

ǯuu-la-wur	*merek-re-n*
house-LOC-REF.POS.PL	return-NONFUT-3SG

'Then they returned to their jurta.'

(124)

hii	*ook-ta*	*tačimar*	*e-ǯi*
you	when-CONJ.CLIT	this_way	not_do-NEG.IMP.2SG

higre-r	*göön-ni*
skin-NEG.CONV	say-NONFUT.3SG

buju-m	*e-ǯi*	*tačimar*
wild reindeer-ACC	not_do-NEG.IMP.2SG	this_way

higi-weeč-te
skin-HABIT-NEG.CONV

'"Don't skin reindeer in such a way", she taught him.'

(125)

erek	*Metele*	*tačimar*	*ereger*	*buju-s-niken*
this	Metele	this_way	always	go hunt-ITER-SIM.CONV

bi-weeči-d-de-n	*buju-m*	*iaa-w*
be-HABIT-PROG-NONFUT-3SG	wild reindeer-ACC	what-ACC

maa-ri	*oo-d-ni*	*tač-ta-n*
kill-NONFUT.PART	become-NONFUT-3SG	get used-NONFUT-3SG

'So Metele learned to hunt reindeer.'

(126)

erek	*nulge-n-niken*	*nulge-n-niken*
this	nomadize-ITER-SIM.CONV	nomadize-ITER-SIM.CONV

bi-ǯ-weeč-te
be-PROG-HABIT-NONFUT.3PL

'So they lived, from time to time nomadizing further.'

(127)

ömneken	*nuulge-riǯii*	*örin-iǯii*
once	nomidize-ANT.CONV	make a camp-ANT.CONV

ñaan-da	*buju-n*
again-CONJ.CLIT	go hunt-NONFUT.3SG

'Once they moved again to a new place and Metele went hunting.'

(128)

erek	*Metele*	*buju-riǯii*
this	Metele	go hunt-ANT.CONV

eme-rge-d-deke-n	*ǯuukčami*	*oo-d-ni*
so-RETR-PROG-COND.DS.CONV-3SG	old camp	become-NONFUT-3SG

ook-kal	*öterep*	*ǯuukčami*	*ureči-n*
when-NONREF.CLIT	old time	old camp	similar-3SG

'When he was going back, he saw rests of a nomad camp.'

(129)

ere-w	*ǯuukčami-l-ba*	*eŋen-ǯen-eke-n*
this-ACC	old camp-PL-ACC	peep-DUR-COND.DS.CONV-3SG

bi-weeči-d-deke-n	*i-le-gel*
be-HABIT-PROG-COND.DS.CONV-3SG	which-LOC-INDEF.CLIT

kuŋa	*hoŋa-n-ni*	*ii-s-ni*
child	cry-NMZR-3SG	sound-NONFUT-3SG

'When he was examining it, he heard a child crying.'

(130)

ere-ŋ-če-mi	*gelet-tiǯii*
this-AL.POS-DIM-REF.POS.SG	look for-ANT.CONV

bak-ra-n	*ömen*	*ǯuukča-n*	*čooŋala-n*
find-NONFUT-3SG	one	old camp-3SG	"kitchen"-3SG

herde-du-n	*hegte-č*	*dasa-p-ča*
under-DAT-3SG	pine-branch(es)-INSTR	cover-MED-PERF.PART

'Looking around, he found a child covered with pine-branches in women's part of the abondoned jurta.'

(131)

ere-w	*kuŋa-w*	*ga-riǯii*
this-ACC	child-ACC	take-ANT.CONV

ǯuu-la-n	*ǯe*	*höru-n*
house-LOC-3SG	Well	bring-NONFUT.3SG

ögn-iǯii	*hin-niǯii*
bear under one's arm-ANT.CONV	thrust-ANT.CONV

'He took that child under his arm and brought it home.'

(132)

iaak-ta	*erek*	*kuŋa-w*	*emen-če*
what-CONJ.CLIT	this	child-ACC	leave-PERF.PA

göö-niken	*ič-teke-n*
say-SIM.CONV	see-COND.DS.CONV-3SG

tara-ŋa-n	*ñari-ka-kan*	*kuŋa*
that-AL.POS-3SG	man-DIM-DIM	child

'"Someone has left the child", he explained to his wife. They looked at the child - the child turned out to be a boy.'

(133) *Gerijen-gerijen* *asi-jan* *Ömček-ken*
Gerijen-gerijen woman-CLIT Omchek-DIM

Gerijen-gerijen *bii-kene* *iaak-a*
Gerijen-gerijen I-DIM what-EPENTH

Gerijen-gerijen *ñari* *hut-ke-wer*
Gerijen-gerijen man child-DES-REF.POS.PL

Gerijen-gerijen *baka-ʒaañ-na-m*
Gerijen-gerijen find-DUR-NONFUT-ACC

'-*Gerijen-gerijen*, my wife Omchek, I've found a child - a boy.'

(134) *Gerijen-gerijen* *ʒuukčami-du* *emen-če-le-n*
Gerijen-gerijen old camp-DAT leave-PERF.PART-LOC-3SG

Gerijen-gerijen *čooŋal-kan-dur*
Gerijen-gerijen "kitchen"-DIM-DAT:REF.POS.PL

Gerijen-gerijen *hegte-ken-ʒur*
Gerijen-gerijen pine-branch(es)-DIM-INSTR:REF.POS.PL

dasa-ʒaañ-ča-l
cover-DUR-PERF.PART-PL

Gerijen-gerijen *göön-ni*
Gerijen-gerijen say-NONFUT.3SG

'"He was covered with pine-branches and left in women's part ("kitchen") of an abondoned jurta", he said.'

(135) *ʒuukčami* *ariŋka-wa-n* *hii* *iaa-ga-j*
old camp devil-ACC-3SG you what-DES-REF.POS.SG

emu-nni *iaa-ri* *kuŋa*
bring-NONFUT.2SG what_do-NONFUT.PART child

iin-ʒi-n *kuŋa-da* *bi-če* *bi-mi*
survive-FUT-3SG child-CONJ.CLIT be-PERF.PART be-COND.CONV

'"Why have you brought the devil-child from the old nomad camp?"'

(136)

iaa-da-j	*emu-nni*	*tiek-mede*
what_do-PURP.CONV-REF.POS.SG	bring-NONFUT.2SG	now-CLIT

maa-li	*göön-ni*
kill-IMP.2SG	say-NONFUT.3SG

'"If it were a human child, it wouldn't survive, go and kill him immediately", the wife says.'

(137)

Gerijen-gerijen	*gužeje-gu*
Gerijen-gerijen	poor-INT.CLIT

Gerijen-gerijen	*iaa-ga-j*	*maa-žaan-ži-m*
Gerijen-gerijen	what-DES-REF.POS.SG	kill-DUR-INSTR-1SG

Gerijen-gerijen	*göö-niken*
Gerijen-gerijen	say-SIM.CONV

'"-*Gerijen-gerijen,* it's a pity for him, why should I kill him?" Metele says.'

(138)

erek	*any*[7]	*erek*	*asi-ŋ-i*
this	well	this	woman-AL.POS-REF.POS.SG

hiačta-mal-la-n-da	*ñaan-da*
whip-ACCEL-NONFUT-3SG-CONJ.CLIT	again-CONJ.CLIT

'He began to beat his wife.'

(139)

erek-že	*erek*	*Ömček*	*bi-mi*	*žöör*	*kuŋa-w*
this-well	this	Omchek	be-COND.CONV	two	child-ACC

ökut-niken-že	*bi-s-ni*
nurse-SIM.CONV-Well	be-NONFUT-3SG

'So Omchek had to suckle two children.'

---

7 < Jak. *аны* 'now, but'. Corrected by DM *to ñaan 'again'*.

(140) *Čimčep-te* *egǯel-le-n*
Chimchep-CONJ.CLIT grow up-NONFUT-3SG
'Her daughter Chimchep grew up.'

(141) *erek* *kuŋa-ŋ-i* *hoŋ-ni-n*
this child-AL.POS-REF.POS.SG cry-PAST-3SG

aji *ǯaa-l-bi* *ǯööri-ke-me-ten*
good relative-PL-REF.POS.SG two.EXHAUST-DIM-ACC-3PL

neeji-weet-te-n
scold-HABIT-NONFUT-3SG

'When the boy was crying Metele scolds his wife and daughter.'

(142) *eñ-me-n-de* *iaa-wa-n-da*
mother-ACC-3SG-CONJ.CLIT what-ACC-3SG-CONJ.CLIT

Čimčep-i-da *hiatta-waat-ta-n*
Chimchep-REF.POS.SG-CONJ.CLIT whip-HABIT-NONFUT-3SG

erek *hut-i* *ñari* *hut-i*
this child-REF.POS.SG man child-REF.POS.SG

mulaa-mi
feel sorry-COND.CONV

'Metele beats his wife and his daughter Chimchep, feeling sorry for the child.'

(143) *erek* *kuŋa-l* *isu-r* *tarpač-ta*
this child-PL grow up-NONFUT.3PL anyway-CONJ.CLIT

egǯe-r *oo-r*
big-PL become-NONFUT.3PL

'The time passes, the children grow up'.

(144) *asačkan* *hunaǯi-n-da* *egǯen*
girl daughter-3SG-CONJ.CLIT big

erek-kene	*ǯuukčami*	*ariŋka-n*	*any*	*e-ti*
this-DIM	old camp	devil-3SG	well	not_do-NONFUT.PART

isu-r	*bi-weeč-te-n*
grow up-NEG.CONV	be-HABIT-NONFUT-3SG

'That is, his daughter is growing up, but the devil-child doesn't grow.'

(145)

Čimčep	*egǯel-le-n*
Chimchep	grow up-NONFUT-3SG

here-če-ŋ-ge-j
embroider-PERF.PART-AL.POS-DES-REF.POS.SG

iaa-ga-j	*here-ǯ-weeč-te-n*
what-DES-REF.POS.SG	embroider-PROG-HABIT-NONFUT-3SG

'Meanwhile his daughter Chimchep learned to do needlework.'

(146)

erek	*ewi-keči-ǯe-mnin*	*ire-ŋ-ge-i*
this	play-DIST-PROG-CONSEC.CONV	which-AL.POS-DES-REF.POS.SG

tara-ŋ-ga-j	*oo-č-waat-ta-n*
that-AL.POS-DES-REF.POS.SG	make-STAT-HABIT-NONFUT-3SG

meen	*oj-ga-j*	*hiŋan-ni*
self's	cloth-DES-REF.POS.SG	embroider-NONFUT.3SG

'As (his daughter) was playing, she learned needlework, made her clothes herself.'

(147)

erek	*ǯuukčami-ŋan*	*ariŋka-n*	*bi-mi*
this	old camp-CLIT	devil-3SG	be-COND.CONV

e-ti	*isu-r*	*erek*	*omolgon*
not_do-NONFUT.PART	grow up-NEG.CONV	this	boy

baka-ǯaaka-n	*hute-n*
find-N.LOC-3SG	child-3SG

'And the devil-child doesn't grow at all.'

(148) *dolbani-nǯa-ka-m* *koŋdas* *hoŋ-mač-ta-n*
night-AUGM-DIM-ACC throughout cry-HABIT-NONFUT-3SG

ineŋi *koŋdas* *hukle-weeč-te-n*
day throughout sleep-HABIT-NONFUT-3SG

'All day long he sleeps, all night long he cries.'

(149) *erek* *eñ-mi-de* *e-ti*
this mother-REF.POS.SG-CONJ.CLIT not_do-NONFUT.PART

hukle-wken *am-mi-da*
sleep-CAUS:NEG.CONV father-REF.POS.SG-CONJ.CLIT

e-ti *hukle-wken* *dolba*
not_do-NONFUT.PART sleep-CAUS:NEG.CONV night

hoŋan-ǯi-j
sob-INSTR-REF.POS.SG

'He doesn't let the parents sleep.'

(150) *erek* *Metele* *haadun* *hut-u* *buten-ne-n-de*
this Metele some time child-1SG sick-NONFUT-3SG CONJ.CLIT

göö-weeč-te-n *haadun*
say-HABIT-NONFUT-3SG some time

asi-ŋ-i-da *göö-weeč-te-n*
woman-AL.POS-REF.POS.SG-CONJ.CLIT say-HABIT-NONFUT-3SG

aji-č *e-se-nni* *ulič-ta*
good-INSTR not_do-NONFUT-2SG feed-NEG.CONV

iaak-ta *göö-niken*
what-CONJ.CLIT say-SIM.CONV

'Metele doesn't know what the matter is: either the child is sick or his wife nurses him badly.'

(151) *tarič* *ömneken-ǯe* *buju-n*
then once-Well go hunt-NONFUT.3SG
'One day Metele went hunting.'

(152) *buju-riǯii* *eme-rge-ǯ-deke-n*
go hunt-ANT.CONV come-RETR-PROG-COND.DS.CONV-3SG

hiisečin *eme-rge-ǯ-deke-n* *ǯuu-n*
evening come-RETR-PROG-COND.DS.CONV-3SG house-3SG

halkamča-kan-du-n *toga-n* *nergi-n*
smoke-hole-DIM-DAT-3SG fire-3SG flame-3SG

ñöö-d-de-n
go out-PROG-NONFUT-3SG

'Returning in the evening, he saw a spark flying out of the smoke-hole of his jurta.'

(153) *ta-la* *araj* *töören* *ii-ǯ-de-n*
this-LOC suddenly voice sound-PROG-NONFUT-3SG

em-neke-n
come-COND.DS.CONV-3SG

'Coming nearer he hears a voice.'

(154) *Geril-geril-geril-gu* *ami-ja-w-da*
Geril-geril-geril-INT.CLIT father-ASSOC-ACC-CONJ.CLIT

ǯeb-ǯi-m-e
eat-FUT-1SG-EPENTH

Geril-geril-geril-gu *eni-je-w-de*
Geril-geril-geril-INT.CLIT mother-EPENTH-1SG-CONJ.CLIT

ǯeb-ǯi-m-e
eat-FUT-1SG-EPENTH

'-*Geril-geril-geril-gu*, I'll eat my father, I'll eat my mother.'

(155) *Geril-geril-geril-gu* *iaak-ta-gal* *udaj-kan-ni*
Geril-geril-geril-INT.CLIT what-CONJ.CLIT-INDEF.CLIT dawdle-DIM-3SG

Geril-geril-geril-gu *ami-ja* *Metele-ñǯe*
Geril-geril-geril-INT.CLIT father-ASSOC Metele-AUGM

Geril-geril-geril-gu *berke-če-nǯe-duki-j*
Geril-geril-geril-INT.CLIT linger-PERF.PART-AUGM-ABL-REF.POS.SG

Geril-geril-geril-gu *iaakman* *e-ti*
Geril-geril-geril-INT.CLIT how long not_do-NONFUT.PART

em-ne
come-NEG.CONV

Geril-geril-geril-gu *iaak-ta-gu* *udaj-kan-ni*
Geril-geril-geril-INT.CLIT what-CONJ.CLIT-INT.CLIT dawdle-DIM-3SG

'Why is he dawdling like that? I can't stand that sluggishness.'

(156) *Geril-geril-geril-gu* *eni-je-de*
Geril-geril-geril-INT.CLIT mother-EPENTH-CONJ.CLIT

gorol-ča-kan *ke* *e-te-n-gu*
move_away-PERF.PART-DIM CLIT not_do-FUT-3SG-INT.CLIT

bi-se-le
be-NONFUT-CLIT

Geril-geril-geril-gu *eki-je-de*
Geril-geril-geril-INT.CLIT elder sister-EPENTH-CONJ.CLIT

Čimčep-čen *gorol-ča-kan* *ke*
Chimchep-DIM move_away-PERF.PART-DIM CLIT

e-te-n-gu *bi-se*
not_do-FUT-3SG-INT.CLIT be-NONFUT

Geril-geril-geril-gu *göö-niken* *töören-ni*
Geril-geril-geril-INT.CLIT say-SIM.CONV voice-3SG

ii-s-ni	*ǯuu*	*doo-la-n*
sound-NONFUT-3SG	house	inside-LOC-3SG

'"My mother and sister are, sure, far away by now," a voice sounded.'

(157)

Geril-geril-geril-gu	*ami-ja-ka-m*	*ǯep-tiǯii*
Geril-geril-geril-INT.CLIT	father-EPENTH-DIM-ACC	eat-ANT.CONV

aj-makan-ǯa	*höče-ǯ-ǯi-m*
good-INTENS-INSTR	chase-PROG-FUT-1SG

Geril-geril-geril-gu	*i-le*	*töör-le*	*ŋen-ǯi-s*
Geril-geril-geril-INT.CLIT	which-LOC	earth-LOC	go-FUT-2PL

Geril-geril-geril-gu	*göön-ni*
Geril-geril-geril-INT.CLIT	say-NONFUT.3SG

'-*Geril-geril-geril-gu*, when I eat my father, I'll chase them too, they cannot escape from me, - the devil-child says.'

(158)

erek	*Metele*	*bi-mi*	*urke-i*	*aaŋa-n*
this	Metele	be-COND.CONV	door-REF.POS.SG	open-NONFUT.3SG

urke-li-j	*eŋen-ni*	*ǯaa*	*iaak*
door-PROL-REF.POS.SG	peep-NONFUT.3SG	child	what

oo-da-nni	*enin-si-de*	*i-le*
become-NONFUT-2SG	mother-2SG.POS-CONJ.CLIT	which-LOC

ŋen-ni-ten	*eken-si-de*	*i-le*
go-PAST-3PL	elder sister-2SG.POS-PURP.CONV	which-LOC

ŋen-ni-ten	*göö-niken*	*hut-tuki-j*
go-PAST-3PL	say-SIM.CONV	child-ABL-REF.POS.SG

ulgeme-me-ssi-l-le-n
inquire-VOL-CONAT-INCH-NONFUT-3SG

'Metele looked into the jurta. "My child, what's wrong with you? Where are your mother and sister?" he asks.'

(159) *erek hute-n iite-n egǯen kuñalda-gčin oo-ča*
this child-3SG teeth-3SG big fang-EQUAT become-PERF.PART

oosta-n egǯen elgelde-gčin oo-ča
nail-3SG big harpoon-hook-EQUAT become-PERF.PART

'[Looking closely Metele saw that] the child became very big, his teeth grew as big as fangs, his nails became as big as harpoon's hooks, his dishevelled hair reached down to the earth.'

(160) *ñuurite-ñǯe-n töör-li is-si arbaŋaja*[8]
hair-AUGM-3SG earth-PROL reach-NONFUT.PART dishevelled

tege-či-d-de-n tog-i
sit_down-STAT-PROG-NONFUT-3SG fire-REF.POS.SG

bi-mi halkamča-kan-du duru-če
be-COND.CONV smoke-hole-DIM-DAT make fire-PERF.PART

'The devil-child hade made a big fire; its flames reached the smoke-hole of the jurta.'

(161) *Geril-geril-geril-gu ama-ran Metele-ken*
Geril-geril-geril-INT.CLIT father-VOCAT Metele-DIM

Geril-geril-geril-gu hin-ke-m ke
Geril-geril-geril-INT.CLIT you-DIM-ACC CLIT

e-se-m alači-d-da-m
not_do-NONFUT-1SG wait-PROG-NONFUT-1SG

Geril-geril-geril-gu hanŋa-ji dulakan-du-n
Geril-geril-geril-INT.CLIT palm-REF.POS.SG middle-DAT-3SG

irge-če-ǯeku-s
raise-STAT-Nloc-2SG

Geril-geril-geril-gu ikeri-ke-me-s
Geril-geril-geril-INT.CLIT bone-DIM-ACC-2SG.POS

8 < Jak. арбаҕар 'dishevelled'. Corrected by DM to nawlaŋaja 'dishevelled'.

Geril-geril-geril-gu	*hökte-j*
Geril-geril-geril-INT.CLIT	guts-REF.POS.SG

mukču-kan-du-n
cecum-DIM-DAT-3SG

Geril-geril-geril-gu	*göli-ǯeen-ǯi-m*
Geril-geril-geril-INT.CLIT	sacrifice-DUR-FUT-1SG

Geril-geril-geril-gu	*göön-ni*
Geril-geril-geril-INT.CLIT	say-NONFUT.3SG

'-*Geril-geril-geril-gu*, my father Metele, I'm just waiting for you. I'll enjoy eating you, you, who nourished me in your bosom, I'll eat you with your bones and guts and all.'

(162)

ǯaa	*iaak*	*oo-da-nni*	*huč-teki-j*
child	what	become-NONFUT-2SG	child-DIR-REF.POS.SG

göö-ssi-n
say-CONAT-NONFUT.3SG

'"My child, what's wrong with you?" Metele asks once more.'

(163)

hute-n	*bi-mi*	*tačin*	*göö-mnin*	*deepki*
child-3SG	be-COND.CONV	so	say-CONSEC.CONV	meeting

tugul-či-n	*ǯeb-ǯi-m*	*göö-niken*
carge-STAT-NONFUT.3SG	eat-FUT-1SG	say-SIM.CONV

'And the devil-child saying "I'll eat you" charged at Metele.'

(164)

erek	*Metele*	*bi-mi*	*erek*	*omolga-čil*
this	Metele	be-COND.CONV	this	boy-COMIT

hulbere-l-le-n	*hötu-meči-l-le-n*
fight-INCH-NONFUT-3SG	chase-REC-INCH-NONFUT-3SG

'Metele started to fight with his son.'

(165)

omolgon	*bi-mi*	*gaadač*	*it-či-de*
boy	be-COND.CONV	ahead	teeth-INSTR-CONJ.CLIT

oosta-ǯii-da	*osi-nikan*
nail-INSTR.SG.REF.POS-CONJ.CLIT	scratch-SIM.CONV

ŋen-ne-n
go-NONFUT-3SG

'And the son bites him with his teeth and tears him with claws.'

(166)

Metele	*erek*	*enin-si-de*
Metele	this	mother-2SG.POS-CONJ.CLIT

eken-si-de	*i-le*	*hör-ri-ten*
elder sister-2SG.POS-CONJ.CLIT	which-LOC	go-PAST-3PL

'"Where are your mother and your sister?" Metele asks.'

(167)

Geril-geril-geril-gu	*eki-je-w-de*
Geril-geril-geril-INT.CLIT	elder sister-EPENTH-ACC-CONJ.CLIT

ǯeb-ǯi-m
eat-FUT-1SG

Geril-geril-geril-gu	*eni-je-w-de*
Geril-geril-geril-INT.CLIT	mother-EPENTH-ACC-CONJ.CLIT

ǯeb-ǯi-m
eat-FUT-1SG

Geril-geril-geril-gu	*hine-nǯe-w-kene*
Geril-geril-geril-INT.CLIT	you-AUGM-ACC-CLIT

mudak-ta-ku
finish-PURP.CONV-1SG.IRR

'-*Geril-geril-geril-gu*, I'll eat my mother, I'll eat my sister after I kill you, - the devil-child answers.'

(168) *Geril-geril-geril-gu* *göö-niken* *erek* *Metele-w*
Geril-geril-geril-INT.CLIT say-SIM.CONV this Metele-ACC

mud-nikan-da *iaa-nikan-da*
gnaw-SIM.CONV-CONJ.CLIT what_do-SIM.CONV-CONJ.CLIT

hulute-l-le-n
chase-INCH-NONFUT-3SG

'He chased Metele, biting and tearing him with his claws.'

(169) *ǯuu-w* *ereli* *ñoo-mač-ta-n*
house-ACC around flee-HABIT-NONFUT-3SG
'He chased Metele around the jurta.'

(170) *ñoo-mat-tiǯii* *this* *kusi-keči-ssi-riǯii-de*
flee-HABIT-ANT.CONV erek fight-DIST-CONAT-ANT.CONV-CONJ.CLIT

any *huč-tii* *dabda-n* *erek*
now child-DAT:REF.POS.SG loose-NONFUT.3SG this

okaata-ŋ-i *ejeki* *ñoon-ni* *gaadač*
river-AL.POS-REF.POS.SG downstream run-NONFUT.3SG ahead

erek *Metele* *bi-mi*
this Metele be-COND.CONV

'Metele realizing that he cannot overwhelm his son, flees the river downstream.'

(171) *erek* *omolgo-dmar* *bi-mi* *osi-nikan*
this boy-CONT be-COND.CONV scratch-SIM.CONV

höč-te-n *hepke-ssi-niken*
chase-NONFUT-3SG catch-CONAT-SIM.CONV

'And his son pursued him, trying to catch him with his claws.'

(172) *tačin* *hoo-ka-m* *goru* *hölu-meč-te-n*
so very-DIM-ACC for_a_long_time chase-REC-NONFUT-3SG

tačin hölu-meči-d-deke-n i-le-de
so chase-REC-PROG-COND.DS.CONV-3SG which-LOC-CONJ.CLIT

i-le töören ii-s-ni bej-ǯi-de
which-LOC voice sound-NONFUT-3SG man-INSTR-CONJ.CLIT

e-s-ni utal-la
not_do-NONFUT-3SG understand-NEG.CONV

'As Metele was fleeing, once he hears a voice from somewhere.'

(173) *Čipitoru-čipitoru ama-ran Metele-ken*
Chipitoru-cipitoru father-VOCAT Metele-DIM

Čipitoru-čipitoru guǯel-li-ke-s omalga-s
Chipitoru-cipitoru love-NONFUT.PART-DIM-2SG son-2SG

hin-ke-me oña-k(a)-ča-kan
you-DIM-ACC how-DIM-DIM-DIM

Čipitoru-čipitoru hin-ke-me oña-k(a)-ča-kan
Chipitoru-cipitoru you-DIM-ACC how-DIM-DIM-DIM

aji-ča baka-lda-n
good-INSTR find-SOC-NONFUT.3SG

Čipitoru-čipitoru iaa-da-j
Chipitoru-cipitoru what_do-PURP.CONV-REF.POS.SG

ñoo-ŋči-ǯeen-ni
flee-STAT-DUR-3SG

'-*Čipitoru-čipitoru*, father Metele, what a nice greeting from your dear son! Why are you running away like that?'

(174) *Čipitoru-čipitoru hoŋ-naka-n mut-u-gu*
Chipitoru-cipitoru cry-COND.DS.CONV-3SG we-ACC-INT.CLIT

hiatta-gra-n-ni
whip-PAST.ITER-ITER-NONFUT.3SG

‘When my mother and I were crying you were beating us.’

(175)

Čipitoru-čipitoru	*amta-li*	*akari-ǯii*[9]
Chipitoru-cipitoru	taste-IMP.2SG	fool-INSTR.SG.REF.POS

Čipitoru-čipitoru	*ǯuukčami-kan*	*ariŋka-wa-n*
Chipitoru-cipitoru	old camp-DIM	devil-ACC-3SG

Čipitoru-čipitoru	*hanŋa-ji*	*dulakan-du-n*
Chipitoru-cipitoru	palm-REF.POS.SG	middle-DAT-3SG

irge-ri-s
raise-PAST-2SG

Čipitoru-čipitoru	*enine-ken*	*Ömček-ke-m*
Chipitoru-cipitoru	mother-DIM	Omchek-DIM-ACC

öku-č-uke-ŋne-nni	*göö-niken*
nurse-STAT-CAUS-PAST.ITER-NONFUT.2SG	say-SIM.CONV

töören	*ii-s-ni*
voice	sound-NONFUT-3SG

‘-Now the day has come to pay for your foolishness. And you made my mother Omchek nurse the devil-child, whom you nourished at your bosom, - a voice sounds.’

(176)

eluken	*ǯuukčami-kan*	*ariŋka-n*	*ariŋka-san*	*hii-kene*
brother	old camp-DIM	devil-3SG	devil-2PL.POS	you-DIM

amŋa-ji	*tura-ǯaan-ni*	*ami-ja-wi*
mouth-REF.POS.SG	open-DUR-NONFUT.3SG	father-EPENTH-1SG

e-dle-s	*ǯebe-ǯ-de*
not_do-NEG.FIN-2SG	eat-PROG-NEG.CONV

eni-je-ke-m	*nooda-ǯ-da-ku*
mother-EPENTH-DIM-ACC	throw-PROG-PURP.CONV-1SG.IRR

9 < Jak. *акаары* ‘stupid, fool’.

amŋa-ñǯa-n	*tura-ǯ-li-la*	*göön-ni*
mouth-AUGM-3SG	open-PROG-IMP.2SG-CLIT	say-NONFUT.3SG

'"My brother-devil, open your mouth wide, before you'll eat the father, I throw you my mother first", Chimchep says.'

(177)

erek	*amŋa-i*	*tur-ra-n*	*erek*	*ǯuukčami*
this	mouth-REF.POS.SG	open-NONFUT-3SG	this	old camp

ariŋka-n	*Metele*	*omolgon*
devil-3SG	Metele	boy

amŋa-i	*tur-ri-ñun-ni*	*ömettu*
mouth-REF.POS.SG	open-NONFUT.PART-COMIT-3SG	together

erek	*iaak-kal*	*iiwden*	*kiŋke-nuken*
this	what-NONREF.CLIT	bow-string	ring-INTENS

ii-s-ni
sound-NONFUT-3SG

'As soon as the devil opened his mouth the sound of a bow-string rang.'

(178)

erek	*Metele*	*ere-w-de*	*e-s-ni*
this	Metele	this-ACC-CONJ.CLIT	not_do-NONFUT-3SG

esen	*e-s-ni-de*
take notice.NEG.CONV	not_do-NONFUT-3SG-CONJ.CLIT

kööje-t-te	*okaata-ŋ-i*
glance-STAT-NEG.CONV	CONV river-AL.POS-REF.POS.SG

ejeki	*gaadač*	*ñoon-ni*
downstream	ahead	run-NONFUT.3SG

'And Metele without even looking back keeps on running down the river.'

(179)

erek	*tut-ča-kan*	*tut-te-n*
this	run-PERF.PART-DIM	run-NONFUT-3SG

erek	*tut-te-n-de*	*señe-n*[10]
this	run-NONFUT-3SG-CONJ.CLIT	strong-3SG

ačča	*oo-ča*
not_exist	become-PERF.PART

bukatyn	*ŋisule-tne-weeč-te-n-de*
all the time	stumble-MULT-HABIT-NONFUT-3SG-CONJ.CLIT

iaa-waač-ta-n-da	*ŋun*	*ŋun-du-n*
what_do-HABIT-NONFUT-3SG-CONJ.CLIT	even	even-DAT-3SG

'He is running and running until exhausted to death, he began stumbling all the time on the level ground.'

(180)

erek	*ariŋka-ñun*	*ariŋka-ŋ-u-ñun*	*e-de-n*
this	devil-CLIT	devil-AL.POS-1SG-CLIT	not_do-PURP.CONV-3SG

bokn-a	*göö-niken*	*ñooŋ-či-n*
catch-NEG.CONV	say-SIM.CONV	flee-STAT-3SG

'"What if I get caught by the devil?" he thinks and flees ahead.'

(181)

tačin	*ŋene-d-deke-n*	*ǯulde-le-n*
so	go-PROG-COND.DS.CONV-3SG	ahead-LOC-3SG

oŋka-ča-kan	*oo-d-ni*
graze-DIM-DIM	become-NONFUT-3SG

ere-w	*oŋka-w*	*ielten-ni*
this-ACC	graze-ACC	pass-NONFUT.3SG

okaat-u	*barda-l-duli-n*	*oŋka-r*	*ora-r*
river-ACC	opposite side-PL-PROL-3SG	graze-NONFUT.3PL	reindeer-PL

'As he is fleeing, he sees a pasture in front of him, a reindeer graze on both sides of the river.'

10 < Jak *сэниэ* 'strength, energy'.

(182) *erek* *bej* *ŋen-ne-n* *okaat* *hööli-li-n*
this man go-NONFUT-3SG river side-PROL-3SG

dikeñ-ket-niken *ŋen-ne-n*
hide-DISTR-SIM.CONV go-NONFUT-3SG

'He's passed the pasture and wandered along the river, hiding here and there.'

(183) *ŋen-če-le-n* *öril-če-ken* *öriŋ-či-n*
go-PERF.PART-LOC-3SG camp-DIM-DIM make a camp-STAT-3SG
'Then he saw in front of him a nomad camp.'

(184) *kööje-t-teke-n* *hoo-kan* *hooja*
glance-STAT-COND.DS.CONV-3SG very-DIM many
'Looking closer he found out that the camp was very big.'

(185) *erek* *Metele* *bi-mi* *erek* *omalga-ǯii*
this Metele be-COND.CONV this son-INSTR.SG.REF.POS

ŋeele-l-če-ǯii *beje-č*
be afraid-INCH-PERF.PART-INSTR.SG.REF.POS man-INSTR

bekeč-či-n *ŋeel-li* *oo-d-ni*
all-INSTR-3SG be afraid-NONFUT.PART become-NONFUT-3SG

ečin *dikeŋ-či-niken* *em-ne-n*
this_way hide-STAT-SIM.CONV come-NONFUT-3SG

'Meanwhile Metele scared by his devil-son grew scary, keeps hiding all the time.'

(186) *erek* *tarič* *ǯugarma-kan* *oo-d-ni*
this then path-DIM become-NONFUT-3SG

tarak *ǯugarma-li* *möö-w* *möö-li-ŋke-ten*
that path-PROL water-ACC water-DIRECT.ITER-Nloc-3PL

'At some distance he saw a path to the watering-place.'

(187)

erek	*e-du*	*tige-č-te-n*
this	this-DAT	lie in ambush-STAT-NONFUT-3SG

tege-č-te-n
sit_down-STAT-NONFUT-3SG

'Metele hid in the ambush there.'

(188)

hiisele-d-deke-n	*ömen*	*asi-kan*
get dark-PROG-COND.DS.CONV-3SG	one	woman-DIM

em-ne-n
come-NONFUT-3SG

ačura-ñ-takan	*tetu-t-te-n*
rag-INSTR-REST.CLIT	wear-STAT-NONFUT-3SG

'When it grew darker, he sees a serving woman wearing the rags.'

(189)

ieeke	*iaalla-n*	*oo-ča*	*ojo-n*	*bekečen*
pot	coal-3SG	become-PERF.PART	cloth-3SG	all

'She was dressed in sooty rags.'

(190)

erek	*ieeke-čen-ǯi*	*möö-w*	*huku-sn-iǯii*
this	pot-DIM-INSTR	water-ACC	scoop-MOM-ANT.CONV

tö-te-d-deke-n	*erek*	*Metele*	*bi-mi*
step-STAT-PROG-COND.DS.CONV-3SG	this	Metele	be-COND.CONV

emkere-ŋ-i	*ojči-han-ǯid-daka-n*
bank-AL.POS-REF.POS.SG	climb-MOM-PROG-COND.DS.CONV-3SG

ieeke-če-me-n	*oǯus*	*taan-ni*
pot-DIM-ACC-3SG	over	pull-NONFUT.3SG

'As she scoops up with her pot water from the river and starts going back, Metele, hiding himself under the river bank, turns the pot over.'

(191)

Ieeke-čen-ni	*öŋkelbe-n*
pot-DIM-3SG	spill-NONFUT.3SG

'The pot turned over.'

(192)

Ieeke-čen	*öŋkelbe-če-le-n*	*ñaan-da*
pot-DIM	spill-PERF.PART-LOC-3SG	again-CONJ.CLIT

möö-w	*huku-sn-a-n*	*muču-riǯii*
water-ACC	scoop-MOM-NONFUT-3SG	return-ANT.CONV

'The serving woman went back to the watering-place, scooped up the water again.'

(193)

erek	*ñaan-da*	*ojči-n*
this	again-CONJ.CLIT	climb-NONFUT.3SG

erek	*Metele*	*ñaan-da*	*taan-ni*	*ieeke-če-me-n*
this	Metele	again-CONJ.CLIT	pull-NONFUT.3SG	pot-DIM-ACC-3SG

möö-ŋ-če-me-n	*ejdu*	*öŋke-wken-ni*
water-AL.POS-DIM-ACC-3SG	all	spill-CAUS-NONFUT.3SG

'But when she was climbing the bank, Metele turned the pot over once again, spilling all the water.'

(194)

Uñdalakaña-uñdalakaña	*ere-gu*	*ootla*	*er-kene*
Un'dalakan'a-un'dalakan'a	this-INT.CLIT	before	now-CLIT

ǯugarma-li
path-PROL

Uñdalakaña-uñdalakaña
Un'dalakan'a-un'dalakan'a

möö-ŋ-ge-j-de-gu
water-AL.POS-DES-REF.POS.SG-CONJ.CLIT-INT.CLIT

möö-li-d-gere-re-m
water-DIRECT.ITER-PROG-PAST.ITER-NONFUT-1SG

Uñdalakaña-uñdalakaña	*ečin*	*ook-ta-gu*
Un'dalakan'a-un'dalakan'a	this_way	when-CONJ.CLIT-INT.CLIT

e-niken-e-gu
not_do-SIM.CONV-EPENTH-INT.CLIT

Uñdalakaña-uñdalakaña	*e-s-ni-kene-gu*
Un'dalakan'a-un'dalakan'a	not_do-NONFUT-3SG-CLIT-INT.CLIT

horni-d-gara-ra
catch on-PROG-PAST.ITER-NEG.CONV

Uñdalakaña-uñdalakaña	*göön-ni*
Un'dalakan'a-un'dalakan'a	say-NONFUT.3SG

'"-*Uñdalakaña-uñdalakaña*, when I was going to the watering-place before the pot never turned over like that", she said.'

(195)

tačin	*göö-niken*	*ili-s-tan*
so	say-SIM.CONV	three-ORD.NUM-3PL

möö-ŋ-ge-j	*mööl-le-n*
water-AL.POS-DES-REF.POS.SG	scoop-NONFUT-3SG

'For the third time she went back for water.'

(196)

erek	*mööl-če-le-n*	*tara-ŋ-i-da*
this	scoop-PERF.PART-LOC-3SG	that-AL.POS-REF.POS.SG-CONJ.CLIT

tö-te-hen-ǯid-deke-n	*öŋke-n*
step-STAT-MOM-PROG-COND.DS.CONV-3SG	spill-NONFUT.3SG

'But when she was climbing back, Metele turned over the pot once again.'

(197)

erek	*utakan*	*tarpač-kan-da*
this	serving woman	anyway-DIM-CONJ.CLIT

emkere-ŋ-i	*heeje-du-n*
bank-AL.POS-REF.POS.SG	top-DAT-3SG

tege-ñde-riǯii	*hoŋan-ǯa-l-la-n*
sit_down-MOM-ANT.CONV	sob-PROG-INCH-NONFUT-3SG

'The serving woman collapsed on the ground (on the cliff) and burst into tears.'

(198) *Uñdalakaña-uñdalakaña* *öötel-tiitel*
Un'dalakan'a-un'dalakan'a ages ago-previously

buw-ja-dii *bi-ŋsi-ke-mi*
country-EPENTH-DAT:REF.POS be-SIM.PAST.CONV-DIM-REF.POS.SG

Uñdalakaña-uñdalakaña *bi-de-kene*
Un'da9lakan'a-un'dalakan'a I-CONJ.CLIT-CLIT

'-*Uñdalakaña-uñdalakaña*, ages ago I used to live so well in my own country.'

(199) *Kagan-ča-kan* *beje-mdes-kene* *bi-ǯ-gere-re-m*
Kagan-DIM-DIM man-SIMIL-DIM be-PROG-PAST.ITER-NONFUT-1SG

Uñdalakaña-uñdalakaña *Kagan-ča-kan*
Un'dalakan'a-un'dalakan'a Kagan-DIM-DIM

Uñdalakaña-uñdalakaña *öril-je-ke-mi*
Un'dalakan'a-un'dalakan'a camp-EPENTH-DIM-REF.POS.SG

utaka-ŋa-n *emu-če-duku-n*
serving woman-DES-3SG bring-PERF.PART-ABL-3SG

Uñdalakaña-uñdalakaña *iaak-ta* *bekečin*
Un'dalakan'a-un'dalakan'a what-CONJ.CLIT all

möje-ǯeeñ-met-te-n
humiliate-DUR-HABIT-NONFUT-3SG

'But Kagankan, the elder, brought me to his nomad camp as a captive and made me his servant. Anyone who feels like it, can humiliate me now.'

(200) *Uñdalakaña-uñdalakaña* *ieeke-če-mu*
Un'dalakan'a-un'dalakan'a pot-DIM-1SG.POS

iaa-kan-a-gu *öŋke-če-ǯeeñ-ne-n*
what-DIM-EPENTH-INT.CLIT spill-STAT-DUR-NONFUT-3SG

Uñdalakaña-uñdalakaña	*bej-ken-gu*	*bi-mi*
Un'dalakan'a-un'dalakan'a	man-DIM-INT.CLIT	be-COND.CONV

ila-d-li-la-gu
stand up-PROG-PROL-CLIT-INT.CLIT

'Who has turned over my pot? If you are a human being, show yourself.'

(201) *Kagankan-a*
Kagankan-EPENTH

Uñdalakaña-uñdalakaña	*čoorami-ǯii*	*em-niǯii*
Un'dalakan'a-un'dalakan'a	staff-INSTR.SG.REF.POS	come-ANT.CONV

Uñdalakaña-uñdalakaña
Un'dalakan'a-un'dalakan'a

miat-ka-mu-da-gu	*kaltaka-nna*
top of the head-DIM-1SG.POS-CONJ.CLIT-INT.CLIT	split-NEC.PART

oo-ǯaañ-na-n
become-DUR-NONFUT-3SG

'Otherwise Kagana will beat me with his staff so hard until my head splits.'

(202)

Uñdalakaña-uñdalakaña	*iaak-ta-gal-a*
Un'dalakan'a-un'dalakan'a	what-CONJ.CLIT-INDEF.CLIT-EPENTH

hilus-kan-ni
torture-DIM-3SG

Uñdalakaña-uñdalakaña	*tunŋan*	*ǯaannu*	*örile-ñǯe-ke-m*
Un'dalakan'a-un'dalakan'a	five	ten	camp-AUGM-DIM-ACC

Uñdalakaña-uñdalakaña	*öme-kke-ken*
Un'dalakan'a-un'dalakan'a	one-DIM-DIM

uli-či-ǯ-weet-te-m
feed-STAT-PROG-HABIT-NONFUT-1SG

Uñdalakaña-uñdalakaña *e-le* *iaak-a-gu*
Un'dalakan'a-un'dalakan'a this-LOC what-EPENTH-INT.CLIT

em-niǯii *kargis-ka-ma*[11] *ilu-ta-ǯaañ-na-n*
come-ANT.CONV trouble-DIM-ACC put-STAT-DUR-NONFUT-3SG

Uñdalakaña-uñdalakaña *göön-ni*
Un'dalakan'a-un'dalakan'a say-NONFUT.3SG

'-What a disaster! I on my own have to cook for five dozens families and now here I've got this trouble with the pot. Come out! she says.'

(203) *erek* *Metele* *tarakam-mak* *hekerkiŋ-či-n*
this Metele then-CLIT out-STAT-NONFUT.3SG

kubdeke-ŋ-duki-j *erek* *Metele* *göön-ni*
cave-AL.POS-ABL-REF.POS.SG this Metele say-NONFUT.3SG

e-le *iaak* *ureči-n* *beji-l* *bi-se*
this-LOC what similar-3SG man-PL be-NONFUT.3PL

'So Metele jumped out from the cave behind the cliff and said: "Who are your people?"'

(204) *er* *beji-l-ǯi* *ŋeel-mi*
now man-PL-INSTR be afraid-COND.CONV

dikeŋ-či-d-de-m
hide-STAT-PROG-NONFUT-1SG

'"I am afraid of everybody, that's why I'm hiding here."'

(205) *Uñdalakaña-uñdalakaña* *tawara-gu* *ieeke-čen-du-wu*
Un'dalakan'a-un'dalakan'a this-INT.CLIT pot-DIM-DAT-1SG

möö-ŋ-ge-wer *huku-sn-iǯii*
water-AL.POS-DES-REF.POS.PL scoop-MOM-ANT.CONV

---

11 *kargis* < Jak. *харгыс* 'obstacle, trouble'.

Uñdalakaña-uñdalakaña	*bi-ken*	*ǯuu-la-wur*
Un'dalakan'a-un'dalakan'a	I-DIM	house-LOC-REF.POS.PL

höre-ǯeeñ-ger-e
go-DUR-IMP.1PL-EPENTH

Uñdalakaña-uñdalakaña	*göön-ni*
Un'dalakan'a-un'dalakan'a	say-NONFUT.3SG

'-*Uñdalakaña-uñdalakaña*, scoop up water into my pot and let's go to my home, - she says.'

(206)

erek	*Metele*	*bi-mi*	*erek*	*utakan*
this	Metele	be-COND.CONV	this	serving woman

ieeke-če-me-n	*ga-riǯii*	*ta-du*
pot-DIM-ACC-3SG	take-ANT.CONV	that-DAT

möö-ŋ-ge-j	*mööl-liǯii*	*erek*
water-AL.POS-DES-REF.POS.SG	scoop-ANT.CONV	this

utakan	*ǯuu-la-n*	*ŋen-ne-n*
serving woman	house-LOC-3SG	go-NONFUT-3SG

'So Metele takes a pot, scoops up water and follows the serving woman to her house.'

(207)

erek	*asi*	*bi-mi*	*gudi*	*herget-či-n*
this	woman	be-COND.CONV	stomach	underneath-INSTR-3SG

ǯepleŋe-č-te-n	*ewte*	*aŋatkan-ǯi-n*
have as food-STAT-NONFUT-3SG	lungs	"orphan"-INSTR-3SG

ǯepleŋe-č-te-n
have as food-STAT-NONFUT-3SG

'The serving woman was usually given some left-overs to eat (like reindeer's stomach and lungs).'

(208)

erek	*beji-l*	*emen-deŋ-u-ten*	*ire-w*
this	man-PL	leave-PAST.PART-ACC-3PL	which-ACC

tara-w	*ǯeb-gere-če-l*
that-ACC	eat-PAST.ITER-PERF.PART-PL

'She fed Metele with the rests of her meal.'

(209)

erek	*Metele*	*ta-du*	*dikeŋ-či-n*
this	Metele	that-DAT	hide-STAT-NONFUT.3SG

'So Metele started to live there, hiding in her jurta.'

(210)

tačin	*hoo-ka-m*	*goru*	*dikeŋ-či-n*
so	very-DIM-ACC	for_a_long_time	hide-STAT-NONFUT.3SG

adi	*ineŋi-w*	*bi-deŋe-n*	*e-s-ni*
how many	day-ACC	be-PAST.PART-3SG	not_do-NONFUT-3SG

haa-w-ra
know-PASS-NEG.CONV

'He hid there for some time, how long - nobody knows.'

(211)

tačin	*dikeŋ-či-d-deke-n*
so	hide-STAT-PROG-COND.DS.CONV-3SG

ukčen-meči-d-di-wu-ten	*dolda-riǯii*	*ömen*
tell-REC-PROG-NONFUT.PART-ACC-3PL	hear-ANT.CONV	one

beltelke	*aman-dula-j*	*Kagana-la*	*tut-tiǯii*
servant	father-LOC-REF.POS.SG	Kagana-LOC	run-ANT.CONV

metu-n
warn-NONFUT.3SG

'Once when they were talking in the jurta, one of Kagana's servants heard them and run to Kagana to warn him about the stranger.'

(212)

Kagana	*bi-mi*	*tara-w*	*dolda-riǯii*	*erek*
Kagana	be-COND.CONV	that-ACC	hear-ANT.CONV	this

Metele-w	*hepken-iǯii*	*hepken-ni*	*erek*	*Metele-w*
Metele-ACC	catch-ANT.CONV	catch-3SG	this	Metele-ACC

‘As soon as Kagana heard it, he ordered to catch Metele.’

(213)

ir-gič	*em-ni-s*	*iaa-duk*	*eme-nni*
which-ELAT	come-PAST-2SG	what-ABL	come-NONFUT.2SG

göö-niken
say-SIM.CONV

‘“Who are you? What place have you come from?” he asks.’

(214)

erek	*Metele*	*oj-wa-n*	*tar-da*	*gudeku*
this	Metele	cloth-ACC-3SG	that-CONJ.CLIT	torn

oj-wa-n	*nuk-rižii*	*ñaan*
cloth-ACC-3SG	take off-ANT.CONV	again

ačura-ñ-takan	*tetu-n*
rag-INSTR-REST.CLIT	put on-NONFUT.3SG

‘He took off Metele’s torn clothes and dressed him as his servant, in sooty clothes made of an old covering (of the top) of the jurta.’

(215)

toobaŋa-ga-n	*böö-n*
axe-DES-3SG	give-NONFUT.3SG

že	*erek*	*Metele*	*dil-wa-n*	*togta-nikan*
Well	this	Metele	head-ACC-3SG	batter-SIM.CONV

moo-w	*moo-li-wči-n*
wood-ACC	wood-DIRECT.ITER-wait-NONFUT.3SG

‘He gave him an axe and battering Metele on the head, sent him to chop wood.’

(216)

erek	*Metele*	*eŋi*	*bej*	*bi-če*	*ureči-n*
this	Metele	strong	man	be-PERF.PART	similar-3SG

ninkat-u	*kubeči-č*	*emu-niken*	*moo-w*
dead tree-ACC	all-INSTR	bring-SIM.CONV	wood-ACC

moo-li-ǯ-weeč-te-n
wood-DIRECT.ITER-PROG-HABIT-NONFUT-3SG

'Metele turned out to be a strong man, pulled alone whole dried trees.'

(217) *tara-ŋ-i* *turku-t-teke-n*
that-AL.POS-REF.POS.SG not able-STAT-COND.DS.CONV-3SG

bi-mi *erek* *Kagana* *em-niken* *ere-w*
be-COND.CONV this Kagana come-SIM.CONV this-ACC

Metele-w *čoorami-čan-ǯii* *dil-wa-n*
Metele-ACC staff-DIM-INSTR.SG.REF.POS head-ACC-3SG

togta-waač-ta-n
batter-HABIT-NONFUT-3SG

'And when he was not quick enough, Kagana beats him on his head whis his staff.'

(218) *tačin* *bi-d-deke-ten* *Metele* *moo-ga-j*
so be-PROG-COND.DS.CONV-3PL Metele wood-DES-REF.POS.SG

ira-ssi-ǯaañ-naka-n *okaata-ŋ-ma-n*
drag-CONAT-DUR-COND.DS.CONV-3SG river-AL.POS-ACC-3SG

hol-gič *nuulge* *iču-n*
upstream-ELAT caravan appear-NONFUT.3SG

'So Metele lives there, cutting wood. Once he sees a reindeer caravan moving downstream.'

(219) *asi-ŋa-n* *eme-ǯeen-ni* *iču-n*
woman-AL.POS-3SG come-DUR-3SG appear-NONFUT.3SG
'Now his wife appeared.'

(220) *erek* *Metele* *tara-w* *it-tiǯii* *oŋka-la*
this Metele that-ACC see-ANT.CONV graze-LOC

ñoon-ni	*dikn-e-n*
run-NONFUT.3SG	hide-NONFUT-3SG

'As soon as Metele recognized her he runs towards the pasture and hides there.'

(221)	*erek*	*asi*	*bi-mi*	*awlan-dula*
	this	woman	be-COND.CONV	meadow-LOC

hie-mnin	*tööre-niken*	*em-ne-n*
appear-CONSEC.CONV	talk-SIM.CONV	come-NONFUT-3SG

'And his wife, approaching the forest meadow, began to sing.'

(222)	*Deñeegu*	*ama-ran*	
	Den'eegu	father-VOCAT	
	Deñeegu	*Kagana-čan*	
	Den'eegu	Kagana-DIM	
	Deñeegu	*bi-ŋen*	*iaaka*
	Den'eegu	I-CLIT	what
	Deñeegu	*berne-ke-mi*	
	Den'eegu	loss-DIM-REF.POS.SG	
	Deñeegu	*gele-te-ǯ-de-m hi-ken*	
	Den'eegu	look for-STAT-PROG-NONFUT-1SG	

'-*Deñee-gu*, father Kagankan, I'm looking for my husband who got lost.'

(223)	*Hi-ken*	*iaa-ri-s*
	you-DIM	what_do-PAST-2SG
	Deñeegu	*iče-d-di-s*
	Den'eegu	see-PROG-PAST-2SG
	Deñeegu	*uǯa-kan-ni*
	Den'eegu	track-DIM-3SG

Deñeegu	*er-je-ke-kle-t*
Den'eegu	this-EPENTH-DIM-DIR-LOC-INST

Deñeegu	*eme-ǯeeñ-ni-n*
Den'eegu	come-DUR-PAST-3SG

Deñeegu	*göö-niken*
Den'eegu	say-SIM.CONV

'-*Deñee-gu*, have you seen him by chance? His traces are leading here.'

(224)

erek	*Metele*	*kööje-č-teke-n*
this	Metele	glance-STAT-COND.DS.CONV-3SG

hunaǯa-n	*ñoog-ra-n*	*hunaǯa-n*	*amarda-la-n*
daughter-3SG	lead-NONFUT-3SG	daughter-3SG	behind-LOC-3SG

ömen	*bej*	*badu-n-ni*	*iču-n*
one	man	ride-NMZR-3SG	appear-NONFUT.3SG

tarak	*amarda-du-n*	*asi-ŋa-n*	*badu-ǯ-da-n*
that	behind-DAT-3SG	woman-AL.POS-3SG	ride-PROG-NONFUT-3SG

bebe-niken	*eme-ǯ-de-n*
nurse-SIM.CONV	come-PROG-NONFUT-3SG

'Metele looked closer and saw: his daughter is leading the caravan. Behind her rides a man, then his wife, holding a cradle.'

(225)

Deñeegu	*ama-ran*
Den'eegu	father-VOCAT

Deñeegu	*Kagana-čan*
Den'eegu	Kagana-DIM

Deñeegu	*em-če*	*bi-seke-n*
Den'eegu	come-PERF.PART	be-COND.DS.CONV-3SG

Deñeegu	*böö-rge-ǯ-li-le*
Den'eegu	give-RETR-PROG-IMP.2SG-CLIT

Deñeegu	*ič-če-s-de-ku*
Den'eegu	see-PERF.PART-2SG-CONJ.CLIT-CLIT

bi-gre-ǯi-n	*göön-ni*
be-PAST.ITER-FUT-3SG	say-NONFUT.3SG

'*-Deñee-gu*, father Kagankan, if my husband is by you, give me him back, you should have seen him.'

(226)

Deñeegu	*Metele-ken*
Den'eegu	Metele-DIM

Deñeegu	*em-če*	*bi-ǯi-n*
Den'eegu	come-PERF.PART	be-FUT-3SG

Deñeegu	*er-ken*	*hii-ken*
Den'eegu	this-DIM	you-DIM

Deñeegu	*oŋka-la-s-a*
Den'eegu	graze-LOC-2SG-EPENTH

Deñeegu	*is-siǯii*
Den'eegu	reach-ANT.CONV

Deñeegu	*uǯa-kan-ni*	*beri-p-te-n*
Den'eegu	track-DIM-3SG	lose-MED-NONFUT-3SG

'Metele must have been here, his traces disappear near your pasture.'

(227)

Iŋe-e	*ačej*	*ömen*	*bej*	*em-ne-n*
OK-EPENTH	daughter(VOC)	one	man	come-NONFUT-3SG

tarak	*eme*	*bi-če*	*bi-ǯi-n*	*göö-niken*	*erek*
that	so	be-PERF..PART	be-FUT-3SG	say-SIM.CONV	this

etiken	*bi-mi*	*öril-mi*	*beket-ke-me-n*
old man	be-COND.CONV	camp-REF.POS.SG	all-DIM-ACC-3SG

gelet-uken-ni
seek-CAUS-NONFUT.3SG

'-Yes, (my) daughter, one stranger had come, - answers Kagana. He sent his people to find Metele.'

(228)

Metele	*bi-mi*	*dikn-e-n*	*ñoon-ni*
Metele	be-COND.CONV	hide-NONFUT-3SG	run-NONFUT.3SG

oŋka-la
graze-LOC

erek	*Metele*	*ilan*	*ineŋi-lken*	*dolbani-wu*	*koŋdas*
this	Metele	three	day-PROPR	night-ACC	throughout

dikeŋ-či-n	*bugin*	*oŋka-du-n*
hide-STAT-NONFUT.3SG	in the forest	graze-DAT-3SG

'And Metele keeps hiding in the forest near the pasture. He spent there three days.'

(229)

Asi-ŋ-ǯi	*ŋeele-l-če-de*
woman-AL.POS-INSTR	be afraid-INCH-PERF.PART-CONJ.CLIT

bi-če	*bi-ǯi-n*
be-PERF.PART	be-FUT-3SG

'He must have been afraid of his wife.'

(230)

ǯe	*tačin*	*gelete-wči-riǯii*	*ǯe*
Well	so	seek-wait for-ANT.CONV	Well

bak-ča-la-tan	*bak-riǯur*	*emu-r*
find-PERF.PART-LOC-3PL	find-ANT.CONV.PL	bring-NONFUT.3PL

'Well, finally he was found and brought back to the camp.'

(231)

erek	*Kagana*	*Metele-du*	*oj-ga-n*	*meen*
this	Kagana	Metele-DAT	cloth-DES-3SG	self's

oj-i	*böö-re-n*
cloth-REF.POS.SG	give-NONFUT-3SG

'Kagana presented him his own dress.'

(232) *erek* *Metele* *Kagana* *oj-wa-n* *tet-teke-n*
this Metele Kagana cloth-ACC-3SG put on-COND.DS.CONV-3SG

bi-mi *ösen* *iečen-duli-n* *oo-d-ni*
be-COND.CONV sleeve elbow-PROL-3SG become-NONFUT-3SG

istan-ni *bujan-ni* *bi-mi* *henŋen-duli-n*
trousers-3SG cuff-3SG be-COND.CONV knee-PROL-3SG

oo-d-ni
become-NONFUT-3SG

'When Metele put that dress on, it turned out to be too short: the sleeves hardly reach his elbows, the trouser cuffs are to his knee.'

(233) *erek* *Kagana* *kučuken* *bi-če* *bi-ǯi-n*
this Kagana little be-PERF.PART be-FUT-3SG

ñiri-n-da *iaa-n-da* *iču-n*
back-3SG-CONJ.CLIT what-3SG-CONJ.CLIT appear-NONFUT.3SG

'Kagana was small, so (when Metele put on his clothes) the back is bare.'

(234) *tar-da* *bi-seke-n* *erek* *Metele*
that-CONJ.CLIT be-COND.DS.CONV-3SG this Metele

ñari *hute-lken* *oo-ča*
man child-PROPR become-PERF.PART

tara-ŋa-n *gerbe-n* *Helniken*
that-AL.POS-3SG name-3SG Helniken

'Meanwhile Metele's wife gave birth to a son. They called him Helniken.'

(235) *erek* *Metele* *bi-mi* *erek* *kuuntek-le*
this Metele be-COND.CONV this field-LOC

galani-wača-d-da-n *örilen* *mudan-du-n*
stroll-HABIT-PROG-NONFUT-3SG camp end-DAT-3SG

örin-ni
make a camp-NONFUT.3SG

'Metele used to stroll in the field, not far from Kagankan's nomad camp.'

(236)

asi-ŋa-n	*em-nižii*	*teeri-žeke-n*
woman-AL.POS-3SG	come-ANT.CONV	both side(s)-Nloc-3SG

žuu-w	*žuuŋ-na-n*
house-ACC	pitch a jurta-NONFUT-3SG

'His wife built a big jurta-tent.'

(237)

kutete-lken	*oo-ča*
brother-in-law-PROPR	become-PERF.PART

'And Metele became a son-in-law [of Kagankan].'

(238)

erek	*gor-ka-m*	*bi-s-ni*	*tačin*
this	long-DIM-ACC	be-NONFUT-3SG	so

bi-ž-weeč-te-n
be-PROG-HABIT-NONFUT-3SG

erek	*Metele*	*bi-mi*	*e-du*	*örilen-du*
this	Metele	be-COND.CONV	this-DAT	camp-DAT

ñaan	*noŋan*	*begen*	*oo-d-ni*
again	(s)he	chief	become-NONFUT-3SG

'Well, so they live, Metele became the chief of this camp.'

(239)

erek	*iaak-ta*	*bej*	*bi-s-ni*
this	what-CONJ.CLIT	man	be-NONFUT-3SG

e-s-ni	*haa-w-ra*
not_do-NONFUT-3SG	know-PASS-NEG.CONV

'Who were these (other) people is not known.'

(240) *ereger tačin bi-weeč-weeč-te-n hut-čen-ni*
tacin so be-HABIT-HABIT-NONFUT-3SG child-DIM-3SG

tarpač-ta mirke-weeče-l-le-n
then-CONJ.CLIT crawl-HABIT-INCH-NONFUT-3SG

girka-waač-ti oo-d-ni
walk-HABIT-NONFUT.PART become-NONFUT-3SG

'As his son is growing up, he first was crawling around then begins to go.'

(241) *tačin goru bi-se*
so for_a_long_time be-NONFUT.3PL
'So they live for a long time.'

(242) *erek ilan niermi bi-s-ni*
this three larch be-NONFUT-3SG
'Near the Kagana's nomad camp grow three big larches.'

(243) *ilan niermi-le iaak-ta ačča*
three larch-LOC what-CONJ.CLIT not_exist
'Still there are no weapons hanging on them.'

(244) *noŋan e-s-ni-de ulgemi-weeč-te*
(s)he not_do-NONFUT-3SG-CONJ.CLIT ask-HABIT-NEG.CONV

bi-ǯ-so-n-ñun-de
be-PROG-ATTEN-3SG-CLIT-CONJ.CLIT

'And Metele doesn't ask anything: "Let it be."'

(245) *tačin bi-ǯ-diǯii bi-ǯ-diǯii*
so be-PROG-ANT.CONV be-PROG-ANT.CONV

hut-čen-ni hurka-w iaa-w hurkat-ti
child-DIM-3SG loop-ACC what-ACC set loops-NONFUT.PART

oo-d-ni naŋ-u-da iaa-w-da
become-NONFUT-3SG trap-ACC-CONJ.CLIT what-ACC-CONJ.CLIT

am-ŋači-mi	*tul-weeč-te-n*
father-EQUAT-REF.POS.SG	set-HABIT-NONFUT-3SG

'Meanwhile his son has grown up, started to make loops and set traps, as his father does.'

(246)

tarič	*ömneken*	*hurka-la-n*	*bi-mi*	*koobaki-kkan*
then	once	loop-LOC-3SG	be-COND.CONV	hare-DIM

hor-ča
get caught-PERF.PART

'Once a little hare got caught in his loop.'

(247)

erek	*koobaki-ŋ-čan-ni*	*bi-mi*
this	hare-AL.POS-DIM-3SG	be-COND.CONV

mekuk-mi	*čiarŋan-nika-ča-kan*
rush about-COND.CONV	screech-SIM.CONV-DIM-DIM

mekuk-re-n
rush about-NONFUT-3SG

'The little hare is rushing about, screeching.'

(248)

tara-ŋ-ča-mi	*illal-liǯii*	*kuŋa-jakan*
that-AL.POS-DIM-REF.POS.SG	take pity-ANT.CONV	child-DIM

tiin-ni	*koobaka-ŋ-ča-mi*
set free-NONFUT.3SG	hare-AL.POS-DIM-REF.POS.SG

'The boy took pity for the hare and set it free.'

(249)

aman-dula-n	*em-niǯii*	*göön-ni*
father-LOC-3SG	come-ANT.CONV	say-NONFUT.3SG

'He came to his father and said.'

(250)

ama	*bi*	*e-te-m-ele*	*hurkat-ta*
father.VOC	I	not_do-FUT-1SG-CLIT	set loops-NEG.CONV

göön-ni
say-NONFUT.3SG

'"Daddy, I shall not set loops any more."'

(251)

kobaka-ŋ-kan-ti	*kuŋa-gčin*	*hoŋ-na-n*
hare-AL.POS-DIM-1PL	child-EQUAT	cry-NONFUT-3SG

göön-ni
say-NONFUT.3SG

tugöömi	*tiine-m*
that's why	set free-NONFUT.2SG

'"The little hare was crying as a baby. I've let it go".'

(252)

erek	*kuŋa*	*iaak*	*taajala-n*	*hurka-la*	*hor-ča-w*
this	child	what	fool-3SG	loop-LOC	get caught-PERF.PART-ACC

iaa-da-j	*tiine-nni?*
what_do-PURP.CONV-REF.POS.SG	set free-NONFUT.2SG

'Metele began to scold him: "How silly of you! Why set the quarry, you caught, free?"'

(253)

maariǯii	*emu-reke-s*	*iaaka*	*göö-niken*
kill-ANT.CONV	bring-COND.DS.CONV-2SG	what	say-SIM.CONV

erek	*hut-i*	*negi-t-te-n*	*erek*
this	child-REF.POS.SG	scold-STAT-NONFUT-3SG	this

kuŋa-jaka-čan	*em-neke-n*
child-DIM-DIM	come-COND.DS.CONV-3SG

'"You should've killed it and brought it here", he scolds the boy.'

(254)

tačin	*neji-w-riǯii*	*berke-m*	*oon-da*
so	scold-PASS-ANT.CONV	bow-trap-ACC	how-CONJ.CLIT

berke-m	*tul-le-n*	*am-mi*
bow-trap-ACC	set-NONFUT-3SG	father-REF.POS.SG

galani-wača-ŋka-du-n	*erek*	*kuŋa*	*bi-mi*
stroll-HABIT-Nloc-DAT-3SG	this	child	be-COND.CONV

'Then the boy took his (self-shooting) bow-trap and set it right on the track where his father used to stroll.'

(255)

erek	*Metele*	*iaa-w*	*iaa-ǯi-n*	*erek*
this	Metele	what-ACC	what_do-FUT-3SG	this

e-s-ni	*haa-r*	*Metele,*	*ia-w*
not_do-NONFUT-3SG	know-NEG.CONV	Metele	what-ACC

oo-ǯak-ka-n
make-Nloc-ACC-3SG

'And Metele hasn't the faintest idea about it.'

(256)

ömneken	*baǯikar*	*galani-waač-na-riǯii*	*Metele*
once	morning	stroll-HABIT-DIRECT-ANT.CONV	Metele

bi-mi	*hut-i*	*berken-dule-n*
be-COND.CONV	child-REF.POS.SG	bow-trap-LOC-3SG

hor-ra-n
get caught-NONFUT-3SG

erek	*berken-dule*	*hor-riǯii*
this	bow-trap-LOC	get caught-ANT.CONV

tege-nde-riǯii	*kuni-ǯa-l-la-n*
sit_down-MOM-ANT.CONV	shout-PROG-INCH-NONFUT-3SG

'Once, as he went strolling, he got caught in the trap he called.'

(257)

ǯa	*hii*	*iaami*	*bej*	*girka-ŋka-du-n*	*berke-m*
child	you	why	man	walk-Nloc-DAT-3SG	bow-trap-ACC

tul-li-s	*göön-ni*
set-PAST-2SG	say-NONFUT.3SG

bi	*erek*	*berken-dule*	*hor-ra-m*	*aj-na-li*
I	this	bow-trap-LOC	get caught-NONFUT-1SG	help-DIRECT-IMP.2SG

'"Sonny, why on earth have you set the bow-trap right on my path, come over and help me. I've got caught".'

(258) *erek* *kuŋa-jakan* *ǯuu-duk* *golaŋka-w*
this child-DIM house-ABL log-ACC

naŋti-sn-a-n-da *erek* *am-mi*
seize-MOM-NONFUT-3SG-CONJ.CLIT this father-REF.POS.SG

dil-wa-n *kampas* *golaŋka-č* *ieeč-te-n*
head-ACC-3SG in two log-INSTR hit-NONFUT-3SG

'But the boy seized a log and cracked the head of his father in two.'

(259) *aman-ni* *iaa-ǯi-n* *köke-ječ-te-n*
father-3SG what_do-FUT-3SG die-DURAT-NONFUT-3SG
'So, Metele died, what else.'

(260) *iaak-kal* *iaak* *huta-nukan-ni*
what-NONREF.CLIT what sparkle-INTENS-3SG

e-s-ni *kisan-na*
not_do-NONFUT-3SG notice-NEG.CONV

golaŋka-j *toga-n*
log-REF.POS.SG fire-3SG

huta-nukan-i-ǯi-n *gerbeč-te-n*
sparkle-INTENS-NONFUT.PART-INSTR-3SG consider-NONFUT-3SG

'When he died, a spark flashed. The boy didn't take any notice, thinking that the spark was from the log.'

(261) *erek* *am-mi* *bi-mi*
this father-REF.POS.SG be-COND.CONV

berke-lke-ke-ñ *ir-ra-n*
bow-trap-PROPR-DIM-INSTR drag-NONFUT-3SG

ǯuu-la-j
house-LOC-REF.POS.SG

'The boy brings his father together with the bow-trap back home.'

(262)	*eñe-e*	*erek*	*bi*	*am'a-w*
	mother_VOC-EPENTH	this	I	dad-ACC

ǯeb-de-wur	*hurka-riǯii*
eat-PURP.CONV-REF.POS.PL	catch with loop-ANT.CONV

emu-re-m	*hor-ča-la-n*	*göön-ni*
bring-NONFUT-1SG	get caught-PERF.PART-LOC-3SG	say-NONFUT.3SG

'"Mammy, here is the quarry I have caught in the trap, let's eat it".'

(263)	*erek*	*am-mi*	*iaa-da-i*
	this	father-REF.POS.SG	what_do-PURP.CONV-REF.POS.SG

maa-nni?	*irek*	*ösi*	*bej*	*am-mi*
kill-NONFUT.2SG	which	previously	man	father-REF.POS.SG

ǯep-ti-we-n	*it-ti-s*	*am-mi*
eat-NONFUT.PART-ACC-3SG	see-PAST-2SG	father-REF.POS.SG

ičin	*ǯebe-nne-s?*
how	eat-NEC.PART-2SG

'The mother says: "Why have you killed your father, where have you seen that people eat their own fathers, how are you going to eat him?"'

(264)	*iaami*	*am'a*	*meenǯi*	*göön-i-n*
	why	father (VOC)	(him)self	say-PAST-3SG

iaak-ta	*hor-raka-n*
what-CONJ.CLIT	get caught-COND.DS.CONV-3SG

e-ǯi	*tii-ŋne-r*	*göön-i-n*
not_do-NEG.IMP.2SG	set free-PAST.ITER-NEG.CONV	say-PAST-3SG

'-What are you saying?! The father has taught me himself: "If anything is in the loop, don't set it free".'

(265)

bi	*koobak*	*hor-ča-w*	*tiin-ča-la-wu*
I	hare	get caught-PERF.PART-ACC	set free-PERF.PART-LOC-1SG

min-u	*neji-ri-n*	*göön-ni*
I-ACC	scold-PAST-3SG	say-NONFUT.3SG

"'When I've set a little hare free, he scolded me", the boy answers.'

(266)

erek	*iaa-ǯi-r*	*ere-w*	*beje-ŋ-ur*
this	what_do-FUT-3PL	this-ACC	man-AL.POS-REF.POS.PL

köke-če-le-n	*ačča-la-n*	*ima-ra*
die-PERF.PART-LOC-3SG	not_exist-LOC-3SG	bury-NONFUT.3PL

'So, what could they do, Metele has died, so they buried him.'

(267)

erek	*kuŋa-jakan*	*egǯen*	*oo-d-ni*
this	child-DIM	big	become-NONFUT-3SG

tarpač-ta	*tute-ne-l-le-n*
anyway-CONJ.CLIT	run-ITER-INCH-NONFUT-3SG

tute-n-niken	*bi-ǯ-weeč-te-n*
run-ITER-SIM.CONV	be-PROG-HABIT-NONFUT-3SG

ewi-ket-niken
play-DISTR-SIM.CONV

'The boy grew up. He is running around, playing all the time.'

(268)

Ömneken	*ewi-keči-d-de-n*	*erek*	*örilen*	*hiisečin*
once	play-DIST-PROG-NONFUT-3SG	this	camp	evening

hiisel-leke-n	*nörge-ne-l-weeč-te*
get dark-COND.DS.CONV-3SG	dance-ITER-INCH-HABIT-NONFUT.3PL

ewi-keči-l-weeč-te
play-DIST-INCH-HABIT-NONFUT.3PL

giaki-č	*ewi-ǯ-weeč-te*
various-INSTR	play-PROG-HABIT-NONFUT.3PL

'Once as they played at dusk the people gathered to dance and play games.'

(269)

kuŋa-jakan	*kööje-č-teke-n*	*araj*	*örilen*
child-DIM	glance-STAT-COND.DS.CONV-3SG	suddenly	camp

mudan-dula-n	*ook-ta*	*e-deŋe-n*
end-LOC-3SG	when-CONJ.CLIT	not_do-PAST.PART-3SG

it-te	*asi*	*em-nižii*	*iču-weeč-te-n*
see-NEG.CONV	woman	come-ANT.CONV	appear-HABIT-NONFUT-3SG

'The boy sees - not far from the camp appeared an unknown woman.'

(270)

erek	*kööje-t-te-n*	*örilen-dule*	*e-niken*
this	glance-STAT-NONFUT-3SG	camp-LOC	not_do-SIM.CONV

em-ne	*bugin-ak*
come-NEG.CONV	in the forest-CLIT

'The boy stays looking at the dancers at a distance, but doesn't dare to come nearer.'

(271)

örilen-dule	*e-s-ni*	*holu-waač-ta*
camp-LOC	not_do-NONFUT-3SG	join-HABIT-NEG.CONV

e-le	*eme-ssi-reke-n*	*beltelke-l*
this-LOC	come-CONAT-COND.DS.CONV-3SG	servant-PL

bi-mi	*kuŋa-jakan*	*deelbi*[12]
be-COND.CONV	child-DIM	very

irka-ŋna-waač-ta
tease-PAST.ITER-HABIT-NONFUT:3PL

'He doesn't play together with the camp youths, because they mock him.'

12 *deelbi* < Jak. *дэлби* 'very'.

(272) *am-mi* *Metele-w* *ǯeb-de-j*
father-REF.POS.SG Metele-ACC eat-PURP.CONV-REF.POS.SG

ñek-ri-s *bej* *etigen* *oo-da-j*
do-PAST-2SG man cannibal become-PURP.CONV-REF.POS.SG

ñeke-nni *ǯeb-de-j* *maa-ri-s*
do-NONFUT.2SG eat-PURP.CONV-REF.POS.SG kill-PAST-2SG

göö-niken
say-SIM.CONV

'"You've killed your own father Metele to eat, you'll become a cannibal!"'

(273) *nar*[13] *tarič* *ineñ-meeč-te*
always then laugh-HABIT-NONFUT.3PL
'So they used to tease him.'

(274) *tarič* *ömnekeñ-ǯe* *tarič* *erek* *mian-ni* *kuŋa-jakan*
then once-CLIT then this wonder-NONFUT.3SG child-DIM

erek *iaa-duk* *em-gere-če*
this what-ABL come-PAST.ITER-PERF.PART

bi-ǯi-n *tawar-ak* *iaak* *bi-če*
be-FUT-3SG that one-CLIT what be-PERF.PART

bi-ǯi-n *göö-niken* *iaa-duk?*
be-FUT-3SG say-SIM.CONV what-ABL

'The boy pondered. "Where does this girl come from? Who is she?"'

(275) *iaa-duk* *erek* *tööre* *amkačan* *herde-le-n*
what-ABL this earth hill under-LOC-3SG

ŋen-niǯii *beri-b-weeč-te-n*
go-ANT.CONV lose-MED-HABIT-NONFUT-3SG

13 *nar* < Jak. *наар* 'always'.

'How come, she goes behind the hill and then suddenly disappears?'

(276) *i-le-de* *ŋen-ni-we-n*
which-LOC-CONJ.CLIT go-NONFUT.PART-ACC-3SG

e-s-ni *ič-weeč-te* *ta-duk*
not_do-NONFUT-3SG see-HABIT-NEG.CONV that-ABL

ñöö-d-deke-n-de
go_out-PROG-COND.DS.CONV-3SG-CONJ.CLIT

e-s-ni *ič-weeč-te*
not_do-NONFUT-3SG see-HABIT-NEG.CONV

'Where she enters and from where she comes out - one cannot see.'

(277) *erek* *ǯe* *beri-be-ŋke-le-n* *dali-la-n* *ereger*
this Well lose-MED-Nloc-LOC-3SG near-LOC-3SG always

hiisen-ten *dalil-la-n* *kööje-t-te-n*
evening-3PL approach-NONFUT-3SG glance-STAT-NONFUT-3SG

'The boy approaches the place where she disappears every day, hides there and starts to watch.'

(278) *ömneken* *hiisečin* *beltelke-l* *nörge-ne-l-če-le-ten*
once evening servant-PL dance-ITER-INCH-PERF.PART-LOC-3PL

Helniken *bi-mi* *aj-maka-ñ*
Helniken be-COND.CONV good-INTENS-INSTR

kööje-t-tiǯii *ǯe* *niiwet* *haač-tu-n*
glance-STAT-ANT.CONV Well dwarf_birch base-DAT-3SG

'When the young people started the dance, Helniken hid in the bushes of dwarf birch-trees, started to watch.'

(279) *bukčeŋ-či-reke-n* *erek* *ǯulde-le-n*
huddle.up-STAT-COND.DS.CONV-3SG this ahead-LOC

niiwete-ŋe-n *urket-ŋečin* *meenken*
dwarf_birch-AL.POS-3SG door curtain-EQUAT (one)self

aaŋa-p-ta-n
open-MED-NONFUT-3SG

'As he watched, in front of him in the bushes (as if) a door-curtain opened.'

(280) *aaŋa-riǯii* *asi-ča-kan* *ñöö-re-n*
open-ANT.CONV woman-DIM-DIM go out-NONFUT-3SG

bukatyn *erek* *kuŋa-jakan* *kööje-t-te-n*
all the time this child-DIM glance-STAT-NONFUT-3SG

erek *örilen-dule* *nörge-ne-d-di-l-dule*
this camp-LOC dance-ITER-PROG-NONFUT.PART-PL-LOC

'And out of it comes the girl, the boy keeps watching goes to join the dancing youths.'

(281) *hör-če-le-n* *erek* *kuŋa-jakan* *bi-mi*
go-PERF.PART-LOC-3SG this child-DIM be-COND.CONV

ǯalupki *ii-re-n*
passing enter-NONFUT-3SG

ǯalupki *ii-riǯii* *e-du* *dikeŋ-či-n*
passing enter-ANT.CONV this-DAT hide-STAT-3SG

'The boy let her pass and hid himself near the entrance of her jurta.'

(282) *erek* *nörge-n-ni-wer*
this dance-ITER-NONFUT.PART-REF.POS.PL

od-ča-la-tan *dolbani* *dulakan-ni*
finish-PERF.PART-LOC-3PL night middle-3SG

ielten-če-le-n *erek* *asi* *ii-re-n*
pass-PERF.PART-LOC-3SG this woman enter-NONFUT-3SG

'When the dance was over, by midnight the girl appears again.'

(283) *erek* *asi* *ii-če-le-n* *bi-mi*
this woman enter-PERF.PART-LOC-3SG be-COND.CONV

erek *Helniken* *bi-mi* *dikeŋ-či-rižii*
this Helniken be-COND.CONV hide-STAT-ANT.CONV

urke-j *das-ča-la-n* *urke-we-n*
door-REF.POS.SG close-PERF.PART-NONFUT-3SG door-ACC-3SG

aaŋa-n *dessi-hen-če-le-n*
open-NONFUT.3SG lie-MOM-PERF.PART-LOC-3SG

'When she came in and drew the door curtain Helniken drew it aside.'

(284) *erek* *giiwun-ži-n* *urket-mi*
this stick-INSTR-3SG curtain-REF.POS.SG

ñaan-da *das-sa-n*
again-CONJ.CLIT close-NONFUT-3SG

'The girl drew it again and barred the door with a stick.'

(285) *das-sižii* *dessi-sn-i-ken-du-n*
close-ANT.CONV lie-MOM-NONFUT.PART-DIM-DAT-3SG

ñaan-da *urket-me-n* *aaŋa-ra-n*
again-CONJ.CLIT curtain-ACC-3SG open-NONFUT-3SG

'As soon as she went to bed, Helniken drew back the double curtain again.'

(286) *kuŋa-jakan* *e-du* *dikeŋ-či-niken*
child-DIM this-DAT hide-STAT-SIM.CONV

adi-da *župti* *urkete-lken*
how many-CONJ.CLIT row curtain-PROPR

tara-ŋ-ča-ma-n *aaŋa-waač-ta-n*
that-AL.POS-DIM-ACC-3SG open-HABIT-NONFUT-3SG

'The hiding boy opened the double curtain again.'

(287) *erek* *asi* *tarpač-kan-da* *ili-s-tan*
this woman anyway-DIM-CONJ.CLIT three-ORD.NUM-3PL

iliw-ra-n *das-sa-n*
do for the third time-NONFUT-3SG close-NONFUT-3SG

ñaan-da *aaŋa-n*
again-CONJ.CLIT open-NONFUT.3SG

'She closed the door for the third time, but he opened it again.'

(288) *tarpač-ta* *erek* *asi* *tööre-ǯe-l-le-n*
anyway-CONJ.CLIT this woman talk-PROG-INCH-NONFUT-3SG

urke-tki-j
door-DIR-REF.POS.SG

'Then the girl addressed her door like that.'

(289) *Kujukeeke* *ereke-gu*
Kujukeeke this-INT.CLIT

Kujukeeke *urketen-ni*
Kujukeeke curtain-3SG

Kujukeeke *iaakam* *nuŋut-mi*
Kujukeeke how long curse-COND.CONV

Kujukeeke *aaŋa-b-na-ǯaan-ni*
Kujukeeke open-MED-ITER-DUR-3SG

'-*Kujukeeke*, who has bewitched my door so that it opens all the time.'

(290) *Kujukeeke* *ere-w* *oo-tla-kan*
Kujukeeke this-ACC become-(NEG)FIN.CONV

Kujukeeke *e-se-nni-de*
Kujukeeke not_do-NONFUT-2SG-CONJ.CLIT

Kujukeeke *aaŋa-b-na-gra-ra*
Kujukeeke open-MED-ITER-PAST.ITER-NEG.CONV

Kujukeeke *erek* *iaaka* *aaŋa-l-ǯi-ǯaañ-na-n*
Kujukeeke this what open-INCH-PROG-DUR-NONFUT-3SG

'-*Kujukeeke*, it hasn't flown open in such a way before.'

(291) *Kujukeeke* *bej-ken* *bi-mi-gu*
Kujukeeke man-DIM be-COND.CONV-INT.CLIT

Kujukeeke *ñöö-ǯeen-sö-li-gu*
Kujukeeke go out-DUR-ATTEN-IMP.2SG-INT.CLIT

Kujukeeke *ii-ǯeen-sö-li-gu*
Kujukeeke enter-DUR-ATTEN-IMP.2SG-INT.CLIT

Kujukeeke *urke-č iaa-wa*
Kujukeeke door-INSTR what-ACC

Kujukeeke *ewi-keče-nni*
Kujukeeke play-DIST-NONFUT.2SG

Kujukeeke *göön-ni*
Kujukeeke say-NONFUT.3SG

'-*Kujukeeke*, if you are a human being, show yourself, why are you playing with the door like that?'

(292) *erek* *kuŋa-jakan* *deeski* *ii-re-n*
this child-DIM upward enter-NONFUT-3SG

erek *tačin* *göön-če-le-n* *erek* *asi*
this so say-PERF.PART-LOC-3SG this woman

kuŋa-ŋ-ča-mi *ǯeb-de-n*
child-AL.POS-DIM-REF.POS.SG eat-PURP.CONV-3SG

öle-č-te-n
cook-STAT-NONFUT-3SG

'The boy came in sight and the girl treated him.'

Metele

(293) *erek* *kuŋa-jakan* *ömen* *ǯigne-ke-m*
this child-DIM one bit-DIM-ACC

amŋa-la-j *hine-sn-e-n*
mouth-LOC-REF.POS.SG thrust-MOM-NONFUT-3SG

ömen *ǯigne-ke-m* *tog-la* *ule-n*
one bit-DIM-ACC fire-LOC throw-NONFUT.3SG

'One bit the boy puts in his mouth another bit he casts into the fire (as an offer-sacrifice).'

(294) *alik-wa-n* *hiru-mken-ni*
dish-ACC-3SG 3SG move-CAUS-NONFUT.3SG
'He has eaten the food, then moved the dishes away.'

(295) *erek* *bej-čen* *e-du* *ǯuuma-či-ǯa-l-la-n*
this man-DIM this-DAT visit-STAT-PROG-INCH-NONFUT-3SG
'Then he spent the night there.'

(296) *erek* *asi* *bi-mi* *ere-w* *kuŋa-jaka-m*
this woman be-COND.CONV this-ACC child-DIM-ACC

e-ti *ñöö-wken* *oo-d-ni*
not_do-NONFUT.PART go out-CAUS:NEG.CONV become-PROG-3SG

'Next morning the girl doesn't let him go.'

(297) *ǯööriǯur* *hiisečin* *ewi-n-ek-le-de*
two_of_them evening play-ITER-Nloc-LOC-CONJ.CLIT

e-s-ni *ñöö-weeč-te*
not_do-NONFUT-3SG go_out-HABIT-NEG.CONV

'From this evening on she does not go to dance any more.'

(298) *ömneken* *erek* *eñen-ni* *atikan* *em-ne-n*
once this mother-3SG old woman come-NONFUT-3SG
'Once her old mother visited that girl.'

(299) *eñen-ni* *atikan* *ǯeb-de-n* *emu-riǯii*
mother-3SG old woman eat-PURP.CONV-3SG bring-ANT.CONV

uli-če-ssi-n
feed-STAT-CONAT-NONFUT.3SG

'She brought some food with her and treated the girl.'

(300) *Kujukeeke* *eñe-ren*
Kujukeeke Mother-VOC

Kujukeeke *bii-ken* *iaak-a*
Kujukeeke I-DIM what-EPENTH

Kujukeeke *meenken-de-gu*
Kujukeeke (one)self-CONJ.CLIT-INT.CLIT

Kujukeeke *ǯeple-ŋ-ge-j-gu*
Kujukeeke food-AL.POS-DES-REF.POS.SG-INT.CLIT

Kujukeeke *iri-te-d-de-ku*
Kujukeeke cook-STAT-PROG-PURP.CONV-1SG.IRR

'-*Kujukeeke*, mother, let me cook myself.'

(301) *Kujukeeke* *iaakman* *huu-ken*
Kujukeeke how_long you (PL)-DIM

Kujukeeke *iri-te-ǯeen-ǯi-s*
Kujukeeke cook-STAT-DUR-FUT-2SG

Kujukeeke *göön-ni*
Kujukeeke say-NONFUT.3SG

'-*Kujukeeke*, you've been cooking for me long enough.'

(302) *erek* *eñ-mi* *iri-t-te-j*
this mother-REF.POS.SG cook-STAT-PURP.CONV-REF.POS.SG

ñeke-ssi-reke-n *e-s-ni*
do-CONAT-COND.DS.CONV-3SG not_do-NONFUT-3SG

iri-t-uken
cook-STAT-CAUS:NEG.CONV

'When the mother wants to go cooking, the girl doesn't let her.'

(303) *erek* *enin-ni* *ǯeple* *aj-di-wa-n* *emu-niken*
this mother-3SG food good-sort-ACC-3SG bring-SIM.CONV

erek *uli-č-weeč-te-n* *hunaǯ-dii*
this feed-STAT-HABIT-NONFUT-3SG daughter-DAT:REF.POS

'The mother has brought the best food, treats her daughter.'

(304) *eñ-mi* *em-neke-n*
mother-REF.POS.SG come-COND.DS.CONV-3SG

kuŋa-ŋ-ča-mi *hulla-ǯii*
child-AL.POS-DIM-REF.POS.SG blanket-INSTR.SG.REF.POS

tiini-niken *das-waač-ta-n* *ǯaj-waač-ta-n*
pull-SIM.CONV close-HABIT-NONFUT-3SG hide-HABIT-NONFUT-3SG

'When the mother comes, the girl covers the boy with a blanket, hides him.'

(305) *tačin* *bi-s-ni*
so be-NONFUT-3SG

hoo-ka-m *goru* *bi-s*
very-DIM-ACC for_a_long_time be-NONFUT.3PL

'So they live for a long time.'

(306) *tačin* *hoo-ka-m* *goru* *bi-če-le-ten*
so very-DIM-ACC for_a_long_time be-PERF.PART-LOC-3PL

ömneken *hiisečin* *bi-d-deke-ten*
once evening be-PROG-COND.DS.CONV-3PL

i-le-de *i-le* *deetle*
which-LOC-CONJ.CLIT which-LOC wing(s)

kiisala-n-ni	*ii-s-ni*
rustle-NMZR-3SG	sound-NONFUT-3SG

'Once in the evening a rustle of wings sounds at a distance.'

(307)

erek	*kuŋa*	*dol'či-raka-n*	*hoo-kan-dula*
this	child	listen-COND.DS.CONV-3SG	very-DIM-LOC

gor-la	*töören*	*ii-s-ni*	*i-le-de*
far-LOC	voice	sound-NONFUT-3SG	which-LOC-CONJ.CLIT

i-le	*ulda-n*
which-LOC	echo-NONFUT.3SG

'Now the boy hears a voice far away, an echoe rings.'

(308)

Kiido-kiido-gu	*ama-ran*	*Kagana-čan*
Kiido-kiido-INT.CLIT	father-VOCAT	Kagana-DIM

Kiido-kiido-gu	*iŋene-č-te*	*hinŋe-re-p*
Kiido-kiido-INT.CLIT	cold-INSTR-CONJ.CLIT	freeze-NONFUT-1PL.INCL

ñaana-ŋ-ka-mar	*hili-ken-du-n*
heaven-AL.POS-DIM-REF.POS.PL	space-DIM-DAT-3SG

Kiido-kiido-gu	*öötiñ-ǯi-de*	*köke-re-p*
Kiido-kiido-INT.CLIT	suffering-INSTR-CONJ.CLIT	die-NONFUT-1PL.INCL

Kiido-kiido-gu
Kiido-kiido-INT.CLIT

'-*Kiido-kiido-gu*, father Kagana, we've been almost frozen to death flying in cold heaven.'

(309)

Kiido-kiido-gu	*ñaan-a*	*iaak-a*	*ukčeneke-lke-r*
Kiido-kiido-INT.CLIT	again-EPENTH	what-EPENTH	story-PROPR-PL

bi-ǯeen-i-s-e
be-DUR-PAST-2SG-EPENTH

Kiido-kiido-gu	*hör-če-duk-u*	*oona-kča-kan*
Kiido-kiido-INT.CLIT	go-PERF.PART-ABL-1SG	how-DIM-DIM

ai-č	*bi-ǯeen-i-s?*
good-INSTR	be-DUR-PAST-2SG

Kiido-kiido-gu	*göön-ni*
Kiido-kiido-INT.CLIT	say-NONFUT.3SG

'What news can you tell us? How are you living, since we left you.'

(310)

Iŋee-de	*aji-č*	*bi-d-de-p*
OK-CONJ.CLIT	good-INSTR	be-PROG-NONFUT-1PL.INCL

Kagana	*göön-ni*
Kagana	say-NONFUT.3SG

'-Oh, we are getting on well.'

(311)

iaak-ta	*ukčenek*	*ačča*	*göö-niken*	*Kagana*
what-CONJ.CLIT	story	not_exist	say-SIM.CONV	Kagana

ǯuu-n	*doo-duku-n*	*bargu-čan-ni*	*ii-s-ni*
house-3SG	inside-ABL-3SG	answer-DIM-3SG	sound-NONFUT-3SG

'"Nothing special has happened", Kagana answers.'

(312)

tog-ja-ka-mi	*duru-ǯ-li-le*
fire-EPENTH-DIM-REF.POS.SG	make_fire-PROG-IMP.2SG-CLIT

'-Make a fire!'

(313)

Kiido-kiido-gu	*ama-ran*	*Kagana-čan*
Kiido-kiido-INT.CLIT	father-VOCAT	Kagana-DIM

Kiido-kiido-gu	ǯööker	bi-mi
Kiido-kiido-INT.CLIT	two together	be-COND.CONV

merin-ǯid-de-p
return-PROG-NONFUT-1PL.INCL

Kiido-kiido-gu	*göön-ni*
Kiido-kiido-INT.CLIT	say-NONFUT.3SG

'Only two of us are coming back.'

(314)

Kagana	*erek*	*iaak*	*bi-ǯi-n*	*göön-ni*
Kagana	this	what	be-FUT-3SG	say-NONFUT.3SG

Ömček	*gerbe*	*asi*	*örin-iǯii*
Omchek	name	woman	make_a_camp-ANT.CONV

bi-ǯ-de-n	*nimeče-č*	*tawar*
be-PROG-NONFUT-3SG	neighbouring-INSTR	that one

awlan	*mudan-dula-n-*	*göö-niken*	*erek*	*Kagana*
meadow	end-LOC-3SG	say-SIM.CONV	this	Kagana

'"Well, what to tell you," Kagana proceeds. "A woman, Omchek, has come here, lives nearby, at the edge of the forest meadow."'

(315)

etiken	*bi-si-n*
old man	be-PAST-3SG

etiken	*köke-ri-n*	*tara-w*	*ima-ri-tan*
old man	die-PAST-3SG	that-ACC	bury-PAST-3PL

'She had a husband, but he died, we've buried him.'

(316)

omalga-lkan	*bi-si-n*	*omolgon*	*beri-p-te-n*
son-PROP	be-PAST-3SG	boy	lose-MED-NONFUT-3SG

un	*bi-ǯe-mnin*	*göö-niken*	*Kagana*
then	be-PROG-CONSEC.CONV	say-SIM.CONV	Kagana

'She had a son, but he suddenly disappeared, Kagana tells (them).'

(317)

erek	*eme-ǯe-mnin*	*tog-u*	*duru-li*
this	come-PROG-CONSEC.CONV	fire-ACC	make fire-IMP.2SG

göö-niken	*bej*	*bi-mi*	*göön-ni*
say-SIM.CONV	man	be-COND.CONV	say-NONFUT.3SG

'The newcomers ask him again to make a fire.'

(318)

tog	*awsa-j*	*tiimne-riǯii*
fire	needle-bag-REF.POS.SG	throw-ANT.CONV

erek	*Kagana*	*tog-i*	*duru-n*
this	Kagana	fire-REF.POS.SG	make_fire-NONFUT.3SG

ureči-n	*awsa-j*	*tiimne-ǯi-n*
similar-3SG	needle-bag-REF.POS.SG	scraps-INSTR-3SG

imte-n	*ureči-n*
fumigate-NONFUT.3SG	similar-3SG

'Kagana made the fire and cast some scraps from the bottom of a woman's hand-bag into the flame to fumigate.'

(319)

Erek	*beji-l*	*hesseki*	*tike-rge-ǯe-mnin*
this	man-PL	downward	fall-RETR-PROG-CONSEC.CONV

ögeski	*ñačala-n-tan*	*ii-s-ni*
upward	rebound-NMZR-3PL	sound-NONFUT-3SG

'The other ones were about to settle down, but then flew up again.'

(320)

Kiido-kiido-gu	*ama-ran*	*Kagana-čan*
Kiido-kiido-INT.CLIT	father-VOCAT	Kagana-DIM

Kiido-kiido-gu	*iaakam-gu-la*
Kiido-kiido-INT.CLIT	how long-INT.CLIT-CLIT

ǯaju-ča-nni
hide-STAT-NONFUT.2SG

Kiido-kiido-gu	*göön-ni*
Kiido-kiido-INT.CLIT	say-NONFUT.3SG

'-*Kiido-kiido-gu*, father Kagana, what are you concealing, why don't you tell us the whole truth?'

(321)

e-se-m	*iaa-w-da*
not_do-NONFUT-1SG	what-ACC-CONJ.CLIT

e-se-m	*ǯaju-t-ta*	*göön-ni*
not_do-NONFUT-1SG	hide-STAT-NEG.CONV	say-NONFUT.3SG

'I am not concealing anything.'

(322) *tar* *beri-p-ti-n* *kuŋa* *körni-i*
that lose-MED-PAST-3SG child naughty-REF.POS.SG

hoo-duku-n *möö-le-de* *iaa-la-da*
very-ABL-3SG water-LOC-CONJ.CLIT what-LOC-CONJ.CLIT

tik-če *bi-ǯi-n*
fall-PERF.PART be-FUT-3SG

tik-če-ke *e-te-n*
fall-PERF.PART-CLIT not_do-FUT-3SG

bi-se *göön-ni*
be-NEG.CONV say-NONFUT.3SG

'-The boy got lost because of his disobedience, he must've fallen into the river and drunk there, - he says.'

(323) *erek* *tačin* *göö-niken* *erek* *bej-ke-r* *bi-mi*
this so say-SIM.CONV this man-DIM-PL be-COND.CONV

ǯööreken *amaski* *toosaŋ-či-r*
two together back jump-STAT-NONFUT.3PL

halkamča-la-wur *isa-ǯa-mnin*
smoke-hole-LOC-REF.POS.PL reach-PROG-CONSEC.CONV

'The other two almost reached the smoke hole of the jurta, but then flew back as if rebounded.'

(324) *Kiido-kiido-gu* *tar-da-wu-la*
Kiido-kiido-INT.CLIT that-CONJ.CLIT-INT.CLIT-CLIT

bi-seke-n-e
be-COND.DS.CONV-3SG-EPENTH

Kiido-kiido-gu *hi-ŋen-e*
Kiido-kiido-INT.CLIT you-CLIT-EPENTH

Kiido-kiido-gu	*beket-ke-me-n*	*aji-č*
Kiido-kiido-INT.CLIT	all-DIM-ACC-3SG	good-INSTR

e-se-nni	*ukčene-ǯ-de*
not_do-NONFUT-2SG	tell-PROG-NEG.CONV

Kiido-kiido-gu	*göö-niken*
Kiido-kiido-INT.CLIT	say-SIM.CONV

'-*Kiido-kiido-gu*, you are still not telling us the whole truth.'

(325)

Kiido-kiido-gu	*eluken-e*	*Ǯajmuk-ka-ran*
Kiido-kiido-INT.CLIT	sister-EPENTH	D'ajmuk-DIM-VOCAT

Kiido-kiido-gu	*beje-ŋ-ke-mi*
Kiido-kiido-INT.CLIT	man-AL.POS-DIM-REF.POS.SG

timinna-kan	*ñöö-ge-t-ŋe-nni*	*göö-niken*
tomorrow-until	go_out-CAUS-STAT-POL.IMP-2SG	say-SIM.CONV

'Sister D'ajmuk, let your husband out tomorrow.'

(326)

Kiido-kiido-gu	*Ǯajmuk-kan-gu*
Kiido-kiido-INT.CLIT	D'ajmuk-DIM-INT.CLIT

ǯaju-ča-ǯ-da-n
hide-STAT-PROG-NONFUT-3SG

Kiido-kiido-gu	*Helnike-ke-m*
Kiido-kiido-INT.CLIT	Helniken-DIM-ACC

Kiido-kiido-gu	*göö-niken*	*erek*	*aknil-ni*
Kiido-kiido-INT.CLIT	say-SIM.CONV	this	brothers-3SG

erek aknil-ni	*tačin*	*göön-ǯid-diǯii-de*
this brothers-3SG	so	say-PROG-ANT.CONV-CONJ.CLIT

tike-rge-n-ni	*ii-s-ni*
fall-RETR-NMZR-3SG	sound-NONFUT-3SG

'"D'ajmuk hides Helniken." (D'ajmuk's) brothers said, as they settled down.'

(327)	*Helniken*	*ǯee*	*iaak*	*beji-l-ni*	*em-ne*
	Helniken	dear	what	man-INCH-3SG	come-NONFUT:3PL

göö-niken	*erek*	*asi-ŋ-duki-j*
say-SIM.CONV	this	woman-AL.POS-ABL-REF.POS.SG

ulgem-ne-n
ask-NONFUT-3SG

'"Who are these people, who arrived?" Helniken asks his wife.'

(328)	*bi*	*akni-l-bu*	*eme-rge-re*	*göön-ni*
	I	(elder) brother-PL-1SG	come-RETR-NONFUT.3PL	say-NONFUT.3SG

hör-deŋe-ten	*goral-la-n*	*göön-ni*
go-PAST.PART-3PL	move_away-NONFUT-3SG	say-NONFUT.3SG

erek	*asi*
this	woman

'"My elder brothers returned. They have left a long time ago", the girl answers.'

(329)	*timinak*	*ñöö-g-ŋe-ndi*	*göön-ni*
	tomorrow	go out-CAUS-POL.IMP-2SG	say-NONFUT.3SG

erek	*bej-čen*	*timinak*	*oo-ri-wa-n*
this	man-DIM	tomorrow	become-NONFUT.PART-ACC-3SG

aran	*alat-ta-n*
hardly	wait-NONFUT-3SG

'Come out tomorrow - challenges one of the brothers. Helniken could hardly wait till morning.'

(330)	*asi-ŋa-n*	*e-ti*
	woman-AL.POS-3SG	not_do-NONFUT.PART

ñöö-wken	*kajit-ta-n*[14]
go out-CAUS:NEG.CONV	hide-NONFUT-3SG

14 < Jak. *хааŭ* 'to lock up, lock in'.

'His wife doesn't let him go, pitying him.'

(331)

hin-u	*maa-da-wur*	*ñek-re*
you-ACC	kill-PURP.CONV-REF.POS.PL	do-NONFUT.3PL

e-ǯi	*ñöö-re*	*göö-niken*
not_do-NEG.IMP.2SG	go out-NEG.CONV	say-SIM.CONV

'"Don't go out, they want to kill you!" she says.'

(332)

erek	*ilan*	*dolbani-w*	*kaji-t-ta-n*
this	three	night-ACC	hide-STAT-NONFUT-3SG

e-ti	*ñöö-wken*
not_do-NONFUT.PART	go out-CAUS:NEG.CONV

'For three days and nights she keeps him shut in, doesn't let him go out.'

(333)

erek	*akni-l-ni*	*eriñe-ssi-weeč-te*
this	(elder) brother-PL-3SG	challenge-CONAT-HABIT-NONFUT.3PL

ñöö-w-li	*göö-niken*
go out-PASS-IMP.2SG	say-SIM.CONV

e-s-ni	*asi*	*töruč*	*e-ti*
not_do-NONFUT-3SG	woman	completely	not_do-NONFUT.PART

ñöö-wken
go out-CAUS:NEG.CONV

'As the brothers challenge him "Let him go", the girl resists, does not let him go out.'

(334)

ǯe	*tarič*	*ilan*	*dolbani-w*	*kajit-tiǯi*	*ǯe*
Well	then	three	night-ACC	spare-STAT-ANT.CONV	Well

ömneken	*ñöö-wken-ni*
once	go out-CAUS-3SG

'Still, on the fourth day she had to let him out.'

(335) *Kiido-kiido-gu* *kutet-jen*[15] *Helnike-ken*
Kiido-kiido-INT.CLIT brother-in-law-VOCAT Helniken-DIM

Kiido-kiido-gu *hin-u* *bi-ken* *iaak* *ureči-n*
Kiido-kiido-INT.CLIT you-ACC I-DIM what similar-3SG

kutete-lken-gu *bi-se-m-e*
brother-in-law-PROPR-INT.CLIT be-NONFUT-1SG-EPENTH

Kiido-kiido-gu *göö-niken*
Kiido-kiido-INT.CLIT say-SIM.CONV

hee-mken-de-j *ilalla-ča-m*
try-CAUS-PURP.CONV-REF.POS.SG thrice-DIM-ACC

eriñe-ǯ-de-m
challenge-PROG-NONFUT-1SG

Kiido-kiido-gu *göön-ni*
Kiido-kiido-INT.CLIT say-NONFUT.3SG

'-*Kiido-kiido-gu*, brother-in-law, Helniken, let us see what a brother-in-law I've got. We have been challenging you for three days.'

(336) *hooni-ka-ma-s* *hooni-mkan-da-j*
mighty-DIM-ACC-2SG mighty-CAUS-PURP.CONV-REF.POS.SG

nöö-ke-mu *ǯajmuk-kan-a*
younger sister-DIM-1SG.POS D'ajmuk-DIM-EPENTH

iaak *ureč-we-n* *kutet-ke-ku*
what similar-ACC-3SG brother-in-law-DES-1SG.IRR

ñek-či-d-de-n *göö-niken*
do-STAT-PROG-NONFUT-3SG say-SIM.CONV

hee-mke-t-te-j *eriñe-d-di-w*
try-CAUS-STAT-PURP.CONV-REF.POS.SG challenge-PROG-PAST-1SG

15 < Jak. *күтүөт* 'brother-in-law, son-in-law'.

göön-ni
say-NONFUT.3SG

'Let us try each others' skill (who is stronger). Let's see what brother-in-law our sister D'ajmuk has found for us.'

(337) *erek* *bej-čen* *beji-ŋe-l-ni* *noŋan* *aman-ni*
this man-DIM man-AL.POS-PL-3SG (s)he father-3SG

galani-wača-ŋka-li-n *kuuntek-li*
stroll-HABIT-Nloc-PROL-3SG field-PROL

galani-wača-d-da *etek-tu-r*
stroll-HABIT-PROG-NONFUT:3PL belt-DAT-REF.POS.PL

ǯaw-riǯur *ǯööker* *bi-mi*
catch-ANT.CONV.PL two together be-COND.CONV

'The youth (Helniken) sees that both men are strolling with the hands on the hips along the field where his father had been strolling before.'

(338) *erek* *Helniken* *ta-la* *ŋen-ne-n* *ta-la*
this Helniken that-LOC go-NONFUT-3SG that-LOC

ŋen-če-le-n *göön-ni*
go-PERF.PART-LOC-3SG say-NONFUT.3SG

'As Helniken approached the brothers, one of them says.'

(339) *Kiido-kiido-gu* *Helnike-ken* *kutet-ken*
Kiido-kiido-INT.CLIT Helniken-DIM brother-in-law-DIM

Kiido-kiido-gu *hooni-ka-mar*
Kiido-kiido-INT.CLIT mighty-DIM-REF.POS.PL

hee-mke-t-ker-e
try-CAUS-STAT-IMP:1PL-EPENTH

Kiido-kiido-gu *göön-ni*
Kiido-kiido-INT.CLIT say-NONFUT.3SG

'-*Kiido-kiido-gu*, brother-in-law Helniken, let's try our skill.'

(340)

ičin	*hee-mke-či-nne-t*	*iaa-č*
how	try-CAUS-STAT-NEC.PART-1PL.INC	what-INSTR

hee-mke-či-nne-t	*göön-ni*
try-CAUS-STAT-NEC.PART-1PL.INC	say-NONFUT.3SG

'-How are we going to try it? - Helniken asks.'

(341)

Kiido-kiido-gu	*tar*	*bargi-la*	*naaldi-kan*
Kiido-kiido-INT.CLIT	that	bank-LOC	estuary-DIM

kuuntek-le-n	*iče-s-li-le*
field-LOC-3SG	see-ATTEN-IMP.2SG-CLIT

Kiido-kiido-gu	*egǯen*	*niermi-ken*	*ila-č-ta-n*
Kiido-kiido-INT.CLIT	big	larch-DIM	stand up-STAT-NONFUT-3SG

Kiido-kiido-gu	*tar-ka-ma*	*nemke-ǯ-li-le*
Kiido-kiido-INT.CLIT	that-DIM-ACC	shoot-PROG-IMP.2SG-CLIT

Kiido-kiido-gu	*göön-ni*
Kiido-kiido-INT.CLIT	say-NONFUT.3SG

'-*Kiido-kiido-gu*, look, on the other side where two rivers meet, there is a big larch, shoot at it.'

(342)

E-e	*gora*	*göön-ni*	*oon*	*ta-la*
Oh-EPENTH	long	say-NONFUT.3SG	how	that-LOC

is-ukan-ǯi-m	*buga-lkan*	*bej*	*huu-je*
reach-CAUS-FUT-1SG	country-PROP	man	you (PL)-ASSOC

ñooga-lla
lead-IMP:2PL

'-It's too far away, how can my arrow reach it?'

(343)

tačin	*göö-niken*	*erek*	*Helniken*	*bi-mi*
so	say-SIM.CONV	this	Helniken	be-COND.CONV

göön-ni	*tarak*	*goro-n*	*hoo-*	*göön-ni*
say-NONFUT.3SG	that	long-3SG	very	say-NONFUT.3SG

'-You are local people (hosts), you shoot first, - Helniken says.'

(344)

bii	*e-mne-wu*	*is-ukan*
I	not_do-PROB-1SG	reach-CAUS:NEG.CONV

'It's too far away, for my arrow to reach.'

(345)

Kiido-kiido-gu	*eluken*	*Kiŋini-ken*
Kiido-kiido-INT.CLIT	brother	Kingini-DIM

oon-di-ča-kan	*bi-gre-nni*
how-sort-DIM-DIM	be-PAST.ITER-NONFUT.2SG

Kiido-kiido-gu	*hii-kene*	*ñooga-ǯ-li-la*
Kiido-kiido-INT.CLIT	you-DIM	lead-PROG-IMP.2SG-CLIT

Kiido-kiido-gu	*kutet-ke-mer*
Kiido-kiido-INT.CLIT	brother-in-law-DIM-REF.POS.PL

Helnike-ken	*iči-ǯ-de-n*	*göön-ni*
Helniken-DIM	see-PROG-NONFUT-3SG	say-NONFUT.3SG

'-*Kiido-kiido-gu*, brother Kingini, shows what you are worth, take the first shot, let our brother-in-law Helniken see (our skills)! - one of the brothers says.'

(346)

erek	*tačin*	*göön-če-le-n*	*erek*	*Kiŋini*
this	so	say-PERF.PART-LOC-3SG	this	Kingini

bi-mi	*ŋaadi-j*	*ga-riǯii*	*erek*
be-COND.CONV	bow-REF.POS.SG	take-ANT.CONV	this

niermi-ñǯe-w	*nemke-n*
larch-AUGM-ACC	shoot-NONFUT.3SG

niermi-ñǯe-w	*nemke-n*	*niermi-ñǯe*
larch-AUGM-ACC	shoot-NONFUT.3SG	larch-AUGM

huure-li-n	*iŋete-n*	*hor-ra-n*	*ñura-n*
top-PROL-3SG	shaft-3SG	get caught-NONFUT-3SG	arrow-3SG

'Kingini took his bow and shot at the larch. The arrow plunged into the tree-top up to the shaft.'

(347)

Kiido-kiido-gu	*ñaan-a*	*bii-ken*
Kiido-kiido-INT.CLIT	again-EPENTH	I-DIM

hee-mken-de-ku
try-CAUS-PURP.CONV-1SG.IRR

Kiido-kiido-gu	*göön-ni*
Kiido-kiido-INT.CLIT	say-NONFUT.3SG

'-*Kiido-kiido-gu*, now I shall try my own skill.'

(348)

Helniken	*ge*	*hee-mke-li*	*göön-ni*	*hii*
Helniken	come on	try-CAUS-IMP.2SG	say-NONFUT.3SG	you

naa-wkan-aka-s	*ñaan*	*bii*	*hee-mken-ǯiŋe-wu*
hit-CAUS-COND.DS.CONV-2SG	again	I	try-CAUS-FUT2-1SG

göön-ni
say-NONFUT.3SG

'"Come on!" - Helniken says, "If you hit the target, I'll shoot too".'

(349)

erek	*Kidani*	*bi-mi*	*eme*	*ŋaadi-j*
this	Kidani	be-COND.CONV	so	bow-REF.POS.SG

nemke-n
shoot-NONFUT.3SG

'Kidani took his bow and shot.'

(350)

ñura-n	*bi-mi*	*dulaka-kli-j*
arrow-3SG	be-COND.CONV	middle-LOC.PROL-REF.POS.SG

ii-riǯii	*niermi*	*dulaka-kla-n*
enter-ANT.CONV	larch	middle-DIR.LOC-3SG

hor-ra-n
get caught-NONFUT-3SG

'The arrow plunged into the middle of the tree up to the half.'

(351) *Giller-giller-gu eregegej*
Giller-giller-INT.CLIT well done

Giller-giller-gu bi-kene ook-ta gor-la
Giller-giller-INT.CLIT be-CLIT when-CONJ.CLIT long-LOC

e-č-u-ken nökle-ǯeeñ-ne
not_do-PERF.PART-1SG-DIM shoot-DUR-NEG.CONV

Giller-giller-gu dali-la nöki-t-kere-re-m
Giller-giller-INT.CLIT near-LOC shoot-STAT-ITER.PAST-NONFUT-1SG

Giller-giller-gu tarwača-mur gor-la
Giller-giller-INT.CLIT like that-REF.POS.PL long-LOC

Giller-giller-gu e-č-u-ken
Giller-giller-INT.CLIT not_do-PERF.PART-1SG-DIM

nöki-če-ǯ-de
shoot-STAT-PROG-NEG.CONV

'-*Giller-giller-gu*, well done! I've never shot so far.'

(352) *keli-nije-le*[16] *hee-mken-ǯid-de-ku*
brother-in-law-PL-CLIT try-CAUS-PROG-PURP.CONV-1SG.IRR

Giller-giller-gu iaa-ǯi-n-da-si
Giller-giller-INT.CLIT what_do-FUT-3SG-CONJ.CLIT-CLIT

Giller-giller-gu göö-niken
Giller-giller-INT.CLIT say-SIM.CONV

'-*Giller-giller-gu*, well, my brothers-in-law, I'll try my own skill now.'

(353) *erek kuŋa-jakan ǯuu-la-j tut-tiǯii*
this child-DIM house-LOC-REF.POS.SG run-ANT.CONV

nööki-j ga-riǯij em-ne-n
arrow-REF.POS.SG take-ANT.CONV come-NONFUT-3SG

16 Corrected by DM to *daa-nil-bu*.

erek	*nööki-j*	*ga-rižij*	*em-nižij*
this	arrow-REF.POS.SG	take-ANT.CONV	come-ANT.CONV

že	*erek*	*niermi-ŋe-nže-we-ten*	*nökle-n*
Well	this	larch-AL.POS-AUGM-ACC-3PL	shoot-NONFUT.3SG

'The youth ran back home, fetched his bow and shot at the larch.'

(354)

erek	*niermi-nže-ke-m*	*huure-duku-n*	*haat-tu-n*	*mudan*
this	larch-AUGM-DIM-ACC	top-ABL-3SG	base-DAT-3SG	end

hiarki-ča-gčin	*ŋen-uken-ni*	*ömnekeje*
lightning strike-PERF.PART-EQUAT	go-CAUS-3SG	at once

'Straightaway his arrow split the larch from top to the bottom as a lightning.'

(355)

Kiido-kiido-gu	*eregegej*	*Helnike-ken*
Kiido-kiido-INT.CLIT	well done	Helniken-DIM

Kiido-kiido-gu	*ajžit*	*aj*	*bej*	*bi-se-nni*
Kiido-kiido-INT.CLIT	really	good	man	be-NONFUT-2SG

'-*Kiido-kiido-gu*, well done! Helniken, you are a real warrior!'

(356)

Kiido-kiido-gu	*bii*	*hunaž-u*	*tiwömi-de*
Kiido-kiido-INT.CLIT	I	daughter-1SG	therefore-CONJ.CLIT

žaju-ča-č-ča
hide-STAT-PROG-PERF.PART

Kiido-kiido-gu	*göön-ni*
Kiido-kiido-INT.CLIT	say-NONFUT.3SG

'-*Kiido-kiido-gu*, that's why the sister didn't want let you out.'

(357)

Kiido-kiido-gu	*gee*	*ñaan-a-gu*
Kiido-kiido-INT.CLIT	come on	again-EPENTH-INT.CLIT

nöki-ke-r-bur
arrow-DIM-PL-REF.POS.PL

Kiido-kiido-gu *okaata-ŋ-ur*
Kiido-kiido-INT.CLIT river-AL.POS-REF.POS.PL

barda-ja-la-n *tuuhan-ǯi-p*
opposite side-EPENTH-LOC-3SG jump-FUT-1PL.INCL

tute-mni-ken
run-CONSEC.CONV-DIM

Kiido-kiido-gu *göön-ni*
Kiido-kiido-INT.CLIT say-NONFUT.3SG

'Now let's go (to the other bank) and take a look at our arrows. Let's take a running jump over the river.'

(358) *tačin* *göön-iǯii* *erek* *ilniǯur* *daran*
so say-ANT.CONV this three together side by side

illiǯur *tute-l-le*
three together run-INCH-NONFUT.3PL

'Well, all three of them ran to the river.'

(359) *erek* *Helniken* *ǯulege-č* *ŋen-ne-n*
this Helniken front-INSTR go-NONFUT-3SG

erek *göön-če-gčin-ni* *okaata-ŋ-ur*
this say-PERF.PART-EQUAT-3SG river-AL.POS-REF.POS.PL

barda-duku-n *barda-la-n* *erek* *Helniken*
opposite side-ABL-3SG opposite side-LOC-3SG this Helniken

tuuhaŋ-či-n *araj*
jump-STAT-NONFUT.3SG suddenly

erek *ǯaa-l-ni* *amarda-du-n* *tuuhañ-kač-ta*
this relative-PL-3SG behind-DAT-3SG jump-DIST-NONFUT:3PL

'Helniken reached the river first, as the brother suggested, jumped over the river, the brothers followed him.'

(360) *erek* *nöki-l-dule* *em-nižur*
this arrow-PL-LOC come-ANT.CONV.PL

iče-ssi-reke-ten *erek* *keli-nil-ni*[17]
see-CONAT-COND.DS.CONV-3PL this this brother-in-law-PL-3SG

nöki-l-ni *ačča* *bi-ken-ni*
arrow-PL-3SG not_exist be-DIM-3SG

hiarka-ča-gčin *ŋen-če*
lightning-PERF.PART-EQUAT go-PERF.PART

'When they looked at their arrows they saw that nothing was left of them [Helniken's arrow] destroyed them as a lightning.'

(361) *Erek* *hagdi* *keli-n*[18] *eerke-že-l-le-n*
this old brother-in-law-3SG praise-PROG-INCH-NONFUT-3SG
'The elder brother-in-law praises him.'

(362) *Kiido-kiido-gu* *Helniken* *eliwen-de* *hooni*
Kiido-kiido-INT.CLIT Helniken really-CONJ.CLIT mighty

bej-ken *bi-že-mne-s-e*
man-DIM be-PROG-PROB-2SG-EPENTH

Kiido-kiido-gu *irek* *öösi* *eči-ken-e*
Kiido-kiido-INT.CLIT which old days so-DIM-EPENTH

nemke-deŋ-me-n *e-se-m* *haa-r*
shoot-PAST.PART-ACC-3SG not_do-NONFUT-1SG know-NEG.CONV

Kiido-kiido-gu *hiarka-tla-gčin*
Kiido-kiido-INT.CLIT lightning-RES.PART-EQUAT

ŋen-uken-ni *nemke-žeen-ni-s*
go-CAUS-NONFUT.3SG shoot-DUR-PAST-2SG

Kiido-kiido-gu *göön-ni*
Kiido-kiido-INT.CLIT say-NONFUT.3SG

---

17 Corrected by DM to *daa-nil-ni* 'brothers-in-law'.
18 Corrected to *daan* 'brother-in-law'.

'-*Kiido-kiido-gu*, you are a real warrior, I've never seen such a good shot before. It was as a lightning.'

(363)

gia-dmar	*bi-mi*	*nöö-dmer*	*bi-mi*
other-CONT	be-COND.CONV	younger brother-CONT	be-COND.CONV

hira-l-la-n	*erek*	*Kiŋini*	*ñur-i*
be angry-INCH-NONFUT-3SG	this	Kingini	arrow-REF.POS.SG

mula-l-liǯii
take pity-INCH-ANT.CONV

'But the younger brother became angry, taking pity of his arrow.'

(364)

Kiŋirukiŋe	*Helniken*
Kingirukinge	Helniken

Kiŋirukiŋe	*mula-ke-e-da*
Kingirukinge	alas-CLIT-EPENTH-CONJ.CLIT

iŋet-ke-mu	*haaju-ǯaañ-ni-s*
arrow-DIM-1SG.POS	destroy-DUR-PAST-2SG

Kiŋirukiŋe	*göö-niken*	*erek*
Kingirukinge	say-SIM.CONV	this

'-*Kiŋiruki-ŋe*, Helniken, alas for my arrow, you've broken my arrow, he says.'

(365)

erek	*akan-ni-ǯe*	*ǯaa-l-bi*	*ǯe*
this	elder brother-3SG-Well	relative-PL-REF.POS.SG	Well

aran	*od-ukan-ni*
hardly	finish-CAUS-3SG

'The elder brother could hardly calm him down.'

(366)

erek	*bej-čen*	*tačin*	*ñeke-d-diǯur*
this	man-DIM	so	do-PROG-ANT.CONV:PL

od-dižur	*bi-d-de*
finish-ANT.CONV:PL	be-PROG-NONFUT.3PL

'So they began to live together.'

(367)

erek	*Helniken*	*aman-ni*	*galani-wača-ŋka*	*kuunteke-ŋ-ni-n*
this	Helniken	father-3SG	stroll-HABIT-Nloc	field-AL.POS-PROL-3SG

daa-nil-čal	*galani-wača-ǯ-waač-ta-n*
brother-in-law-PL-COMIT.REF	stroll-HABIT-PROG-HABIT-NONFUT-3SG

'Helniken strolls with his brothers-in-law along the meadow of his father.'

(368)

tačin	*ereger*	*hoo-kan*	*goru*	*bi-ǯ-de*
so	always	very-DIM	for_a_long_time	be-PROG-NONFUT.3PL

'So they lived for a long time.'

(369)

tačin	*bi-d-dižur*	*ömneken*	*hiisečin*	*tačin*
so	be-PROG-ANT.CONV:PL	once	evening	so

girka-waači-ǯ-dižur	*hiisečin*	*em-nižur*
walk-HABIT-PROG-ANT.CONV:PL	evening	come-ANT.CONV.PL

hukle-hen-če-le-ten	*dolba-jakan*
sleep-MOM-PERF.PART-LOC-3PL	night-DIM

töören	*ii-l-le-n*	*ñan-da*
voice	sound-INCH-NONFUT-3SG	again-CONJ.CLIT

'Once in the evening when they came back home after a walk and were about to go asleep, a voice sounded at a distance.'

(370)

Hiler-hiler-gu	*maata-l-a*	*Kidani-ja*
Hiler-hiler-INT.CLIT	hero-PL-EPENTH	Kidani-EPENTH

Kiŋeni-je
Kingeni-EPENTH

Hiler-hiler-gu	*bii-ken*	*iaaka*	*eleken-de*
Hiler-hiler-INT.CLIT	I-DIM	what	enough-CONJ.CLIT

höč-če-sen	*bi-ǯi-n-gu*	*göö-niken*
rest-RES-IMIT	be-FUT-3SG-INT.CLIT	say-SIM.CONV

daača-ǯaañ-na-m
chase-DUR-NONFUT-1SG

Hiler-hiler-gu	*Gelilej*	*ojin*	*oo-lla*
Hiler-hiler-INT.CLIT	Come_on	upwards	become-IMP:2PL

Hiler-hiler-gu	*ama-ra*	*Kagana-kan*
Hiler-hiler-INT.CLIT	father-VOCAT	Kagana-DIM

öril-ke-mi	*ogin*	*oo-wka-li*
camp-DIM-REF.POS.SG	upwards	become-CAUS-IMP.2SG

göön-ni
say-NONFUT.3SG

göö-niken	*töören*	*ii-s-ni*
say-SIM.CONV	voice	sound-NONFUT-3SG

'*-Hiler-hiler-gu*, warriors Kidani and Kingini, I think, you've rested enough, I've come here for your sake. Arise, father Kagana, have your people arise!'

(371)

erek	*bieruse-l-e*	*ögin*	*oo-lla*
this	servant-PL-EPENTH	upwards	become-IMP:2PL

köke-re-p	*göö-niken*	*erek*	*Kagana*
die-NONFUT-1PL.INCL	say-SIM.CONV	this	Kagana

öril-mi	*beltelke-l-bi*	*ögin*
camp-REF.POS.SG	servant-PL-REF.POS.SG	upwards

oo-wkan-ni
become-CAUS-NONFUT.3SG

'Kagana says to his people: "Arise or else we'll perish".'

(372)

erek	*bej*	*bi-mi*	*ere-w*	*örile-m*
this	man	be-COND.CONV	this-ACC	camp-ACC

tunŋarakan	*tookara-sn-a-n*[19]
five_times	circle-MOM-NONFUT-3SG

'That stranger circling five times around the camp, shot dead all the inhabitants.'

(373)

Hiler-hiler-gu	*tunŋan*	*ǯaannu-kan*	*örilen*
Hiler-hiler-INT.CLIT	five	dozen-DIM	clan

asun	*bi-ǯi-n*	*ñaan-a*	*iaa-lkan*
how many	be-FUT-3SG	again-EPENTH	what-PROP

bi-se-p-e
be-NONFUT-1PL.INCL-EPENTH

'-*Hiler-hiler-gu*, as if five dozens families (clans) is much enough. [Whom else can I fight?]'

(374)

Ǯajmuk	*asi*	*min-ŋi-t-kke*
D'ajmuk	woman	I-POS.PROP-CLIT-SPEC.CLIT

e-te-n	*oo-ǯaañ-na-la*
not_do-FUT-3SG	become-DUR-NEG.CONV-CLIT

Hiler-hiler-gu	*göön-ni*
Hiler-hiler-INT.CLIT	say-NONFUT.3SG

'D'ajmuk will be mine anyway.'

(375)

Ömček-ken	*Čimčap-kene*	*mian-a*	*ǯaannu*	*öril-ke-mu*
Omchek-DIM	Chimchep-DIM	ten-EPENTH	dozen	clan-DIM-1SG.POS

ǯeb-de-ten	*iri-č-ti-s-e*
eat-PURP.CONV-3PL	cook-STAT-PAST-2SG-EPENTH

möö-ŋe-ten	*mööli-ǯi-s-e*
water-AL.POS-3PL	go for water-FUT-2PL-EPENTH

19 Cf. Ewk: *tokor-* 'circle, swirl'.

utakan-da	*kamag*	*bi-gre-n*
serving_woman-CONJ.CLIT	short_of	be-PAST.ITER-3SG

'Omchek and Chimchep will serve me, cooking for my fifty families, going for water, we are always short of servants.'

(376)

Hiler-hiler-gu	*Čimčewul-ken*	*hii-de*
Hiler-hiler-INT.CLIT	Chimchewul-DIM	you-CONJ.CLIT

iaa-ǯ-da-j	*bi-ǯi-nni*
what_do-PROG-PURP.CONV-REF.POS.SG	be-FUT-2SG

ögin	*oo-li*
upwards	become-IMP.2SG

Hiler-hiler-gu	*göö-niken*	*töören*	*ii-s-ni*
Hiler-hiler-INT.CLIT	say-SIM.CONV	voice	sound-NONFUT-3SG

'-*Hiler-hiler-gu*, and you, Chimchevul, why are you sitting like that, arise! the voice sounded.'

(377)

erek	*beje-l*	*ilniǯur*	*tuuhañ-kač-ta*
this	man-PL	three together	jump-DIST-NONFUT:3PL

erek	*kusi-ǯe-l-le*
this	fight-PROG-INCH-NONFUT.3PL

kusi-ǯe-n-ten	*ii-weeč-te-n*
fight-PROG-NMZR-3PL	sound-HABIT-NONFUT-3SG

'These people, all three of them began to fight with the stranger, only the noise of the battle is heard.'

(378)

sin	*gor-ka-m*	*kusi-ket-tiǯur*
meanwhile	long-DIM-ACC	fight-DIST-ANT.CONV:PL

buga-lka-r	*beji-l*	*dabda-ra*
country-PROP-PL	man-PL	loose-NONFUT.3PL

'They fight so for a long time, nevertheless the local men began to yield after some time.'

(379)	*Kiido-kiido-gu*	*kutet-jen*	*Helnike-ken*
	Kiido-kiido-INT.CLIT	brother-in-law-VOCAT	Helniken-DIM

hi-ka	*iaa-wa*	*alač-či-nni*
you-CLIT	what-ACC	wait-FUT-2SG

'-*Kiido-kiido-gu*, Helniken, what are you waiting for?'

(380)	*eluken-i*	*Šajmuk-kan-a*	*beje-ŋ-ke-mi*
	sister-EPENTH	D'ajmuk-DIM-EPENTH	man-AL.POS-DIM-REF.POS.SG

iaa-gda-w-takan	*bilgu-ǯa-nni*
what-DELIM-ACC-REST.CLIT	caress-PROG-2SG

Kiido-kiido-gu	*ǯoosa-čakan*	*oo-daŋ-kan-ni*
Kiido-kiido-INT.CLIT	perdition-DIM	become-PAST.PART-DIM-3SG

Kiido-kiido-gu	*göö-niken*	*töören*	*ii-s-ni*
Kiido-kiido-INT.CLIT	say-SIM.CONV	voice	sound-NONFUT-3SG

'"How long, sister D'ajmuk, are you going to caress your husband, while we are doomed to death?!" he says.'

(381)	*erek*	*dabda-ča-l*	*beji-l*	*asu-m*
	this	*loose-PERF.PART-PL*	*man-PL*	*how many-AČČ*

goru	*kusi-ǯi-r*	*dabda-ri-mdasa-l*
for_a_long_time	fight-FUT-3PL	loose-NONFUT.PART-SIMIL-PL

ootin-tan	*ii-s-ni*
despair-3PL	sound-NONFUT-3SG

'The local men couldn't resist any more, they fought moaning and exhausted.'

(382)	*Kiido-kiido-gu*	*Čimčewul-ken*
	Kiido-kiido-INT.CLIT	Chimchewul-DIM

Kiido-kiido-gu	*tiek-e-le*
Kiido-kiido-INT.CLIT	now-EPENTH-CLIT

Kiido-kiido-gu *hin-u-de*
Kiido-kiido-INT.CLIT you-ACC-CONJ.CLIT

elsu-čen-e *gerbet-ti-wu* *göö-niken*
strong enough-DIM-EPENTH consider-PAST-1SG say-SIM.CONV

kusi-keči-ǯe-n-ten *ii-weeč-te-n*
fight-DIST-PROG-NMZR-3PL sound-HABIT-NONFUT-3SG

'-*Kiido-kiido-gu*, Chimchevul, and I hoped that you could overwhelm him.'

(383) *erek* *aawasa-dmar-da* *Čimčewul*
this uncle-CONT-CONJ.CLIT Chimchewul

ooti-ǯa-n-ni *ii-si-mdes*
despair-PROG-NMZR-3SG sound-NONFUT.PART-SIMIL

bi-weeč-te-n
be-HABIT-NONFUT-3SG

'The battle is going on, their brother-in-law, Chimchewul, is fighting straining all his forces.'

(384) *erek* *kuŋa-jakan* *ñöö-de-j*
this child-DIM go out-PURP.CONV-REF.POS.SG

ičin-de *töleski* *ñöö-de-j*
like.this-CONJ.CLIT outside go out-PURP.CONV-REF.POS.SG

ñeke-ssi-mi *turku-n* *asi-ŋa-n*
do-CONAT-COND.CONV not able-NONFUT.3SG woman-AL.POS-3SG

kajič-waač-ta-n
lock-HABIT-NONFUT-3SG

'The youth, Helniken, wants to go out - but his wife doesn't let him go.'

(385) *ösömiken* *urultin-ǯi-de* *iaa-ǯi-da*
even belt-INSTR-CONJ.CLIT what-INSTR-CONJ.CLIT

uj-či-weeč-te-n	*ere-w*	*Helnike-m*
tie-STAT-HABIT-NONFUT-3SG	this-ACC	Helniken-ACC

erek	*asi*	*erek*	*ǯajmuk*
this	woman	this	D'ajmuk

'D'ajmuk has even bound him with the belts in order to keep him inside.'

(386)

Nikoj-gu	*bener-jen*
Nikoj-INT.CLIT	brother-in-law-VOCAT
Nikoj-gu	*Helnike-ken*
Nikoj-INT.CLIT	Helniken-DIM
Nikoj-gu	*iaa-gda-w-takan*
Nikoj-INT.CLIT	what-DELIM-ACC-REST.CLIT
Nikoj-gu	*dikeŋ-či-nni*
Nikoj-INT.CLIT	hide-STAT-2SG

'-*Nikoj-gu*, brother-in-law Helniken, how long are you going to hide yourself?'

(387)

Nikoj-gu	*hin-u-ñun-de*	*iñit-te-p*
Nikoj-INT.CLIT	you-ACC-CLIT-CONJ.CLIT	hope-NONFUT-1PL.INCL

Nikoj-gu	*erteken-de*
Nikoj-INT.CLIT	like this-CONJ.CLIT
Nikoj-gu	*bi-deŋ-ken-ti*
Nikoj-INT.CLIT	be-PAST.PART-DIM-1PL.INC.POS
Nikoj-gu	*eñe-de*
Nikoj-INT.CLIT	hurt(s)-CONJ.CLIT
Nikoj-gu	*ǯoosa-čakan*
Nikoj-INT.CLIT	perdition-DIM
Nikoj-gu	*oo-daŋ-kan-ni*
Nikoj-INT.CLIT	become-PAST.PART-DIM-3SG

Nikoj-gu *göö-niken*
Nikoj-INT.CLIT say-SIM.CONV

erek *uŋen* *Helnike-mi-de*
this well Helniken-REF.POS.SG-CONJ.CLIT

erine-n-ni *ii-s-ni*
call-NMZR-3SG sound-NONFUT-3SG

'"You are our last hope, or else we are doomed to death!", Chimchevul calls.'

(388) *aawasa-ǯmar* *tarpač-ta* *tarpač-ta* *erek* *beji-l*
uncle-CONT anyway-CONJ.CLIT anyway-CONJ.CLIT this man-PL

bi-mi *miir-du-ten* *egǯen* *koobak* *köörbe-ten*
be-COND.CONV shoulder(s)-DAT-3PL big hare male-3PL

dii-n *čoglika* *čoglina-sn-a-n* *ewetle-ten*
size-3SG lather foam-MOM-NONFUT-3SG rib-3PL

ǯapka-li-n *ewte-ten* *iču-n*
between-PROL-3SG lungs-3PL appear-NONFUT.3SG

'(Helniken sees) his brothers-in-law foam with lather (as thick as a male hare) like overdriven reindeer, they are so exhausted that one can see their lungs through their ribs.'

(389) *ŋisule-tne-niken* *kusi-se-ǯ-de* *tačin*
stumble-MULT-SIM.CONV fight-ITER-PROG-NONFUT.3PL so

kusi-d-deke-ten *iaak-kal* *kurelen*
fight-PROG-COND.DS.CONV-3PL what-NONREF.CLIT whirlwind

ii-s-ni *ösömiken* *meenken*
sound-NONFUT-3SG even (one)self

kiŋgergi-t-ti-mdes-te
ring-STAT-NONFUT.PART-SIMIL-CONJ.CLIT

iaa-ri-mdas-ta
what_do-NONFUT.PART-sort of-CONJ.CLIT

'While they are fighting a droning of a whirlwind sounds.'

(390) *erek asi eŋen-eke-n araj*
this woman peep-COND.DS.CONV-3SG suddenly

okaata-ŋ-ma-n holgiča-kan bej-čeken
river-AL.POS-ACC-3SG downstream-DIM man-DIM

em-ne-n kiŋne-č
come-NONFUT-3SG ski-INSTR

'Helniken's wife looked around: downstream along the river there came a man skiing.'

(391) *ösömi kiŋne-n meenken buutu-meeč-te-n*
even ski-3SG (one)self slide-HABIT-NONFUT-3SG
'It looks as if the skies move themselves.'

(392) *erek asi kööje-č-teke-n*
this woman glance-STAT-COND.DS.CONV-3SG

Helnike-duku-n bukatyn nooda-dmar bej
Helniken-ABL-3SG all the time beautiful-CONT man

'She sees - this man looks even better than her husband Helniken.'

(393) *meenken hiñan-ǯi-i hetku-n*
(one)self shadow-INSTR-REF.POS.SG jump from-NONFUT.3SG
'(He is) so adroit, that his own shadow cannot follow him.'

(394) *erek asi bi-mi göön-ni*
this woman be-COND.CONV say-NONFUT.3SG

Ö-ö nooda-kke bej köke-mel-le-n
Oh-EPENTH beautiful-SPEC.CLIT man die-ACCEL-NONFUT-3SG

göö-niken ere-w kajiča-ǯak-i
say-SIM.CONV this-ACC lock-PART-REF.POS.SG

beje-ŋ-i	*ñöö-w-re-n*
man-AL.POS-REF.POS.SG	go out-CAUS-NONFUT-3SG

'She thinks: "Oh, such a handsome man, what if he perishes?" And then she finally let her husband out.'

(395)

erek	*hol-gič*	*eme*	*bej*	*bi-mi*	*kiŋne-n*
this	upstream-ELAT	newcomer	man	be-COND.CONV	ski-3SG

meenken	*butu-meeč-te-n*	*ereger*
(one)self	move-HABIT-NONFUT-3SG	always

'As for the stranger, he is rushing ahead so quickly, as if his skies are moving by themselves.'

(396)

erek	*beje-ŋe-ten*	*bi-mi*	*eme*	*beje-ŋe-ten*
this	man-AL.POS-3PL	be-COND.CONV	newcomer	man-AL.POS-3PL

bi-mi	*bej-u*	*Hilini-v*	*nemke-če-l-le-n*
be-COND.CONV	man-ACC	Hilini-ACC	shoot-STAT-INCH-NONFUT-3SG

'Then he starts to shoot at Hilini.'

(397)

Kiido-kiido-gu	*Meŋnuni-ken*
Kiido-kiido-INT.CLIT	Mengnuni-DIM

Kiido-kiido-gu	*mannu-ja-t-li*
Kiido-kiido-INT.CLIT	make effort(s)-ASP-STAT-IMP.2SG

Kiido-kiido-gu	*ooti-gda-ǯur*
Kiido-kiido-INT.CLIT	despair-DELIM-INSTR:REF.POS.PL

Kiido-kiido-gu	*ewi-ǯeeñ-ne-p*
Kiido-kiido-INT.CLIT	play-DUR-NONFUT-1PL.INCL

Kiido-kiido-gu	*göö-niken*
Kiido-kiido-INT.CLIT	say-SIM.CONV

'-*Kiido-kiido-gu*, Mengnuni, help us, this fight (lit. play) is a sheer torture!'

(398)

erek	*buga-lka-r*	*beji-l*	*ilniǯur*
this	country-PROP-PL	man-PL	three together

ǯuu-la-wur	*mirke-sn-e*
house-LOC-REF.POS.PL	crawl-MOM-NONFUT:3PL

'The local warriors, all three of them crawled back to their jurta.'

(399)

erek	*eme*	*bej*	*bi-mi*	*bukatyn*
this	newcomer	man	be-COND.CONV	all the time

erek	*Hilini-ñun*	*nemke-t-meče-l-le-n*
this	Hilini-COMIT	shoot-STAT-REC-INCH-NONFUT-3SG

'The newcomer keeps fighting with Hilini.'

(400)

ösömiken	*hebgere-n*	*iige-lken*	*bi-weeč-te-n*
even	skiing_stick-3SG	sound-PROPR	be-HABIT-NONFUT-3SG

beje-nǯe	*nemke-reke-n*
man-AUGM	shoot-COND.DS.CONV-3SG

hebger-ǯi	*tög-weeč-te-n*
skiing_stick-INSTR	parry-HABIT-NONFUT-3SG

'When Hilini shoots he parries his arrows with his skiing stick.'

(401)

Kiŋer-gu	*Hilini-ken-i*
Kinger-INT.CLIT	Hilini-DIM-EPENTH

Kiŋer-gu	*e-le-gu*	*töör-le*
Kinger-INT.CLIT	this-LOC-INT.CLIT	earth-LOC

Kiŋer-gu	*ikeri-ke-mi*
Kinger-INT.CLIT	bone-DIM-REF.POS.SG

Kiŋer-gu	*göli-de-j*	*eme-ǯeeñ-ni-s*
Kinger-INT.CLIT	sacrifice-PURP.CONV-REF.POS.SG	come-DUR-PAST-2SG

Kiŋer-gu	*göö-niken*
Kinger-INT.CLIT	say-SIM.CONV

'*-Kinger-gu* Hilini, you shouldn't have come here, you lay your bones here.'

(402) *erek asi bi-mi Helnike-mi*
this woman be-COND.CONV Helniken-REF.POS.SG

ñöö-w-ri-n erek bej em-če-le-n
go out-PASS-PAST-3SG this man come-PERF.PART-LOC-3SG

'D'ajmuk let Helniken out when the stranger appeared.'

(403) *erek Helniken ñöö-riǯii*
this Helniken go out-ANT.CONV

nemke-meči-ǯe-l-leke-n Meŋnuni
shoot-REC-PROG-INCH-COND.DS.CONV-3SG Mengnuni

bi-mi kiŋne-ji iaa-ji
be-COND.CONV ski-REF.POS.SG what-REF.POS.SG

nuk-riǯii alla-ǯi-n nee-riǯii
take off-ANT.CONV calm-INSTR-3SG put-ANT.CONV

erek Ömček ǯuu-la-n ii-re-n
this Omchek house-LOC-3SG enter-NONFUT-3SG

'As Helniken starts to fight with Hilini, Mengnuni takes off calmly his skies, puts them carefully aside and enters Omchek's house.'

(404) *erek bej bi-mi Helnike-ñun*
this man be-COND.CONV Helniken-COMIT

kusi-ǯe-l-le
fight-PROG-INCH-NONFUT.3PL

'And Helniken keeps fighting with Hilini.'

(405) *Hiler-hiler-gu Ǯajmuk asi*
Hiler-hiler-INT.CLIT D'ajmuk woman

Hiler-hiler-gu Helnike-m ǯaju-ča-ǯ-diǯii
Hiler-hiler-INT.CLIT Helniken-ACC hide-STAT-PROG-ANT.CONV

tiin-ǯiǯe-nni
set free-PROG-NONFUT.2SG

Hiler-hiler-gu *göö-niken*
Hiler-hiler-INT.CLIT say-SIM.CONV

erek *kusi-keči-ǯe-l-le-n* *Helnike-ñun*
this fight-DIST-PROG-INCH-NONFUT-3SG Helniken-COMIT

'-*Hiler-hiler-gu*, D'ajmuk-maid has been hiding Helniken all the time, only now she let him out.'

(406) *Helniken-de* *elekes*
Helniken-CONJ.CLIT for the first time

kusi-keče-le-d-di *göö-mi*
fight-DIST-INCH-PROG-NONFUT.PART say-COND.CONV

e-nne *naa-w-ra*
not_do-NEC.PART hit-PASS-NEG.CONV

'Helniken, although he is fighting for the first time, doesn't let the arrows strike him.'

(407) *erek* *Hilini* *bi-ǯeke-gde-we-n* *nemke-weeč-te-n*
this Hilini be-Nloc-DELIM-ACC-3SG shoot-HABIT-NONFUT-3SG
'When Hilini shoots his arrows come too late, hit the place where Helniken stood before.'

(408) *Hiler-hiler-gu* *eregegej*
Hiler-hiler-INT.CLIT well done

Hiler-hiler-gu *Helnike-ken*
Hiler-hiler-INT.CLIT Helniken-DIM

Hiler-hiler-gu *ajǯit*
Hiler-hiler-INT.CLIT really

Hiler-hiler-gu *er* *aja* *gaasani*
Hiler-hiler-INT.CLIT now good rival

iču-le-d-di	*uret-ken-ni*	*ootla*
appear-INCH-PROG-NONFUT.PART	similar-DIM-3SG	before

erweč-ke-me-n	*bej-u*	*e-č-u*
like this-DIM-ACC-3SG	man-ACC	not_do-PERF.PART-1SG

bakalda-r
meet-NEG.CONV

'-*Hiler-hiler-gu*, well done, Helniken, you are a worthy rival for me, I've never met such a rival before.'

(409)

Hiler-hiler-gu	*tar-da*	*bi-seke-n*
Hiler-hiler-INT.CLIT	that-CONJ.CLIT	be-COND.DS.CONV-3SG

eŋnije	*e-ǯi*	*hoowla-gra-ra*
too much	not_do-NEG.IMP.2SG	boast-PAST.ITER-NEG.CONV

nona-kan	*beje*	*bekečin*	*hin-geči-ken*
at first-DIM	man	all	you-EQUAT-DIM

hiña-kan-ǯur	*hetku-ri-l*
shadow-DIM-INSTR:REF.POS.PL	jump-NONFUT.PART-PL

bi-ǯ-gere-re
be-PROG-PAST.ITER-NONFUT.3PL

Hiler-hiler-gu	*eregegej*
Hiler-hiler-INT.CLIT	well done

Hiler-hiler-gu	*Ǯajmuk*	*asi*	*tiwömi*
Hiler-hiler-INT.CLIT	D'ajmuk	woman	therefore

Helniken-du	*bilgu-ǯaan-ča*
Helniken-DAT	caress-DUR-PERF.PART

Hiler-hiler-gu	*göö-niken*
Hiler-hiler-INT.CLIT	say-SIM.CONV

Hiler-hiler-gu	*göö-niken*
Hiler-hiler-INT.CLIT	say-SIM.CONV

'-*Hiler-hiler-gu*, no wonder that your wife D'ajmuk loves you so. But still, don't be arrogant. The others were at first fast too, faster than their own shadows.'

(410) | *erek* | *Helnike-m* | *ömniken-de* | *e-ti* |
|---|---|---|---|
| this | Helniken-ACC | once-CONJ.CLIT | not_do-NONFUT.PART |

naa-wkan	*erek*	*bi-leke-gde-we-n*	*nemke-weeč-te-n*
hit-CAUS	this	be-Nloc-DELIM-ACC-3SG	shoot-HABIT-NONFUT-3SG

'Hilini still shoots not quick enough to hit Helniken.'

(411) | *iči-čeken-de* | *ǯupti-č* | *nemke-weeč-te-n* |
|---|---|---|
| which-DIM-CONJ.CLIT | row-INSTR | shoot-HABIT-NONFUT-3SG |

erek	*Helniken*	*bi-leke-gde-n*	*bi-weeč-te-n*
this	Helniken	be-Nloc-DELIM-3SG	be-HABIT-NONFUT-3SG

'Now he shoots two arrows at a time, but still hits only the place where Helniken stood before.'

(412) | *hoo-ka-m* | *goru* | *kusi-keč-te* |
|---|---|---|
| very-DIM-ACC | for_a_long_time | fight-DIST-NONFUT.3PL |

'So they fight for a long time.'

(413) | *Meŋnuni-de* | *e-s-ni* | *kisan-na*[20] |
|---|---|---|
| Mengnuni-CONJ.CLIT | not_do-NONFUT-3SG | notice-NEG.CONV |

'As for Mengnuni, he doesn't care.'

(414) | *omolga-j* | *kusi-ǯe-l-če-le-n* |
|---|---|
| boy-REF.POS.SG | fight-PROG-INCH-PERF.PART-LOC-3SG |

ǯuu-la-j	*ii-ri-n*
house-LOC-REF.POS.SG	enter-PAST-3SG

'Since his son (Helniken) has joined the fight, he stays in the house.'

20 < Jak. *кыһан* 'care (for smb)'.

(415)

Hiler-hiler-gu	*Meŋnuni-ken*	*omolga-ji*
Hiler-hiler-INT.CLIT	Mengnuni-DIM	boy-REF.POS.SG

iniče-l-liǯii	*ajmakañǯa*	*asi-ŋ-dii*
hope-INCH-ANT.CONV	properly	woman-AL.POS-DAT:REF.POS

bilgu-ǯa-nni
caress-PROG-NONFUT.2SG

'-*Hiler-hiler-gu*, Mengnuni, you set your hopes on your son, you don't fight, amusing yourself with your wife.'

(416)

Metele-duk	*ire-ŋ-duku-n*	*kiran-duku-n*
Metele-ABL	which-AL.POS-ABL-3SG	edge-ABL-3SG

erwet-ken-ni	*bej-ken*	*balda-ri-n*
like this-DIM-3SG	man-DIM	be borne-PAST-3SG

Hiler-hiler-gu	*mannu-li-la*
Hiler-hiler-INT.CLIT	make effort(s)-IMP.2SG-CLIT

Hiler-hiler-gu	*göö-niken*
Hiler-hiler-INT.CLIT	say-SIM.CONV

'How come that Metele has turned into such a warrior (lit.: from what edge of Metele could such a man jump out). Still beware!'

(417)

erek	*Helniken*	*tarpač-kan-da*	*ere-w*	*Hilini*
this	Helniken	anyway-DIM-CONJ.CLIT	this-ACC	Hilini

oj-wa-n	*čöreke-l-le-n*
cloth-ACC-3SG	tear-INCH-NONFUT-3SG

beje-ŋe-n	*aǯgu-ŋa-da*
man-AL.POS-3SG	dodge-NEG.MOD.CONV-CONJ.CLIT

turku-či-l-le-n	*ureči-n*
not able-STAT-INCH-NONFUT-3SG	similar-3SG

'And Helniken has already torn Hilini's clothes with his arrows, the latter cannot dodge anymore.'

(418) *Hiler-hiler-gu* *iaakman-da* *e-te-n*
Hiler-hiler-INT.CLIT how long-CONJ.CLIT not_do-FUT-3SG

ad-da *adi* *ñur-u*
wear out-NEG.CONV how many arrow-ACC

kisna-ǯaka-n *oj-jaka-mu*
hit-Nloc-3SG cloth-DIM-1SG.POS

Hiler-hiler-gu *göön-ni*
Hiler-hiler-INT.CLIT say-NONFUT.3SG

'-*Hiler-hiler-gu*, how can my clothes look well, if the arrows tear them.'

(419) *tačin* *göön-ǯid-di-w* *gaad*
so say-PROG-NONFUT.PART-ACC half

gajsa-ŋ-i *čelges* *nemke-n*
pad-AL.POS-REF.POS.SG apart shoot-NONFUT.3SG

'While Hilini was saying that, Helniken splintered his leg with an arrow.'

(420) *Hiler-hiler-gu* *gaad-a* *tiri*
Hiler-hiler-INT.CLIT half-EPENTH garter

hegder-ri-ǯi-n *iaa-ǯi-n-da-si*
break off-NONFUT.PART-INSTR-3SG what-INSTR-3SG-CONJ.CLIT-CLIT

öse-ǯeen-ǯi-m *göö-niken*
not able-DUR-FUT-1SG say-SIM.CONV

'-*Hiler-hiler-gu*, what does it matter, if my (fur) boot belt is torn.'

(421) *un-de* *tačin* *göö-niken*
then-CONJ.CLIT so say-SIM.CONV

tuuhan-kači-d-di-w *erek* *bej-čen* *gaad*
jump-DIST-PROG-NONFUT.PART-ACC this man-DIM half

huraki-ŋ-i *čelges* *nemke-n*
wing's "forearm"-AL.POS-REF.POS.SG breaking shoot-NONFUT.3SG

'While he was saying that, Helniken pierced him the forearm with his arrow.'

(422)

Hiler-hiler-gu	*eregegej*	*Helnike-ken*
Hiler-hiler-INT.CLIT	well done	Helniken-DIM

Hiler-hiler-gu	*eliwen-de*	*hooni-kan*
Hiler-hiler-INT.CLIT	really-CONJ.CLIT	mighty-DIM

bi-mne-ge-s-e	*ilan*	*töör-du*
be-PROB-EPENTH-2SG-EPENTH	three	earth-DAT

gaas-ŋa-ji	*e-č-u*	*baka-ǯaañ-na*
rival-DES-REF.POS.SG	not_do-PERF.PART-1SG	find-DUR-NEG.CONV

'-*Hiler-hiler-gu*, valient Helniken, you are a real warrior, I've never met such a warrior in all the three worlds.'

(423)

Hiler-hiler-gu	*eregegej*	*mannu-ǯ-li-la*
Hiler-hiler-INT.CLIT	Well done	make_effort-PROG-IMP.2SG-CLIT

Hiler-hiler-gu	*eri-č-ke*	*iaa-ǯi-m*
Hiler-hiler-INT.CLIT	this-INSTR-CLIT	what_do-FUT-1SG

öse-ǯi-m
not able-FUT-1SG

Hiler-hiler-gu	*göö-niken*
Hiler-hiler-INT.CLIT	say-SIM.CONV

'-*Hiler-hiler-gu*, still beware! Should I fail because of this?!'

(424)

tarkilaki	*tuuhan-kači-d-da-n*	*gaad*	*böödel-ǯi*
like this	jump-DIST-PROG-NONFUT-3SG	half	feet-INSTR

tačin	*tuuhana-d-di-w*	*gaad*	*böödele-ŋ-i*
so	jump-PROG-NONFUT.PART-ACC	half	feet-AL.POS-REF.POS.SG

čelges	*nemke-n*	*ömen*	*ömčen*	*eme-p-če*
breaking	shoot-NONFUT.3SG	one	single	leave-MED-PERF.PART

'As he was jumping like that on one foot, Helniken cut his other leg off with an arrow.'

(425) *Hiler-hiler-gu* *teeri* *tiri*
Hiler-hiler-INT.CLIT both side(s) garter

hegder-ri-ken-ǯi-n
break off-NONFUT.PART-DIM-INSTR-3SG

iaa-ǯi-n-da-si *öse-ǯi-m*
what-INSTR-3SG-CONJ.CLIT-CLIT not able-FUT-1SG

'*-Hiler-hiler-gu*, what does it matter, if both boot-belts (suspenders) are torn.'

(426) *Hiler-hiler-gu* *gelile* *kata*[21] *e-te-m*
Hiler-hiler-INT.CLIT come_on better not_do-FUT-1SG

hiwse-tne-r *ač* *hönki-le-č*
stumble-MULT-NEG.CONV without toe-NEG.PROP-INSTR

tuuhana-bgan *oo-ča* *bi-ǯi-n*
jump-good_for become-PERF.PART be-FUT-3SG

Hiler-hiler-gu *göö-niken*
Hiler-hiler-INT.CLIT say-SIM.CONV

'*-Hiler-hiler-gu*, if you have no feet, you have nothing to stumble over.'

(427) *erek* *eŋeñe-gde* *bi-niken* *beje-ŋe-n*
this trunk-DELIM be-SIM.CONV man-AL.POS-3SG

tarak-at *heejuk-re-n*
that-CLIT dodge-NONFUT-3SG

'Hilini being a trunk, still tries to dodge from Helniken's arrows.'

---

21 < Jak. *xama* 'but, rather, better'.

(428)

erek	*Helniken*	*bi-mi*	*abalan-niʒi*[22]
this	Helniken	be-COND.CONV	get_angry-ANT.CONV

ñaan-da	*gaad*	*isaki-ŋ-i*
again-CONJ.CLIT	half	shoulder-blade-AL.POS-REF.POS.SG

eʒe-s	*nemke-n*
rip-CONV	shoot-3SG

'Helniken getting cross with him, smashed him another shoulder blade.'

(429)

eregegej	*Hiler-hiler-gu*	*Helnike-ken*
well done	Hiler-hiler-INT.CLIT	Helniken-DIM

Hiler-hiler-gu	*ereger*	*aji-č*	*bi-se-nni-le*
Hiler-hiler-INT.CLIT	always	good-INSTR	be-NONFUT-2SG-CLIT

Hiler-hiler-gu	*e-nikeken*
Hiler-hiler-INT.CLIT	not_do-SIM.CONV:DIM

heči-ʒeeñ-ne	*bakalda-ča*	*bi-mi*	*keni*
get tired-DUR-NEG.CONV	meet-PERF.PART	be-COND.CONV	CLIT

eliwen-de	*aj-kan*	*gaasan*	*bi-če*	*bi-mče-s*
really-CONJ.CLIT	good-DIM	rival	be-PERF.PART	be-SUBJ-2SG

Hiler-hiler-gu	*göö-niken*
Hiler-hiler-INT.CLIT	say-SIM.CONV

'-*Hiler-hiler-gu*, indeed you are a mighty hero! If I were not exausted, when I met you, we could have been worthy rivals.'

(430)

erek	*eŋeñe-gde*	*oo-riʒii*
this	trunk-DELIM	become-ANT.CONV

tuuhañ-kači-ʒa-l-la-n
jump-DIST-PROG-INCH-NONFUT-3SG

---

22 < Jak. cf. *аба* 'grief, annoyance'.

'So his (Hilini's) trunk keeps jumping around.'

(431)

tačin-da	*tuuhana-d-di-w*	*Helniken*
so-CONJ.CLIT	jump-PROG-NONFUT.PART-ACC	Helniken

bi-mi	*dila-ŋ-i*	*pompos*
be-COND.CONV	head-AL.POS-REF.POS.SG	cutting

nemke-n
shoot-NONFUT.3SG

'While Hilini's trunk is still jumping, Helniken cut finally his head off with an arrow.'

(432)

dila-ŋa-n	*okaata-ŋ-ma-n*	*ejeki*
head-AL.POS-3SG	river-AL.POS-ACC-3SG	downstream

čööndu-ne-sn-e-n
roll-ITER-MOM-NONFUT-3SG

'Hilihi's head rolled down the river.'

(433)

erek	*Helniken*	*dila-ŋ-i*	*höč-te-n*
this	Helniken	head-AL.POS-REF.POS.SG	chase-NONFUT-3SG

'Helniken pursued it.'

(434)

dila-ŋ-i	*bi-mi*	*ereger*	*heki-niken*
head-AL.POS-REF.POS.SG	be-COND.CONV	always	kick-SIM.CONV

er-teki-de	*heki-s-weeč-te-n*
this-DIR-CONJ.CLIT	kick-ITER-HABIT-NONFUT-3SG

tar-taki-da	*heki-s-weeč-te-n*
that-DIR-CONJ.CLIT	kick-ITER-HABIT-NONFUT-3SG

'Catching up, he kicks the head to and fro like a ball'.

(435)

dila-ŋ-ǯii	*ewi-niken*
head-AL.POS-INSTR.SG.REF.POS	play-SIM.CONV

tute-l-le-n *gaadač*
run-INCH-NONFUT-3SG ahead

'He runs on, kicking the head.'

(436) *hoo-ka-m* *goru* *ŋen-ne-n*
very-DIM-ACC for_a_long_time go-NONFUT-3SG
'So he chased the head for a long time.'

(437) *Hiler-hiler-gu* *ejemdi-ǯi* *oo-ǯaañ-na-m*
Hiler-hiler-INT.CLIT easy-INSTR become-DUR-NONFUT-1SG

Hiler-hiler-gu *i-li-ken-e*
Hiler-hiler-INT.CLIT which-PROL-DIM-EPENTH

böödel-ǯii *horni-ǯaan-ǯa-m*
feet-INSTR.SG.REF.POS stumble-DUR-FUT-1SG

Hiler-hiler-gu *göö-niken*
Hiler-hiler-INT.CLIT say-SIM.CONV

'-*Hiler-hiler-gu*, how splendid to travel light. No danger to stumble over something.'

(438) *erek* *beje-ŋe-n* *i-du-da* *e-s-ni*
this man-AL.POS-3SG which-DAT-CONJ.CLIT not_do-NONFUT-3SG

horu-waač-ta *dila-ŋa-n* *gaadač*
get caught-HABIT-NEG.CONV head-AL.POS-3SG ahead

čööndun-ne-n *erek* *bokn-iǯii* *dila-ŋ-i*
roll-NONFUT-3SG this catch-ANT.CONV head-AL.POS-REF.POS.SG

heki-s-weeč-te-n *gor-ja-la*
kick-ITER-HABIT-NONFUT-3SG long-EPENTH-LOC

'The man's head keeps rolling on, and the boy keeps chasing and kicking it.'

(439) *Giller-giller-gu* *erek* *dila-nǯa* *hebǯen-ne-ken-ni*
Giller-giller-INT.CLIT this head-AUGM fun-EPENTH-DIM-3SG

Giller-giller-gu	*oo-ǯaañ-na-n*
Giller-giller-INT.CLIT	become-DUR-NONFUT-3SG

'-*Giller-giller-gu*, how amusing is the head.'

(440)

er-mel-ken-ǯi	*ewi-ket-niken*
this-LOC.SPEC-DIM-INSTR	play-DISTR-SIM.CONV
Giller-giller-gu	*tööre-ŋ-jeke-mi*
Giller-giller-INT.CLIT	earth-AL.POS-DIM-REF.POS.SG
hoommi-ǯaan-da-ku	
go_round-DUR-PURP.CONV-1SG.IR	
Giller-giller-gu	*göö-niken*
Giller-giller-INT.CLIT	say-SIM.CONV

'I will go playing with it like that across the world.'

(441)

erek	*dila-ŋ-i*		*ŋene-ǯ-de-n*		
this	head-AL.POS-REF.POS.SG	kick-SIM.CONV	go-PROG-NONFUT-3SG		
hoo-kan	*goru*	*ŋen-niǯii*	*erek*	*bej*	*ömneken*
very-DIM	for_a_long_time	go-ANT.CONV	this	man	once
dila-ŋ-i		*ögeski*	*titakan-ni*		
head-AL.POS-REF.POS.SG		upward	toss-NONFUT.3SG		

'[Helniken] catching up kicks it forth. As Helniken was chasing Hilini's head, he kicked the head upwards.'

(442)

dila-nǯa-kan	*ögeski*	*ŋen-niǯii*	*okaat-la*
head-AUGM-DIM	upward	go-ANT.CONV	river-LOC
hör-re-n	*okaat-taki*	*tik-re-n*	*okaat*
go-NONFUT-3SG	river-DIR	fall-NONFUT-3SG	river
tik-re-n			
fall-NONFUT-3SG			

'The head then fell into the river.'

(443)

erek	*Helniken*	*bi-mi*	*dila-ŋ-i*
this	Helniken	be-COND.CONV	head-AL.POS-REF.POS.SG

amarda-du-n	*tut-te-n*	*okaat-la*	*tuuhaŋ-či-n*
behind-DAT-3SG	run-NONFUT-3SG	river-LOC	jump-STAT-NONFUT.3SG

erek	*dila-ŋ-i*	*dila-ŋ-čal*	*ömettu*
this	head-AL.POS-REF.POS.SG	head-AL.POS-COMIT.REF	together

okaat-la	*eje-sn-e-n*	*gaadač*	*okaat-u*
river-LOC	go downstream-MOM-NONFUT-3SG	ahead	river-ACC

ejeki
downstream

'Helniken also jumped into the river following it, swims chasing the head.'

(444)

hoo-kan	*goru*	*ejen-ni*
very-DIM	for_a_long_time	go downstream-NONFUT.3SG

'So they drift downstream for some time.'

(445)

Hiler-hiler-gu	*Helnike-ken*
Hiler-hiler-INT.CLIT	Helniken-DIM

Hiler-hiler-gu	*mannu-ǯ-li-la*
Hiler-hiler-INT.CLIT	make effort(s)-PROG-IMP.2SG-CLIT

Hiler-hiler-gu	*eči-ken*	*ŋene-d-deke-t*
Hiler-hiler-INT.CLIT	so-DIM	go-PROG-COND.DS.CONV-1PL.INC

Hiler-hiler-gu	*kargis*	*hooja*	*bi-ǯi-n-e-le*
Hiler-hiler-INT.CLIT	danger	many	be-FUT-3SG-EPENTH-CLIT

hooni-ka-ma-s	*hee-mke-či-d-de-ku*
mighty-DIM-ACC-2SG	try-CAUS-STAT-PROG-PURP.CONV-1SG.IRR

Hiler-hiler-gu	*göö-niken*
Hiler-hiler-INT.CLIT	say-SIM.CONV

‘-*Hiler-hiler-gu*, come on, many perils are waiting for us, let us try each other, see what each other are worth.’

(446)

un	*ejen-ǯiǯe-mnin*	*iaa-du-gal*
then	go downstream-PROG-CONSEC.CONV	what-DAT-INDEF.CLIT

hor-ra
get_caught-NONFUT.3PL

e-du	*hor-či-ǯaañ-na*
this-DAT	get caught-STAT-DUR-NONFUT:3PL

‘Well, as they were drifting downstream, they got caught on something and stuck fast.’

(447)

hiisečin	*araj*	*die-giǯi-tan*	*teŋke-duk*
evening	suddenly	up (on the mountain)-ELAT-3PL	giant tree-ABL

egǯen	*teŋke*	*dii-n*	*bej*	*hie-re-n*
big	giant tree	size-3SG	man	appear-NONFUT-3SG

‘In the evening a giant, bigger than a huge tree, came down from the river bank.’

(448)

osta-n	*egǯen*	*elgelde-gčin*	*iite-n*	*egǯen*	*kuñalda-gčin*
nail-3SG	big	harpoon-hook-EQUAT	teeth-3SG	big	fang-EQUAT

‘His claws are like harpoon hooks, teeth as big as fangs.’

(449)

Ö-ö	*alagda*	*erek*	*uuki-le-wu*[23]
Oh-EPENTH	delicious	this	weir-LOC-1SG

iaak-ta	*e-deŋe-n*	*hor-ra*
what-CONJ.CLIT	not_do-PAST.PART-3SG	get_caught-NEG.CONV

goral-la-n
move_away-NONFUT-3SG

23 *ukii* ‘(fishing) weir, dam’; Rus. ‘закол для ловли рыбы’.

'Oh, delicious, I haven't caught anything like that with my fishing-tackle for a long time.'

(450)

ere-w	*hiiseči-m*	*tireŋke-wur*
this-ACC	evening-ACC	hunger-REF.POS.PL

kañara-nna-l	*oo-ča-l*
assuage-NEC.PART-INCH	become-PERF.PART-PL

bi-se-p
be-NONFUT-1PL.INCL

'I'll enjoy eating these titbits tonight, fill myself properly.'

(451)

erek	*Hewejke-nǯe*	*ere-w*	*keŋere-lke-ke-ñ*
this	Hewejken-AUGM	this-ACC	fishing_basket-PROPR-DIM-INSTR

uuki-duku-j	*ga-riǯii*
weir-ABL-REF.POS.SG	take-ANT.CONV

beje-ŋe-l-bi	*huru-n*
man-AL.POS-PL-REF.POS.SG	bring-NONFUT.3SG

'The cannibal giant unfastened his fishing basket from the fishing-weir and brought them to his house.'

(452)

Teŋke	*dulakan-dula-n*	*egǯen*	*uute-mker*
giant tree	middle-LOC-3SG	big	log hut-AUGM2

ila-č-ta-n
stand up-STAT-NONFUT-3SG

'The house was built of big logs in the heart of the forest.'

(453)

ta-la	*emu-re-n*	*asa-l-a*
that-LOC	bring-NONFUT-3SG	woman-PL-EPENTH

hejkeče-ŋ-če-mur	*iri-lle*	*göön-ni*
fry-AL.POS-DIM-REF.POS.PL	cook-IMP:2PL	say-NONFUT.3SG

'Coming home says: "Women! Cook these small fishes!"'

(454) *bi ñaan-da tul-ne-de-ku göö-niken*
I again-CONJ.CLIT set-DIRECT-PURP.CONV-1SG.IRR say-SIM.CONV
'I'll go set my net again.'

(455) *erek dil-u ñaan ere-w bej-u Helnike-m*
this head-ACC again this-ACC man-ACC Helniken-ACC

böö-riǯii keŋere-ñǯe-j
give-ANT.CONV fishing-basket-AUGM-REF.POS.SG

tul-ne-n
set-DIRECT-NONFUT.3SG

'He gave Helniken and the Hilini's head to his domestics and left.'

(456) *erek kiaŋunǯa-l*[24] *bi-mi e-du*
this cannibal woman-PL be-COND.CONV this-DAT

iri-te-ǯe-l-le-n gia
cook-STAT-PROG-INCH-NONFUT-3SG other

unta-ñǯa-j takusa-si-ǯ-da-n
fur_boot-AUGM-REF.POS.SG mend-ASP-PROG-NONFUT-3SG

gia bi-mi moo-ga-j taw-na-n
other be-COND.CONV wood-DES-REF.POS.SG gather-DIRECT-3SG

erek hejkeče-ŋe-l-bi iri-de-j
this fry-AL.POS-PL-REF.POS.SG cook-PURP.CONV-REF.POS.SG

'One of the giant women set the pot cooking; the other mended the fur boots. The first one went meanwhile to gather fire wood, in order to cook the pray.'

(457) *erek hewej-ken keŋer-i tul-ne-n*
this cannibal giant-DIM fishing-basket-REF.POS.SG set-DIRECT-3SG
'The cannibal giant left to set a fishing basket(again).'

---

24 Cf. Ewk. *kengmak* 'witch'.

(458) *erek* *ieeke-ten* *hökele-ǯ-de-n*
this pot-3PL warm up-PROG-NONFUT-3SG
'The pot warmed up.'

(459) *erek* *bej* *bi-mi* *Helniken* *ieeke-čen-di*
this man be-COND.CONV Helniken pot-DIM-DAT:REF.POS.SG

tege-č-te-n *gia-ji* *kööje-t-niken*
sit_down-STAT-NONFUT-3SG other-REF.POS.SG glance-STAT-SIM.CONV

dila-ŋ-i *kööje-t-niken*
head-AL.POS-REF.POS.SG glance-STAT-SIM.CONV

'Helniken is sitting inside together with Hilini's head, watching it.'

(460) *dila-ŋa-n* *bi-mi* *gia-tki-j*
head-AL.POS-3SG be-COND.CONV other-DIR-REF.POS.SG

tööre-ǯe-l-le-n *dil* *dila-n* *bi-niken*
talk-PROG-INCH-NONFUT-3SG head head-3SG be-SIM.CONV

'Now, the head addressed [Helniken]'.

(461) *Hiler-hiler-gu* *Helnike-ken*
Hiler-hiler-INT.CLIT Helniken-DIM

Hiler-hiler-gu *iaa-kan-ǯa* *mergen-ǯii*
Hiler-hiler-INT.CLIT what-DIM-INSTR thought-INSTR.SG.REF.POS

Harkila-kan *ieeke-nǯe-du-n* *tege-če-nni*
Harkilan-DIM pot-AUGM-DAT-3SG sit_down-STAT-NONFUT.2SG

Hiler-hiler-gu *ečin* *kubeči-č* *iri-riǯur*
Hiler-hiler-INT.CLIT this_way all-INSTR cook-ANT.CONV.PL

ǯebe-ǯeen-ǯi-r
eat-DUR-FUT-3PL

'-*Hiler-hiler-gu*, what are you pondering over, sitting inside Harkilan's pot. If we keep sitting like that, they will cook us.'

(462) *Hiler-hiler-gu* *Harkila-kan* *ere-w* *hiiseči-m*
Hiler-hiler-INT.CLIT Harkilan-DIM this-ACC evening-ACC

tireŋke-ji *kañara-ǯ-ǯi-n*
hunger-REF.POS.SG assuage-PROG-FUT-3SG

Hiler-hiler-gu *göö-niken* *e-duk*
Hiler-hiler-INT.CLIT say-SIM.CONV this-ABL

e-seke-t *ñoon-a*
not_do-COND.DS.CONV-1PL.INC run.NEG.CONV-EPENTH

göön-ni
say-NONFUT.3SG

'-*Hiler-hiler-gu*, Harkilan will enjoy eating us, if we do not escape.'

(463) *erek* *kiaŋunǯa* *bi-mi* *tara-w-da*
this cannibal woman be-COND.CONV that-ACC-CONJ.CLIT

e-ti-mdes *dolda-r*
not_do-NONFUT.PART-SIMIL hear-NEG.CONV

unta-j *haŋana-si-d-da-n*
fur_boot-REF.POS.SG sew-ASP-PROG-NONFUT-3SG

'The cannibal woman, who was watching the pot, apparently didn't hear it, kept on patching the fur boots.'

(464) *ǯuu-j* *haan-saka-n* *iaasal-i*
house-REF.POS.SG smoke-COND.DS.CONV-3SG eye(s)-REF.POS.SG

hik-niken
rub-SIM.CONV

'The fire smoked. The house being full of fumes, she rubbed her sore eyes.'

(465) *hii-kene* *ičin* *ñoo-nna-s* *bi* *hin-u-ñun*
you-DIM how flee-NEC.PART-2SG I you-ACC-CLIT

etu-re-m *göön-ni*
watch-NONFUT-1SG say-NONFUT.3SG

'"I'll watch how you escape".'

(466) *hii* *ñoon-aka-s* *ñoon-ǯi-m*
you run-COND.DS.CONV-2SG run-FUT-1SG

e-seke-s-te *hin-ñun*
not_do-COND.DS.CONV-2SG-CONJ.CLIT you-COMIT

e-du *ir-ǯi-m*
this-DAT cook-FUT-1SG

'If you manage escaping, I'll manage as well, if not, we shall cook together here in Harkilan's pot.'

(467) *eregegej* *Hiler-hiler-gu* *tačimar* *ñaan-a*
well done Hiler-hiler-INT.CLIT this_way again-EPENTH

göön-ǯid-mi-ken *ajmakañǯa* *kööje-či-d-li*
say-PROG-COND.CONV-DIM properly glance-STAT-PROG-IMP.2SG

ǯelu-ǯike-s
miss-PREV-2SG

Hiler-hiler-gu *e-ǯi-meken* *ǯelu-re-le*
Hiler-hiler-INT.CLIT not_do-NEG.IMP.2SG-CLIT miss-NEG.CONV-CLIT

Hiler-hiler-gu *göön-ni*
Hiler-hiler-INT.CLIT say-NONFUT.3SG

'-Well said. Then be on your guard. Do not miss your chance.'

(468) *aji-č* *kööje-t-li* *ǯelu-mi-ñun*
good-INSTR glance-STAT-IMP.2SG miss-COND.CONV-CLIT

eme-b-ǯi-nni *e-du*
leave-MED-FUT-2SG this-DAT

'If you overlook how shall I escape, you will remain here,'

(469) *tačin* *göön-ǯiǯe-mnin* *erek* *dila-n*
so say-PROG-CONSEC.CONV this head-3SG

dila-ŋa-ñǯa-n *halkamča-li* *tuuhaŋ-či-n*
head-AL.POS-AUGM-3SG smoke-hole-PROL jump-STAT-NONFUT.3SG

'Saying that the head as it was jumped outside through the smoke-hole.'

(470) *erek* *bej-de* *dilaŋi* *amarda-du-n*
this man-CONJ.CLIT head-AL.POS-REF.POS.SG behind-DAT-3SG

tuuhaŋčin
jump-STAT-NONFUT.3SG

'Helniken leaped after the head in the same way.'

(471) *erek-ǯe* *hööt-meč-ti-ten*
this-CLIT chase-REC-PAST-3PL
'He began to chase it again.'

(472) *erek* *kiaŋunǯa* *bi-mi* *unta-j*
this cannibal woman be-COND.CONV fur_boot-REF.POS.SG

haŋana-ssi-ǯaan-naka-n *Hewejken* *em-ne-n*
sew-CONAT-DUR-COND.DS.CONV-3SG Hewejken come-NONFUT-3SG

keŋere-j[25] *tul-liǯii*
fishing-basket-REF.POS.SG set-ANT.CONV

'The giant-woman was still mending boots, when the cannibal-giant, having set his net, returned.'

(473) *Keruwke* *asi-jan*
Keruwke woman-VOCAT

Keruwke *Čulpuk-kan*
Keruwke Chulpuk-DIM

---

25 Cf. Ewk. *kenger~kunger* 'fishing basket (верша).'

Keruwke *i-le-je-ke-t*
Keruwke which-LOC-EPENTH-CLIT-CLIT

Keruwke *iaa-ra-n* *ir-re-n*
Keruwke what_do-NONFUT-3SG cook (itr)-NONFUT-3SG

'-*Keruvke*, wife Chulpuk, is the meal ready?'

(474) *Keruwke* *töl-gižii* *em-nižii* *ieeke-j*
Keruwke outside-ELAT come-ANT.CONV pot-REF.POS.SG

iči-ssi-reke-n *iaak-ta* *ačča* *ieeke*
see-CONAT-COND.DS.CONV-3SG what-CONJ.CLIT not_exist pot

doo-la-n
pot inside-LOC-3SG

'Going outside, he peeped into the pot and found out that it was empty.'

(475) *Keruwke* *hejkeče-ŋ-ke-r-ti*
Keruwke fry-AL.POS-DIM-PL-1PL.INC.POS

Keruwke *i-le* *ŋen-ni-ten*
Keruwke which-LOC go-PAST-3PL

Keruwke *iaaŋ-ni-san-a*
Keruwke what_do-PAST-2PL.POS-EPENTH

Keruwke *huu-ken* *iaak-a*
Keruwke you (PL)-DIM what-EPENTH

Keruwke *e-du* *bi-d-niken*
Keruwke this-DAT be-PROG-SIM.CONV

Keruwke *žebe-sen-če-l*
Keruwke eat-MOM-PERF.PART-PL

Keruwke *bi-se-s-e*
Keruwke be-NONFUT-2PL-EPENTH

Keruwke	*göö-niken*
Keruwke	say-SIM.CONV

‘-*Keruvke*, where are my young fishes gone? You have remained here, you must have eaten them.’

(476)

E-e	*bi*	*e-č-u*	*ǯep-te*
Oh-EPENTH	I	not_do-PERF.PART-1SG	eat-NEG.CONV

göön-ni	*tawar*	*Toosañ*	*iri-te-ǯe-mnin*
say-NONFUT.3SG	that_one	Toosan‘	cook-STAT-PROG-CONSEC.CONV

ǯebe-sn-iǯur	*ñöö-če*	*bi-ǯi-n*
eat-MOM-ANT.CONV.PL	go out-PERF.PART	be-FUT-3SG

moo-ga-j	*taw-na-san*	*bi-niken*
wood-DES-REF.POS.SG	gather-DIRECT-IMIT	be-SIM.CONV

‘No, I haven’t - said Chulpuk. - Your sister Tosan’ did the cooking, she must have eaten, pretending to go after fire wood.’

(477)

Hujelkiñ	*ook-a*	*ǯebe-d-ǯi-m-a*
Hujelkin’	when-EPENTH	eat-PROG-FUT-1SG-EPENTH

Hujelkiñ	*er*	*unta-i*
Hujelkin’	this	fur_boot-REF.POS.SG

Hujelkiñ	*taku-sa-ǯ-da-m*
Hujelkin’	mend-ITER-PROG-NONFUT-1SG

Hujelkiñ	*Toosañ-kana*
Hujelkin’	Toosan’-DIM

Hujelkiñ	*ta-la-wara*
Hujelkin’	that-LOC-CLIT

Hujelkiñ	*ieeke-če-mi*
Hujelkin’	pot-DIM-REF.POS.SG

Hujelkiñ	*iaaru-ta-ǯ-di-n*
Hujelkin’	check-STAT-PROG-PAST-3SG

Metele

Hujelkiñ	*göön-ni*
Hujelkin’	say-NONFUT.3SG

‘-*Hujelkiñ*, when could I eat them, I was too busy mending the shoes, Tosan’ did the cooking, - said Chulpuk.’

(478)

göö-niken	*erek*	*tačin*	*göö-meči-d-deke-ten*
say-SIM.CONV	this	so	say-REC-PROG-COND.DS.CONV-3PL

erek	*Toosañ*	*ii-n*	*moo-j*	*ŋaal-nikan*
this	Toosan’	enter-NONFUT.3SG	wood-REF.POS.SG	bear-SIM.CONV

‘When they were quarrelling like that, Tosan’ returned bringing the firewood.’

(479)

erek	*any*	*Toosañ-ur*	*oj-la-n*	*tik-re*
this	now	Toosan’-REF.POS.PL	above-LOC-3SG	fall-NONFUT.3PL

‘The other attacked her without any ado.’

(480)

Geriñču	*bi*	*e-č-u*
Gerin’cu	I	not_do-PERF.PART-1SG

Geriñču	*ǯebe-ǯ-de*
Gerin’cu	eat-PROG-NEG.CONV

Geriñču
Gerin’cu

‘-*Gerin’chu*, I haven’t eaten, [said Tosan’].’

(481)

erek	*ǯöör*	*kiaŋunǯa-l*	*any*	*tarič*	*meer*
this	two	cannibal woman-PL	now	then	REF.PL

doo-li	*hutu-meči-l-le*	*ñuurit-tuk-ur*
inside-PROL	chase-REC-PL-NONFUT.3PL	hair-ABL-REF.POS.PL

‘The two cannibal women started to fight, pulling each other by hair.’

(482)	*Keruwke*	*e-ǯi-lle-le*	
	Keruwke	not_do-NEG.IMP.2SG-IMP:2PL-CLIT	
	Keruwke	*kusi-keč-te*	
	Keruwke	fight-DIST-NEG.CONV	
	Keruwke	*ge*	*hun-ke-me*
	Keruwke	come_on	you (PL)-DIM-ACC
	Keruwke	*iči-ǯ-de-ku*	
	Keruwke	see-PROG-PURP.CONV-1SG.IRR	
	Keruwke	*eweski-ke*	
	Keruwke	here(DIR)-CLIT	
	Keruwke	*eme-lle-le*	
	Keruwke	come-IMP:2PL-CLIT	
	Keruwke	*göön-ni*	
	Keruwke	say-NONFUT.3SG	

'-*Keruvke*, stop fighting, I shall check both of you, come over here.'

(483)	*Geriñču*	*aka-ran*		
	Gerin'cu	(elder) brother-VOCAT		
	Geriñču	*Harkilan*		
	Gerin'cu	Harkilan		
	Geriñču	*bi*	*e-č-u*	
	Gerin'cu	I	not_do-PERF.PART-1SG	
	Geriñču	*ǯebe-ǯ-de*		
	Gerin'cu	eat-PROG-NEG.CONV		
	Geriñču	*e-č-u*		*e-č-u*
	Gerin'cu	not_do-PERF.PART-1SG		not_do-PERF.PART-1SG
	Geriñču	*ǯebe-ǯ-de*		
	Gerin'cu	eat-PROG-NEG.CONV		

'-*Gerin'chu*, brother Harkilan, I haven't eaten, I swear!'

(484) *Geriñču* *Čulpuk* *öji*
Gerin'cu Chulpuk sister-in-law

Geriñču *eme-p-ti-n*
Gerin'cu come-MED-PAST-3SG

Geriñču *noŋan-kke* *e-te-n*
Gerin'cu (s)he-SPEC.CLIT not_do-FUT-3SG

Geriñču *ǯep-če* *bi-se*
Gerin'cu eat-PERF.PART be-NEG.CONV

Geriñču *göö-niken*
Gerin'cu say-SIM.CONV

'Your wife Chulpuk stayed here, she must have eaten.'

(485) *Harkilan* *bi-mi* *erek* *hinŋapan-ǯa-j*
Harkilan be-COND.CONV this sword-INSTR-REF.POS.SG

ga-riǯii *uru-we-n* *Čulpuk* *höki-sn-e-n*
take-ANT.CONV belly-ACC-3SG Chulpuk rip-MOM-NONFUT-3SG

'Harkilan hearing this, takes a sword and cuts Chulpuk's belly.'

(486) *Čulpuk-le-n* *iaa-duk* *bi-ǯi-n* *iaa-w-da*
Chulpuk-LOC-3SG what-ABL be-FUT-3SG what-ACC-CONJ.CLIT

e-če *ǯep-te* *ur-le-n*
not_do-PERF.PART eat-NEG.CONV belly-LOC-3SG

iak-ta *ačča*
what-CONJ.CLIT not_exist

'But Chulpuk's belly is empty, why should there be anything inside.'

(487) *Keruwke* *mulakja-da*
Keruwke alas-CONJ.CLIT

Keruwke *atika-mu*
Keruwke old woman-1SG.POS

Keruwke *maa-wkana-nni*
Keruwke kill-CAUS-NONFUT.2SG

Keruwke *eluken* *Toosañ-kan*
Keruwke sister Toosan'-DIM

Keruwke *göö-niken*
Keruwke say-SIM.CONV

nöö-tki-j *iaa-n*
younger sister-DIR-REF.POS.SG what_do-NONFUT.3SG

nöö-j *ur-we-n* *höki-n*
younger sister-REF.POS.SG belly-ACC-3SG rip-NONFUT.3SG

'-*Keruvke*, what a pity, you had me kill my wife, my sister Tosan', - said Harkilan and cut his sister's belly too.'

(488) *nöö-n* *ur-le-n* *ačča*
younger sister-3SG belly-LOC-3SG not_exist
'But there is nothing inside either.'

(489) *Keruwke* *eregegej*
Keruwke well done

Keruwke *ere-ŋe-l-bi*
Keruwke this-AL.POS-PL-REF.POS.SG

Keruwke *tireŋke-j*
Keruwke hunger-REF.POS.SG

Keruwke *kañara-ǯ-ǯi-m*
Keruwke assuage-PROG-FUT-1SG

Keruwke *göö-niken*
Keruwke say-SIM.CONV

'-*Keruvke*, all right, I shall fill myself with these two.'

(490) *erek* *Harkila-ñǯa* *kiaŋuñǯa-ŋa-l-bi*
this Harkilan-AUGM cannibal_woman-AL.POS-PL-REF.POS.SG

bej-mel-u-ten *öle-t-niken*
man-LOC.SPEC-ACC-3PL cook-STAT-SIM.CONV

ǯebe-ǯe-l-le-n *erek* *noŋan* *ǯebe-ǯ-de-n*
eat-PROG-INCH-NONFUT-3SG this (s)he eat-PROG-NONFUT-3SG

'Harkilan cooked up the giant women, and started to devour them.'

(491) *erek* *Helniken* *bi-mi* *dila-ŋ-i*
this Helniken be-COND.CONV head-AL.POS-REF.POS.SG

hulu-niken *gaadač* *hör-re-n*
chase-SIM.CONV ahead go-NONFUT-3SG

'As for Helniken, he kept on chasing the head as before.'

(492) *er* *ičin* *ŋen-ni-n-de* *tačin*
now like.this go-PAST-3SG-CONJ.CLIT so

ŋen-meč-te-n *heke-niken-de*
go-HABIT-NONFUT-3SG kick-SIM.CONV-CONJ.CLIT

iaa-nikan-da
what_do-SIM.CONV-CONJ.CLIT

'Catching up, he kicked it to and fro.'

(493) *Hiler-hiler-gu* *e-ǯi-ge-le*
Hiler-hiler-INT.CLIT not_do-NEG.IMP.2SG-EPENTH-CLIT

menu-ǯeeñ-ne *isa-nna-la-wur*
hurry-DUR-NEG.CONV reach-NEC.PART-LOC-REF.POS.PL

ook-ta-wu-la *bi-seke-n*
when-CONJ.CLIT-INT.CLIT-CLIT be-COND.DS.CONV-3SG

isa-ǯaan-ǯa-p
reach-DUR-FUT-1PL.INCL

Hiler-hiler-gu *tiek-e* *iaaka*
Hiler-hiler-INT.CLIT now-EPENTH what

dalbala-d-di-l *ureč-ken-ti*
approach-PROG-NONFUT.PART-PL similar-DIM-1PL.INC.POS

Hiler-hiler-gu *göö-niken*
Hiler-hiler-INT.CLIT say-SIM.CONV

'-*Hiler-hiler-gu*, do not be in such a hurry, soon we shall reach the place we are making our way to, it looks as if we are approaching it.'

(494) *erek* *Helniken* *tara-w* *e-s-ni*
this Helniken that-ACC not_do-NONFUT-3SG

dolda-waač-ta *sin bir* *heke-niken*
hear-HABIT-NEG.CONV anyway kick-SIM.CONV

hulu-weeč-te-n
chase-HABIT-NONFUT-3SG

'Helniken didn't care, chased him as before.'

(495) *tačin* *hulu-meči-d-deke-ten*
so chase-REC-PROG-COND.DS.CONV-3PL

oŋka-ča-kan *oo-d-ni*
graze-DIM-DIM become-NONFUT-3SG

hoo-kan *hooja* *oron* *oŋka-ča*
very-DIM many reindeer graze-PRF.PART

'In this way they approached the pasture, with a lot of reindeer grazing.'

(496) *erek* *oŋka* *doo-li-n* *ŋen-ne-n* *gaadač*
this graze inside-PROL-3SG go-NONFUT-3SG ahead

oŋka *doo-li-n* *ŋene-d-niken* *oŋka*
graze inside-PROL-3SG go-PROG-SIM.CONV graze

mudan-dula-n *čaaski* *oŋka-w* *ielten-če-le-ten*
end-LOC-3SG further graze-ACC pass-PERF.PART-LOC-3PL

ojiñǯa-mkar *moo-w* *huutu-si-ǯeeñ-ne-n*
woodcutter-AUGM2 wood-ACC carry (off)-ASP-DUR-NONFUT-3SG

'Passing the pasture, Helniken saw at the far edge of the pasture a woodcutter dragging wood.'

(497) *egǯen* *tenmek* *dii-n* *dila-lkan* *mirke-ǯeeñ-ne-n*
big boulder size-3SG head-PROP crawl-DUR-NONFUT-3SG
'He came dragging, almost crawling, with his huge head as big as a boulder.'

(498) *ninkata-ŋ-ga-n* *teke-lke-ke-ñ*
dead tree-AL.POS-DES-3SG root-PROPR-DIM-INSTR

iaa-lka-ka-ñ *ira-ǯ-da-n*
what-PROP-DIM-INSTR drag-PROG-NONFUT-3SG

'He dragged whole dead trees with their roots and all.'

(499) *Hiler-hiler-gu* *ojinǯa-kan* *boliñǯa-kan*
Hiler-hiler-INT.CLIT woodcutter-DIM servant-DIM

oon-di-čakan *bi-gre-nni*
how-sort-DIM be-PAST.ITER-NONFUT.2SG

ooti-gda-ǯur *eme-ǯeeñ-ne-m*
despair-DELIM-INSTR:REF.POS.PL come-DUR-NONFUT-1SG

Hiler-hiler-gu *er-teken-te*
Hiler-hiler-INT.CLIT this-REST-CONJ.CLIT

bi-deŋ-ken-ti
be-PAST.PART-DIM-1PL.INC.POS

Hiler-hiler-gu *göö-niken*
Hiler-hiler-INT.CLIT say-SIM.CONV

'*-Hiler-hiler-gu*, my servant-woodcutter, what a miserable sight, I return suffering too, what a misfortune!'

(500)

erek	*bej*	*moo-ŋ-i*	*ir-nikan*
this	man	wood-AL.POS-REF.POS.SG	drag-SIM.CONV

huutu-si-d-di-w	*hiakita-ŋa-nʒa-n*
carry-ASP-PROG-NONFUT.PART-ACC	tree-AL.POS-AUGM-3SG

Helniken	*ninkata-ŋa-n*	*huure-du-n*	*töö-re-n*
Helniken	dead_tree-AL.POS-3SG	top-DAT-3SG	step on-NONFUT-3SG

'As the wood-cutter was dragging the tree, Helniken tread on its top.'

(501)

erek	*noŋan-da*	*bi-mi*
this	(s)he-CONJ.CLIT	be-COND.CONV

binara-ssi-mi	*turku-n*
pull-CONAT-COND.CONV	not able-NONFUT.3SG

'The other one drugged straining all his strength, digging his heels into the ground, but still could not move it.'

(502)

erek	*dila-ŋa-n*	*gaadač*	*ejeki*	*hör-re-n*
this	head-AL.POS-3SG	ahead	downstream	go-NONFUT-3SG

'As for (Hilini's) head, it went ahead downstream.'

(503)

erek	*ojinʒa-kan*	*ñaan-da*	*binar-ra-n*
this	woodcutter-DIM	again-CONJ.CLIT	pull-NONFUT-3SG

nider-re-n	*ösömiken*	*henŋe-kli-i*
plunge-NONFUT-3SG	even	knee-LOC.PROL-REF.POS.SG

'The woodcutter plants his feet so firmly that they sank into the ground up to his knees.'

(504)

erek	*Tenmendeñ-Tenmendeñ*	*iaak-ta-gal-a*
this	Tenmenden'-Tenmenden'	what-CONJ.CLIT-INDEF.CLIT-EPENTH

hinar-kan-ni[26]	*oo-ǯaañ-na-n*
nuisance-DIM-3SG	become-DUR-NONFUT-3SG

Tenmendeñ-Tenmendeñ	*bej-ken*	*ečin*	*oo-raka-n*
Tenmenden'-Tenmenden'	man-DIM	this_way	become-COND.DS.CONV-3SG

Tenmendeñ-Tenmendeñ	*iaak*	*bekečin*	*kirgis*
Tenmenden'-Tenmenden'	what	all	trouble

oo-waač-ta-n
become-HABIT-NONFUT-3SG

Tenmendeñ-Tenmendeñ	*göö-niken*
Tenmenden'-Tenmenden'	say-SIM.CONV

binar-ra-n	*turku-n*
pull-NONFUT-3SG	not able-NONFUT.3SG

'-*Tenmendeñ-Tenmendeñ*, what a nuisance! Living so, I am having trouble all the time. - He pulled the tree with all his force, still cannot move it.'

(505)

erek	*turku-riǯii*	*tarpač-ta*
this	not able-ANT.CONV	anyway-CONJ.CLIT

moo-ŋa-ñǯa-j	*ule-mnin*
wood-AL.POS-AUGM-REF.POS.SG	throw-CONSEC.CONV

esen-ǯid-di-w
glance (back)-PROG-NONFUT.PART-ACC

erek	*bej-čen*	*bi-mi*	*amar-gič*	*ojinǯa*
this	man-DIM	be-COND.CONV	behind-ELAT	woodcutter

dil-wa-n	*hinŋapan-ǯi*	*kaltas*	*hoona-sn-a-n*
head-ACC-3SG	sword-INSTR	splitting	cut-MOM-NONFUT-3SG

'Annoyed, he flung the tree on the ground and was about to turn around, when Helniken cut off him the head with his sword.'

26 Ewk. *henni-* 'get angry'.

(506)

ojinǯa	*čajda-duku-n*	*čajda-la-n*	*bej*	*bej-ǯi*
woodcutter	behind-ABL-3SG	behind-LOC-3SG	man	man-INSTR

tuuhaŋ-či-n
jump-STAT-NONFUT.3SG

'All at once there jumped another man out of the wood-cutter.'

(507)

Tenmendeñ-Tenmendeñ	*er-ken*	*ñaan-a*
Tenmenden'-Tenmenden'	this-DIM	again-EPENTH

ir-giči-ken-ǯi	*eme-le-nni*
which-ELAT-DIM-INSTR	come-INCH-NONFUT.2SG

Tenmendeñ-Tenmendeñ	*bi-de-wul*
Tenmenden'-Tenmenden'	be-CONJ.CLIT-INT.CLIT

eme-ken	*bej*	*bi-se-m-e*
newcomer-DIM	man	be-NONFUT-1SG-EPENTH

Tenmendeñ-Tenmendeñ	*göö-niken*
Tenmenden'-Tenmenden'	say-SIM.CONV

erek	*beje-ŋe-n*	*kusi-keče-l-le-n*
this	man-AL.POS-3SG	fight-DIST-INCH-NONFUT-3SG

'-*Tenmendeñ-Tenmendeñ*, where have you come from, I myself am a stranger in this land. - The wood-cutter started to fight with Helniken.'

(508)

erek	*ojinǯa-ñun*	*ŋuneke-m*	*kusi-keč-te-n*
this	woodcutter-COMIT	some time-ACC	fight-DIST-NONFUT-3SG

e-s-ni	*tači-kan*	*goru*	*kusi-r*
not_do-NONFUT-3SG	like that-DIM	for_a_long_time	fight-NEG.CONV

'Helniken didn't fight with the woodcutter for a long time.'

(509)

erek	*eŋeñ-me-n*	*pompas*	*nemke-n*
this	waist-ACC-3SG	cutting	shoot-NONFUT.3SG

'After a while he shot an arrow through his breast.'

Metele

(510) *Tenmendeñ-Tenmendeñ* *Neeruk* *asi* *iig-je-le-n*
Tenmenden'-Tenmenden' Neeruk woman rumour-EPENTH-LOC-3SG

em-niʒii *moo-ŋ-ga-n-da-wur*
come-ANT.CONV wood-AL.POS-DES-3SG-CONJ.CLIT-CLIT

mooli-d-da-m *dabda-riʒii*
go for wood-PROG-NONFUT-1SG loose-ANT.CONV

'-*Tenmendeñ-Tenmendeñ*, I had come here attracted by Neruk-maiden's fame. After losing (to her brothers), I had to stay here, serving as a wood-cutter.'

(511) *Tenmendeñ-Tenmendeñ* *hi-da-gu* *bi-mi-ken*
Tenmenden'-Tenmenden' you-CONJ.CLIT-INT.CLIT be-COND.CONV-DIM

Tenmendeñ-Tenmendeñ *iaaka-gu-de* *degerek-čen*
Tenmenden'-Tenmenden' what-INT.CLIT-CONJ.CLIT equal-DIM

tere-ʒi-nni
overwhelm-FUT-2SG

Tenmendeñ-Tenmendeñ *göö-mnin*
Tenmenden'-Tenmenden' say-CONSEC.CONV

beje-ŋe-nʒe-n *tik-re-n*
man-AL.POS-AUGM-3SG fall-NONFUT-3SG

'-*Tenmendeñ-Tenmendeñ*, anyhow, you'll lose too, - saying so he collapsed on the ground.'

(512) *erek* *bej* *ieeltes* *hör-re-n*
this man past go-NONFUT-3SG
'Helniken went ahead.'

(513) *tačin* *tute-l-le-n* *ʒuleski*
so run-INCH-NONFUT-3SG ahead

tačin *tute-ʒ-deke-n* *i-le-gel*
so run-PROG-COND.DS.CONV-3SG which-LOC-INDEF.CLIT

i-le	*untun*	*direlen-ni*	*ii-s-ni*
which-LOC	tambourine	clink-3SG	sound-NONFUT-3SG

'As he was running ahead, he heard the clink of shaman's tambourine.'

(514)

Neril-Neril	*eluken-e*	*Hilini-ken*	
Neril-Neril	brother-EPENTH	Hilini-DIM	
Neril-Neril	*eregej*	*bi-ŋen*	*iaaka*
Neril-Neril	well done	I-CLIT	what

e-mne-ke-mu	*tere-ǯeeñ-ne*
not_do-PROB-DIM-1SG.POS	overwhelm-DUR-NEG.CONV

'-*Neril-Neril*, brother Hilini, daring warrior, I cannot overwhelm Helniken.'

(515)

Neril-Neril	*ǯal-ǯi-da*	*e-ǯi*
Neril-Neril	mood-INSTR-CONJ.CLIT	not_do-NEG.IMP.2SG

ǯawa-ǯ-da-la
catch-PROG-NEG.CONV-CLIT

Neril-Neril	*Helnike-ke-m*	*ejel-diǯi*
Neril-Neril	Helniken-DIM-ACC	like-ANT.CONV
Neril-Neril	*e-se-nni*	*aj-či-ǯaañ-na*
Neril-Neril	not_do-NONFUT-2SG	help-STAT-DUR-NEG.CONV
Neril-Neril	*göö-niken*	
Neril-Neril	say-SIM.CONV	
Neril-Neril	*e-ǯi-le*	*köömele-ǯ-de*
Neril-Neril	not_do-NEG.IMP.2SG-CLIT	be disappointed-PROG-CONJ.CLIT

'-*Neril-Neril*, don't be cross with me, don't think: "She wouldn't help me, because she fell in love with Helniken."'

(516)

Neril-Neril	*depki-kene*	*iči-sn-eke-n*
Neril-Neril	against-DIM	see-MOM-COND.DS.CONV-3SG

Neril-Neril *depki-keken* *iče-sn-eke-n*
Neril-Neril against-DIM see-MOM-COND.DS.CONV-3SG

ǯaja-tna-ra-m
hide-MULT-NONFUT-1SG

Neril-Neril *iaasal-kan-ni* *tog-kan-ni* *emer-ken-ni*
Neril-Neril eye(s)-DIM-3SG fire-DIM-3SG sharp-DIM-3SG

Neril-Neril *ösömiken* *hujalkin-na-n*
Neril-Neril even shine-NONFUT-3SG

'-*Neril-Neril*, Believe me, I cannot stand Helniken's keen gaze, his eyes are sharp as sparkles.'

(517) *Neril-Neril* *eregegej*
Neril-Neril well done

Neril-Neril *e-mne-ke-mu* *tere-ǯeeñ-ne*
Neril-Neril not_do-PROB-DIM-1SG.POS overwhelm-DUR-NONFUT

Neril-Neril *mut-ŋen* *iaak-a*
Neril-Neril we-CLIT what-EPENTH

tere-nne-l-e *bi-seke-t-e*
overwhelm-NEC.PART-PL-EPENTH be-COND.DS.CONV-1PL.INC-EPENTH

Neril-Neril *untu-nǯe-ken* *iluri-tle-j*
Neril-Neril tambourine-AUGM-DIM dry-RES.PART-REF.POS.SG

ilu-gre-re-n-gu *tiek-e-gu*
dry-PAST.ITER-NONFUT-3SG-INT.CLIT now-EPENTH-INT.CLIT

Neril-Neril *untu-nǯe-t*
Neril-Neril tambourine-AUGM-1PL.INC

derbu-ǯeen-če[27]
get_damp-DUR-PERF.PART

27 Cf. Ewk. *derbi-* 'become damp'.

‘I cannot resist him. If I could, my (shaman’s) tambourine would have been dry. But now it is damp, wouldn’t sound as it should.’

(518) *Neril-Neril Hilini-keken tar-da-man bi-seke-n*
Neril-Neril Hilini-DIM that-CONJ.CLIT-CLIT be-COND.DS.CONV-3SG

Neril-Neril ǯal-ǯi-da e-ǯi
Neril-Neril mood-INSTR-CONJ.CLIT not_do-NEG.IMP.2SG

ǯaw-gara-r
catch-PAST.ITER-NEG.CONV

Neril-Neril göö-niken töören ii-s-ni
Neril-Neril say-SIM.CONV voice sound-NONFUT-3SG

‘-Hilini, don’t be cross with me, - said shaman-maiden Neruk, Hilini’s elder sister.’

(519) *erek bej-čen e-s-ni kihan-na*[28]
this man-DIM not_do-NONFUT-3SG take notice-NEG.CONV
‘Helniken doesn’t take any notice of her words.’

(520) *tööre-ǯ-li-gul iaa-li-gul*
talk-PROG-IMP.2SG-INT.CLIT what_do-IMP.2SG-INT.CLIT

isa-nna-j is-či-m
reach-NEC.PART-REF.POS.SG reach-FUT-1SG

göön-i-gčin ǯuleski-tte tuč-te-n
say-NONFUT.PART-EQUAT ahead-CLIT run-NONFUT-3SG

‘“Let her chatter ahead, whatever she wants, I shall make my way anyhow.” He rushes forth.’

(521) *Hiler-hiler-gu bieruse-l-e ögin oo-lla*
Hiler-hiler-INT.CLIT servant-PL-EPENTH upwards become-IMP:2PL

Hiler-hiler-gu eregegej Neruk eki-ken
Hiler-hiler-INT.CLIT well done Neruk elder sister-DIM

28 Corrected by DM to: a*wdatta* ‘take notice’.

Hiler-hiler-gu	*erek*	*iaa-nni*
Hiler-hiler-INT.CLIT	this	what_do-NONFUT.2SG

Hiler-hiler-gu	*enile-čen*	*e-se-nni-gu*
Hiler-hiler-INT.CLIT	really-DIM	not_do-NONFUT-2SG-INT.CLIT

deepke-ne-le
defy-NEG.CONV-CLIT

Hiler-hiler-gu	*göön-ni*
Hiler-hiler-INT.CLIT	say-NONFUT.3SG

'-*Hiler-hiler-gu*, my men arise! My sister Neruk, are you actually trying to do me no harm?'

(522)

tačin	*göön-i-ñun-ni*	*untu-ŋe-n*
so	say-NONFUT.PART-COMIT-3SG	tambourine-AL.POS-3SG

iige-n	*beri-p-te-n*
sound-3SG	lose-MED-NONFUT-3SG

'As he said so, the tambourine's thunder died away.'

(523)

erek	*bej*	*ŋen-neken*	*bukatyn*	*deepki*	*mian*	*ǯaannu*
this	man	go-COND.DS.CONV	all the time	meeting	ten	ten

örilen	*ila-č-ta-n*	*bekeči-nǯe-n*	*deepki*
camp	stand up-STAT-NONFUT-3SG	all-AUGM-3SG	meeting

nemke-le-mnin	*erek*	*bej-čen*	*ere-w*
shoot-INCH-CONSEC.CONV	this	man-DIM	this-ACC

örile-nǯe-w	*miarakaja*	*tookara-sn-a-n*
camp-AUGM-ACC	ten times	circle-MOM-NONFUT-3SG

'When Helniken approached, all population of the settlement, ten dozen families lined up. Helniken circling around them ten times, laid all of them low.'

(524)

Hiler-hiler-gu	*eluken*	*Hergenmej-ken*	*mannu-li-la*
Hiler-hiler-INT.CLIT	brother	Hergenmej-DIM	try-IMP.2SG-CLIT

Hiler-hiler-gu	*iaa-ka-ma*	*alača-nni*
Hiler-hiler-INT.CLIT	what-DIM-ACC	wait-NONFUT.2SG

Hiler-hiler-gu	*e-seke-s*	*ñaan-a*
Hiler-hiler-INT.CLIT	not_do-COND.DS.CONV-2SG	again-EPENTH

maatama-ǯ-da	*köömel-ǯi-n*
visit-PROG-NEG.CONV	be disappointed-FUT-3SG

Hiler-hiler-gu	*göö-niken*
Hiler-hiler-INT.CLIT	say-SIM.CONV

'-*Hiler-hiler-gu*, my (younger) brother, Hergenmej, come on, try your strength, what are you waiting for? If you won't go to meet the guest in a proper way, he will be disappointed.'

(525)

huulu-ǯeke-n	*bej*	*töören-ni*	*ii-s-ni*	*egǯen*	*keerkete*
chase-Nloc-3SG	man	voice-3SG	sound-NONFUT-3SG	big	spacy

ǯuu	*ila-č-ta-n*	*örilen*	*dulakan-dula-n*
house	stand up-STAT-NONFUT-3SG	camp	middle-LOC-3SG

ta-la	*ǯuu-la*	*töören-ni*	*ii-s-ni*
that-LOC	house-LOC	voice-3SG	sound-NONFUT-3SG

'There sounded Hilini's voice from the big jurta-house in the middle of the encampment.'

(526)

erek	*iaa-ǯi-n*	*erek*	*bej*	*kusi-keče-l-le-n*
this	what_do-FUT-3SG	this	man	fight-DIST-INCH-NONFUT-3SG

'Well his brother had to go out to fight Helniken.'

(527)

Hiñöögu	*bej-kene*
Hin'öögu	man-DIM

Hiñöögu	*Helnike-ken*
Hin'öögu	Helniken-DIM

Hiñöögu	*ureči-l-e*
Hin'öögu	similar-PL-EPENTH

Hiñöögu	*ilamat-ka-r*		
Hin'öögu	of the same age-DIM-PL		
Hiñöögu	*bi-se-p-e*		
Hin'öögu	be-NONFUT-1PL.INCL-EPENTH		

'-*Hiñöögu* Helniken, it looks like we, youths, are of the same age.'

(528)	*Hiñöögu*	*awag-čan-ke*		
	Hin'öögu	which-DIM-CLIT		
	Hiñöögu	*hooni-la*	*bi-ǯi-n*	
	Hin'öögu	mighty-CLIT	be-FUT-3SG	
	Hiñöögu	*hooni-ka-mar*		
	Hin'öögu	mighty-DIM-REF.POS.PL		
	Hiñöögu	*heemke-lde-ger*		
	Hin'öögu	try-SOC-IMP.1PL		

'Let us try each other's skill, who proves to be stronger.'

(529)	*Hiñöögu*	*tawagara*	*ŋiaajda-la-n*	
	Hin'öögu	that one	downhill-LOC-3SG	
	Hiñöögu	*niermi-le*	*Hiñöögu*	*tawara*
	Hin'öögu	larch-LOC	Hin'öögu	this
	Hiñöögu	*asi-ŋ-kan-si*		
	Hin'öögu	woman-AL.POS-DIM-2SG.POS		
	Hiñöögu	*akan-ni*		
	Hin'öögu	elder brother-3SG		
	Hiñöögu	*Giakčawal-kan*		
	Hin'öögu	Giakcawal-DIM		
	Hiñöögu	*dil-kan-ni*		
	Hin'öögu	head-DIM-3SG		

Hiñöögu *noku-ča-ǯ-da-n*
Hin'öögu hang-STAT-PROG-NONFUT-3SG

'Downhill, by the foot of the mountain, there stands a huge larch, there hangs the head of your brother-in-law, Giakchavul.'

(530) *Hiñöögu* *e-le* *em-če*
Hin'öögu this-LOC come-PERF.PART

Hiñöögu *bej-kene*
Hin'öögu man-DIM

Hiñöögu *öösi* *öösi-du-n*
Hin'öögu old days old days-DAT-3SG

Hiñöögu *e-se-p*
Hin'öögu not_do-NONFUT-1PL.INCL

Hiñöögu *muču-gra-r*
Hin'öögu return-PAST.ITER-NEG.CONV

Hiñöögu *göö-niken*
Hin'öögu say-SIM.CONV

'It never happened that strangers returned alive from here.'

(531) *erek* *bej-čen* *Hergenmej* *nemke-l-li-j*
this man-DIM Hergenmej shoot-INCH-NONFUT.PART-REF.POS.SG

haa-ra-n *ere-w* *bej-u*
know-NONFUT-3SG this-ACC man-ACC

erek *bej* *Helniken-de* *iaa-ǯi-n*
this man Helniken-CONJ.CLIT what_do-FUT-3SG

nemke-le-w-če *bej* *nemke-meči-l-le-n*
shoot-INCH-PASS-PERF.PART man shoot-REC-INCH-NONFUT-3SG

'This man, Hergenmej, keeps on shooting at Helniken. What should Helniken do? He started to shoot back.'

(532)

erek	*kusi-ket-tiǯii*	*e-s-ni*	*tači-kan*
this	fight-DIST-ANT.CONV	not_do-NONFUT-3SG	like that-DIM

goru	*kusi-ǯ-de*	*asun-da*
for_a_long_time	fight-PROG-NEG.CONV	how many-CONJ.CLIT

kusi-deŋ-i	*de*	*e-s-ni*
fight-PAST.PART-REF.POS.SG	CONJ.CLIT	not_do-NONFUT-3SG

haa-ra
know-NEG.CONV

‘So they fought for a while, however not very long.’

(533)

erek	*beje-ŋ-i*	*gaasimi-wa-n*
this	man-AL.POS-REF.POS.SG	side-ACC-3SG

niŋi-n	*ta-duk*	*tik-re-n*
cut-NONFUT.3SG	that-ABL	fall-NONFUT-3SG

‘Soon Helniken split the man with his arrow in twos, the other one collapsed.’

(534)

Hiñöögu	*hökče-sn-e-nni*
Hin’öögu	surprise-MOM-NONFUT-2SG

Hiñöögu	*eeŋut-tiǯii*
Hin’öögu	miss-ANT.CONV

Hiñöögu	*er-kene*
Hin’öögu	this-DIM

Hiñöögu	*eči-ken*
Hin’öögu	so-DIM

Hiñöögu	*oo-ǯaañ-na-m*
Hin’öögu	become-DUR-NONFUT-1SG

Hiñöögu	*göön-ni*
Hin’öögu	say-NONFUT.3SG

'-*Hiñöögu*, you have taken me by surprise, I was unaware of your shot, therefore I have to die like that.'

(535) *tačin* *göö-niken* *iaa-d-daka-n*
so say-SIM.CONV what_do-PROG-COND.DS.CONV-3SG

ñaan-da *ömen* *bej* *tuuhaŋ-či-n* *ǯuu-duk*
again-CONJ.CLIT one man jump-STAT-NONFUT.3SG house-ABL

'As he was talking like that, another man jumped out of the jurta.'

(536) *ñaan-da* *nemke-meči-ǯe-l-le-n*
again-CONJ.CLIT shoot-REC-PROG-INCH-NONFUT-3SG
'The fight started anew.'

(537) *Kewlirö* *bi-kene*
Kewlirö I-DIM

Kewlirö *Hiñani-kan*
Kewlirö Hin'ani-DIM

Kewlirö *gerbe-mu*
Kewlirö name-1SG.POS

Kewlirö *bi-kene*
Kewlirö be-DIM

Kewlirö *bi-gre-re-n*
Kewlirö be-PAST.ITER-NONFUT-3SG

'-*Kevlirö*, my name is Hin'ani.'

(538) *Kewlirö* *Helniken*
Kewlirö Helniken

Kewlirö *mannu-li-la*
Kewlirö try-IMP.2SG-CLIT

Kewlirö *awag-čan-ke*
Kewlirö which-DIM-CLIT

Kewlirö *hooni-la* *bi-ǯe-n*
Kewlirö mighty-CLIT be-FUT-3SG

Kewlirö *gu* *tiek-e-le*
Kewlirö INT.CLIT now-EPENTH-CLIT

Kewlirö *göö-niken*
Kewlirö say-SIM.CONV

erek *nemke-meči-l-li-j* *haa-n*
this shoot-REC-INCH-NONFUT.PART-REF.POS.SG know-NONFUT.3SG

'"Helniken, come on, let us see who is stronger," saying so Hin'ani kept on shooting.'

(539) *Erek* *bej-čen* *Hiñani-w* *bi-mi*
this man-DIM Hin'ani-ACC be-COND.CONV

e-s-ni *goru* *nemke-č-te*
not_do-NONFUT-3SG for_a_long_time shoot-STAT-NEG.CONV

eŋeñe-ŋ-i *čikas* *nemke-n*
trunk-AL.POS-REF.POS.SG cutting shoot-NONFUT.3SG

'Helniken, however, didn't fight with Hin'ani long either, shot an arrow through his waist.'

(540) *Kewlirö* *aka-ran*
Kewlirö (elder) brother-VOCAT

Kewlirö *Hilini-ken*
Kewlirö Hilini-DIM

Kewlirö *beedne-če-de*
Kewlirö yield-PERF.PART-PURP.CONV

Kewlirö *gu* *bi-se-nni*
Kewlirö INT.CLIT be-NONFUT-2SG

Kewlirö *dila-nǯa-ji*
Kewlirö head-AUGM-REF.POS.SG

Kewlirö	*čiki-w-ri-s*
Kewlirö	cut-PASS-PAST-2SG

'-*Kevlirö*, brother Hilini, no surprise that you could not endure either, had you head cut off.'

(541)

Kewlirö	*min-ke-m*	*iaaka*
Kewlirö	I-DIM-ACC	what

Kewlirö	*etek-ke-mu*	*čikak-ra-n*
Kewlirö	belt-DIM-1SG.POS	cut-NONFUT-3SG

'He has also shot me through the waist (lit. belt).'

(542)

Kewlirö	*göö-niken*
Kewlirö	say-SIM.CONV

erek	*bej-čen*	*tik-če-le-n*	*ñaan-da*
this	man-DIM	fall-PERF.PART-LOC-3SG	again-CONJ.CLIT

doo-duku-n	*ömen*	*bej*	*ñöö-re-n*
inside-ABL-3SG	one	man	go out-NONFUT-3SG

ñaan-da	*nemke-meče-l-le-n*
again-CONJ.CLIT	shoot-REC-INCH-NONFUT-3SG

'Saying so, he collapsed on the ground. Another man rushed out of the jurta, charged at Helniken.'

(543)

Dekiiru-Deeke	*mulakja-da*
Dekiiru-Deeke	alas-CONJ.CLIT

nöö-ŋi-ke-r-bu	*mudala-nni*
younger brother-AL.POS-DIM-PL-ACC.1SG	finish-NONFUT.2SG

tawara	*ač*	*hawka-la-l-bu*	*elekes*
this	without	wise-NEG.PROP-PL-ACC	for the first time

ilamata-l	*bi-mi-ken*	*eeŋuči-ǯ-de*
growing up-PL	be-COND.CONV-CLIT	miss-PROG-NONFUT.3PL

‘*-Dekiiru-de-Deeke*, Alas for my brothers! Young unexperienced warriors, they have missed the arrow. You took them by surprise (unaware).’

(544)	*Dekiiru-Deeke*	*mannu-ǯ-li-la*	*e-le*
	Dekiiru-Deeke	make effort(s)-PROG-IMP.2SG-CLIT	this-LOC

em-če-w	*e-le*	*em-če-w*
come-PERF.PART-ACC	this-LOC	come-PERF.PART-ACC

bej-ke-mi	*e-se-p-meje*
man-DIM-REF.POS.SG	not_do-NONFUT-1PL.INCL-CLIT

amaski	*muču-w-gara-r*
back	return-PASS-PAST.ITER-NEG.CONV

Dekiiru-Deeke	*göö-niken*	*nemke-meči-l-le-n*
Dekiiru-Deeke	say-SIM.CONV	shoot-REC-INCH-NONFUT-3SG

‘*-Dekiiru-Deeke*, Come on, we are not going to let the strangers return alive from here.’

(545)	*erek*	*tačin*	*nemke-meči-d-diǯii*	*ere-w-de*
	this	so	shoot-REC-PROG-ANT.CONV	this-ACC-CONJ.CLIT

bej-u	*e-s-ni*	*goru*	*nemke-re*
man-ACC	not_do-NONFUT-3SG	for_a_long_time	shoot-NEG.CONV

nöö-ŋi-l-duk-i-ñun	*aran*
younger_brother-AL.POS-PL-ABL-REF.POS.SG-CLIT	hardly

hoo-dma-kan	*ureči-n*	*erek*	*beje-ŋ-i*
very-CONT-DIM	similar-3SG	this	man-AL.POS-REF.POS.SG

ñaan-da	*gaasimi-wa-n*	*nemke-n*
again-CONJ.CLIT	sides-ACC-3SG	shoot-NONFUT.3SG

‘So Helniken fought with this new man for a while, however not very long. He turned out to be just a little stronger than his brothers. Helniken split this man in twos.’

(546)	*Dekiiru-de-Deeke*	*akni-ja-la*	
	Dekiiru-CONJ.CLIT-Deeke	elder_brother-PL-CLIT	
	Dekiiru-de-Deeke	*er-teken-te*	
	Dekiiru-CONJ.CLIT-Deeke	now-REST-CONJ.CLIT	
	bi-deŋ-ken-ti	*göön-ni*	
	be-PAST.PART-DIM-1PL.INC.POS	say-NONFUT.3SG	
	Dekiiru-de-Deeke	*Helnike-ken*	
	Dekiiru-CONJ.CLIT-Deeke	Helniken-DIM	
	Dekiiru-de-Deeke	*dulan*	*töör-du*
	Dekiiru-CONJ.CLIT-Deeke	middle	middle earth-DAT
	Dekiiru-de-Deeke	*gaas-ŋa-ji*	
	Dekiiru-CONJ.CLIT-Deeke	rival-AL.POS-REF.POS.SG	
	Dekiiru-de-Deeke	*e-mne-ken-ni*	
	Dekiiru-CONJ.CLIT-Deeke	not_do-PROB-DIM-3SG	
	Dekiiru-de-Deeke	*baka-ǯaañ-na*	
	Dekiiru-CONJ.CLIT-Deeke	find-DUR-NEG.CONV	

'-*Dekiiru-de-Deeke*, brothers, alas for us, what a misery, what a misfortune! Before I could not find a worthy rival in all the three worlds!'

(547)	*Dekiiru-de-Deeke*	*eregegej*
	Dekiiru-CONJ.CLIT-Deeke	well done
	Dekiiru-de-Deeke	*nood-la-kan-ni*
	Dekiiru-CONJ.CLIT-Deeke	beautiful-CLIT-DIM-3SG
	Dekiiru-de-Deeke	*borkat-kan-ni*
	Dekiiru-CONJ.CLIT-Deeke	graceful-DIM-3SG
	Dekiiru-de-Deeke	*ölleč-ken-si*
	Dekiiru-CONJ.CLIT-Deeke	handsome-DIM-2SG.POS
	Dekiiru-de-Deeke	*ösömiken*
	Dekiiru-CONJ.CLIT-Deeke	even

e-ti-mdes-ken	*miña-tna-r*[29]
not_do-NONFUT.PART-SIMIL-DIM	be in a hurry-MULT-NEG.CONV

'Well done, valiant warrior! What a handsome graceful man you are! (He) appears not to be in a hurry at all.'

(548) *Dekiiru-de-Deeke* *er-kene*
Dekiiru-CONJ.CLIT-Deeke now-DIM

Dekiiru-de-Deeke *Neeruk* *eki*
Dekiiru-CONJ.CLIT-Deeke Neeruk elder_sister

Dekiiru-de-Deeke *er-teken-te*
Dekiiru-CONJ.CLIT-Deeke now-REST-CONJ.CLIT

Dekiiru-de-Deeke *köke-re-p*
Dekiiru-CONJ.CLIT-Deeke die-NONFUT-1PL.INCL

Dekiiru-de-Deeke *Helnike-m* *ejel-ližii*
Dekiiru-CONJ.CLIT-Deeke Helniken-ACC like-ANT.CONV

Dekiiru-de-Deeke *e-se-nni-ken-de*
Dekiiru-CONJ.CLIT-Deeke not_do-NONFUT-2SG-CLIT-CONJ.CLIT

deepki-žeen-ne *göö-niken*
resist-DUR-NEG.CONV say-SIM.CONV

Dekiiru-de-Deeke
Dekiiru-CONJ.CLIT-Deeke

'My sister Neruk, my time has come to perish. You must have fallen in love with Helniken, that's why you don't resist him (with witchcraft).'

(549) *tačin* *göö-niken* *erek* *ač* *gaasimi-la-č*
so say-SIM.CONV this without (two) side(s)-NEG.PROP-INSTR

mirke-weeči-ssi-že-l-le-n
crawl-HABIT-CONAT-PROG-INCH-NONFUT-3SG

29 Cf. Ewk: *min'a-* 'get confused, embarassed'.

'Saying so, he crept aside to die.'

(550) *tarpač-kan-da* *digitan* *beje-ŋe-ten* *ñöö-re-n*
anyway -DIM-CONJ.CLIT fourth man-AL.POS-3PL go out-NONFUT-3SG
'The fourth man appeared.'

(551) *Ilgooj-kene* *Ilgooj-kene* *eregegej*
Ilgooj-DIM Ilgooj-DIM well done

Ilgooj-kene *Ilgooj-kene* *mulakja-da*
Ilgooj-DIM Ilgooj-DIM alas-CONJ.CLIT

nöö-ŋi-ke-r-bu *aččalta-nni*
younger brother-AL.POS-DIM-PL-1SG annihilate-NONFUT.2SG

tiek-e *oon-a* *beji-l* *oo-gra-n*
now-EPENTH how-EPENTH man-PL become-PAST.ITER-NONFUT.3SG

Ilgooj-kene *Ilgooj-kene* *tači-ka-mar*
Ilgooj-DIM Ilgooj-DIM like that-DIM-REF.POS.PL

gaasimi-tan *nemke-w-če*
(two) side(s)-3PL shoot-PASS-PERF.PART

Ilgooj-kene *Ilgooj-kene* *mulakja-da*
Ilgooj-DIM Ilgooj-DIM alas-CONJ.CLIT

nöö-ŋi-ke-r-bu
younger_brother-POS.PROP-DIM-PL-1SG

Ilgooj-kene *Ilgooj-kene* *hiilgi-ǯaan-ni*
Ilgooj-DIM Ilgooj-DIM torture-DUR-NONFUT.3SG

'-*Ilgooj-kene*, Alas for my brothers, how they could live on, crippled, with one half of the body shot off.'

(552) *er* *oo-tla-kan*
now become-LIMIT.CONV-DIM

Ilgooj-kene *Ilgooj-kene* *er* *mut-u* *eči-ken-i*
Ilgooj-DIM Ilgooj-DIM now we-ACC so -DIM-EPENTH

e-s-ten *hüilge-ǯ-gere-r*
not_do-NONFUT-3PL torture-PROG-PAST.ITER-NEG.CONV

Ilgooj-kene *Ilgooj-kene* *hooja-w* *bej-u*
Ilgooj-DIM Ilgooj-DIM many-ACC man-ACC

hoŋi-mkin-dur *haǯipka-du-n*[30]
torment-Nloc-DAT:REF.POS.PL curse-DAT-3SG

haǯi-la-w-ra-p
curse-INCH-PASS-NONFUT-1PL.INCL

Ilgooj-kene *Ilgooj-kene* *göö-niken*
Ilgooj-DIM Ilgooj-DIM say-SIM.CONV

'-*Ilgooj-kene*, Previously, nobody tormented us like this. We must have been doomed to death by curses of people we have injured or killed.'

(553) *erek* *bej-čen* *kusi-keči-ǯe-l-le-n*
this man-DIM fight-DIST-PROG-INCH-NONFUT-3SG

erek *hoo-kan* *goru* *kusi-keč-te-n*
this very-DIM for_a_long_time fight-DIST-NONFUT-3SG

'So the fight began anew, and fought for a long time.'

(554) *erek* *beje-ŋ-i* *oj-wa-n*
this man-AL.POS-REF.POS.SG cloth-ACC-3SG

tarpač-kan-da *čöreke-l-le-n* *erek*
anyway-DIM-CONJ.CLIT tear-INCH-NONFUT-3SG this

Helniken *bi-mi*
Helniken be-COND.CONV

'After a while Helniken tore this man's clothes with his arrows to pieces.'

30 Cf. Ewk. *haadi-* 'curse, condemn'.

(555)

erek	*bej*	*aǯgu-ŋa-da*
this	man	dodge-NEG.MOD.CONV-CONJ.CLIT

turku-če-l-le-n
not able-PERF.PART-INCH-NONFUT-3SG

'The other one couldn't dodge Helniken's arrows anymore.'

(556)

Ilgooj-kene	*Ilgooj-kene*	*eregegej*	*Helnike-ken*
Ilgooj-DIM	Ilgooj-DIM	well done	Helniken-DIM

nood-duku-n-a	*iimka-ča-n-dii*
beautiful-ABL-3SG-EPENTH	aim-STAT-NMZR-DAT:REF.POS

Ilgooj-kene	*Ilgooj-kene*	*nemke-nne-j*
Ilgooj-DIM	Ilgooj-DIM	shoot-NEC.PART-REF.POS.SG

omŋa -riǯij	*ila-t-mi*
forget-ANT.CONV	stand up-STAT-COND.CONV

Ilgooj-kene	*Ilgooj-kene*	*eči-ken*	*e-nike-ken*
Ilgooj-DIM	Ilgooj-DIM	so-DIM	not_do-SIM.CONV-DIM

adaga-ǯ-da	*oj-ka-mi*	*čöreke-ŋčin*
dodge-PROG-NEG.CONV	cloth-DIM-REF.POS.SG	tear-EQUAT

nemke-weeč-te-n
shoot-HABIT-NONFUT-3SG

'-*Ilgooj-kene*, Delighted with Helniken's daring, I remembered neither to aim properly, nor to dodge; he shot my clothes to rags.'

(557)

Ilgooj-kene	*Ilgooj-kene*	*eregegej*	*Helnike-ken*
Ilgooj-DIM	Ilgooj-DIM	well done	Helniken-DIM

Ilgooj-kene	*Ilgooj-kene*	*Ömček*	*asi*
Ilgooj-DIM	Ilgooj-DIM	Omchek	woman

ir-gide-gu	*kiran-duku-n*	*erweeč-ken-ni*
which-LOCAT-INT.CLIT	edge-ABL -3SG	like this-DIM-3SG

nood-a	*bej-ken*	*balda-daŋa-n*
beautiful-EPENTH	man-DEMIN	be borne-PAST.PART-3SG

erweeč-ken-ni	*hooni*	*bej-ken*	*balda-ǯaañ-ni-n?!*
like this-DIM-3SG	mighty	man-DIM	be borne-DUR-PAST-3SG

'-*Ilgooj-kene*, well done! How come that Omchek has given birth to such a valiant son?!'

(558)

Ilgooj-kene	*Ilgooj-kene*	*eregegej*	*aki-jakan*
Ilgooj-DIM	Ilgooj-DIM	well done	elder brother-DIM

Hilini-kan	*beedne-če-ken*	*bi-se-nni*
Hilini-DIM	yield-PERF.PART-DIM	be-NONFUT-2SG

Ilgooj-kene	*Ilgooj-kene*	*eñe-de-men*	*tikuña-da*
Ilgooj-DIM	Ilgooj-DIM	hurt(s)-CONJ.CLIT-CLIT	rage-CONJ.CLIT

Ilgooj-kene	*Ilgooj-kene*	*ooti-gda-ǯur*
Ilgooj-DIM	Ilgooj-DIM	despair-DELIM-INSTR:REF.POS.PL

ewi-ǯeeñ-ne-p
play-DUR-NONFUT-1PL.INCL

'-*Ilgooj-kene*, And my elder brother Hilini couldn't overwhelm him. So suffering in impotent rage, we perish.'

(559)

Ilgooj-kene	*Ilgooj-kene*	*ama-ran-i*	*Ñuŋeje-ken*
Ilgooj-DIM	Ilgooj-DIM	father-VOCAT-EPENTH	N'ungeje-DIM

Ilgooj-kene	*Ilgooj-kene*	*er-teken-te*
Ilgooj-DIM	Ilgooj-DIM	this-REST-CONJ.CLIT

bi-deŋ-ken-ti
be-PAST.PART-DIM-1PL.INC.POS

Ilgooj-kene	*Ilgooj-kene*	*hagdi*	*bej-e*	*iaa-kana-w*
Ilgooj-DIM	Ilgooj-DIM	old	man-EPENTH	what-DIM-ACC

Ilgooj-kene	*Ilgooj-kene*	*ičin-ner-de*
Ilgooj-DIM	Ilgooj-DIM	like.this-INDEF.CLIT-CONJ.CLIT

awaŋči-li
entertain-IMP.2SG

'My father, N'ungeje, although you are an old man still try to entertain our guest somehow.'

(560) *Ilgooj-kene* *Ilgooj-kene* *eregegej* *hisak-takan*
Ilgooj-DIM Ilgooj-DIM well done bone-flesh-REST.CLIT

ulle-ke -mu *ačča* *oo-kan* *nemke-ǯeeñ-ne-n*
meat-DIM-1SG.POS not_exist become-until shoot-DUR-NONFUT-3SG

Ilgooj-kene *Ilgooj-kene* *göö-niken* *erek* *bej*
Ilgooj-DIM Ilgooj-DIM say-SIM.CONV this man

dabda-riǯii *ŋisule-tne-niken* *ǯuu-tki-j*
loose-ANT.CONV stumble-MULT-SIM.CONV house-DIR-REF.POS.SG

mirka-sn-a-n
crawl-MOM-NONFUT-3SG

'-Well done, Helniken! He has shot all my the flesh from my bones! - saying that the loosing man, crawled home.'

(561) *Čoorami* *ǯawu-t -nikan* *etiken* *ñöö-re-n*
staff hold-STAT-SIM.CONV old man go out-NONFUT-3SG

erek *Ñuŋeje*
this N'ungeje

'An old man appeared holding his staff.'

(562) *Ŋisulañ* *ǯaadini*
Ngisulan' son:VOCAT

Ŋisulañ *Helniken*
Ngisulan' Helniken

Ŋisulañ *hi-ŋen iaaka*
Ngisulan' you-CLIT what

Ŋisulañ	*nösegče-r*
Ngisulan'	youth-PL

Ŋisulañ	*beje-l*
Ngisulan'	man-PL

Ŋisulañ	*huseli-če-ten*
Ngisulan'	bully-PERF.PART-3PL

Ŋisulañ	*iaa-n-da*	*hiannu-s*	*bi-ǯi-n*
Ngisulan'	what-3SG-CONJ.CLIT	offence-2SG	be-FUT-3SG

'- *Ngisulan*', sonny, why are you starting a quarrel with my youths, bully them? What's the reason (the insult)?'

(563)

Ŋisulañ	*mannu-li*
Ngisulan'	try-IMP.2SG

Ŋisulañ	*bi-de-kene*
Ngisulan'	I-CONJ.CLIT-DIM

Ŋisulañ	*öötel-titel*
Ngisulan'	previously

Ŋisulañ	*nösegčen-di*
Ngisulan'	youth-DAT:REF.POS.SG

Ŋisulañ	*hi-ŋečin-de*
Ngisulan'	you-EQUAT-CONJ.CLIT

Ŋisulañ	*gaas-ŋa-j*	*e-č-u*
Ngisulan'	rival-AL.POS-REF.POS.SG	not_do-PERF.PART-1SG

Ŋisulañ	*baka-ǯ-da-la*
Ngisulan'	find-PROG-NEG.CONV-CLIT

Ŋisulañ	*göö-niken*
Ngisulan'	say-SIM.CONV

'Come one, fight, beware, in my old days, I, just like you now, could not find a worthy rival!'

(564) *etiken* *ñöö-d-de-n*
old man go out-PROG-NONFUT-3SG

tar-da *bi-niken* *ookarap* *naawta*
that-CONJ.CLIT be-SIM.CONV long ago moss

hie-če *ŋaadi-nǯa-j* *ga-riǯij*
appear-PERF.PART bow-AUGM-REF.POS.SG take-ANT.CONV

nemke-ǯe-l-le-n
shoot-PROG-INCH-NONFUT-3SG

'The old man comes out, takes his moss-grown bow and starts to shoot at Helniken.'

(565) *Ŋisulañ* *eŋnije* *e-ǯi*
Ngisulan' too much not_do-NEG.IMP.2SG

Ŋisulañ *ojli-gra-ra*
Ngisulan' boast-PAST.ITER-NEG.CONV

Ŋisulañ *ǯaadini*
Ngisulan' son:VOCAT

Ŋisulañ *bi-ŋene*
Ngisulan' I-CLIT

Ŋisulañ *hooni-ka-ma-s*
Ngisulan' mighty-DIM-ACC-2SG

Ŋisulañ *heemke-či-d-de-m*
Ngisulan' try-STAT-PROG-NONFUT-1SG

'-*Ngisulan'*, don't boast of your strength, don't put on airs, let's try each other's skill!'

(566) *Ŋisulañ* *oon-di* *bej-ken*
Ngisulan' what man-DIM

Ŋisulañ *bi-ǯeeñ-ni-s*
Ngisulan' be-DUR-PAST-2SG

Metele

Ŋisulañ	*oon-di*	*bej-ken*
Ngisulan'	how-sort	man-DIM

Ŋisulañ	*bi-ǯeeñ-ni-s*
Ngisulan'	be-DUR-PAST-2SG

'-*Ngisulan*', let me see what you are worth!'

(567)

Ŋisulañ	*tiek*	*esikun*
Ngisulan'	now	recent

Ŋisulañ	*diksamna-kan*
Ngisulan'	suckling-DIM

Ŋisulañ	*mannu-li*
Ngisulan'	try-IMP.2SG

Ŋisulañ	*e-duk-te*	*ǯuleski*
Ngisulan'	this-ABL-CONJ.CLIT	ahead

Ŋisulañ	*hooja-wa*
Ngisulan'	many-ACC

Ŋisulañ	*bakalda-ǯa-nni*
Ngisulan'	meet-PROG-NONFUT.2SG

Ŋisulañ	*hooja-wa*
Ngisulan'	many-ACC

Ŋisulañ	*bakaldu-t-či-nni*
Ngisulan'	meet-STAT-FUT-2SG

Ŋisulañ	*göö-niken*
Ngisulan'	say-SIM.CONV

nemke-če-l-le-n	*erek*	*etiken*
shoot-STAT-INCH-NONFUT-3SG	this	old man

"'Come on, suckling, I shall teach you a lesson!' (Saying that) the old man keeps on shooting.'"

(568) *erek etike-ŋ-n heŋe-č ereger bej-ñun*
this old man-AL.POS-3SG bold-INST always man-COMIT

nemke-meči-l-le-n
shoot-REC-INCH-NONFUT-3SG

'Being old, he is still adroit, shoots arrows all the time.'

(569) *Giller-giller-gu oona-di-gu nemke-ǯeen-ǯa-m*
Giller-giller-INT.CLIT how-sort-INT.CLIT shoot-DUR-FUT-1SG

Giller-giller-gu ama-ran Ñuŋej-keken
Giller-giller-INT.CLIT father-VOCAT N'ungeje-DIM

Giller-giller-gu mannu-gu-jat-li
Giller-giller-INT.CLIT make effort(s)-INT.CLIT-ASP-IMP.2SG

Giller-giller-gu göö-niken
Giller-giller-INT.CLIT say-SIM.CONV

erek Helniken bi-mi e-niken
this Helniken be-COND.CONV not_do-SIM.CONV

nemke-r etiken Ñuŋeje ŋaadi-wa -n[31] *ñura-ma-n*
shoot-NEG.CONV old man N'ungeje bow-ACC-3SG arrow-ACC-3SG

iečeñ-ǯi-n al-či-ǯa-l-la-n
elbow-INSTR-3SG reach (out)-STAT-PROG-INCH-NONFUT-3SG

'-*Giller-giller-gu*, father N'ungeje, how can I shoot at the old man, - saying so, Helniken doesn't shoot back. He parries with his elbow N'ungeje's arrows.'

(570) *Eǯereǯej*
well done!

Giller-giller-gu irek-ke öösi
Giller-giller-INT.CLIT which-CLIT old days

---

31 Cf. Ewk. *ngaade* 'bow'.

Giller-giller-gu *hagdi-kana* *deepken-deŋ-me-ni*
Giller-giller-INT.CLIT old-DIM defy-PAST.PART-ACC-3SG

dolda-ǯ-diǯii
hear -PROG-ANT.CONV

Giller-giller-gu *mannu-li-la*
Giller-giller-INT.CLIT try-IMP.2SG-CLIT

oon-da-kana *deepken-ǯi-ǯeen-ǯi-m*
how-CONJ.CLIT-DIM resist-PROG-DUR-FUT-1SG

'-*Giller-giller-gu*, well done, it is unheard that the young should fight with the old one. How can I attack the old man? Come on!'

(571) *tar-da* *bi-seke-n* *ǯal-ǯi*
that-CONJ.CLIT be-COND.DS.CONV-3SG mood-INSTR

e-miken *ǯawa-ǯaañ-na*
not_do-NEG.FUT.IMP catch-DUR-NEG.CONV

Giller-giller-gu *hii-ŋen* *iaaka*
Giller-giller-INT.CLIT you-CLIT what

ŋaača-ǯ-daka-s *oon-da-kana*
challenge-PROG-COND.DS.CONV-2SG how-CONJ.CLIT-DIM

Giller-giller-gu *ila-ča-n-ǯa-m*
Giller-giller-INT.CLIT stand up-STAT-ITER-FUT-1SG

irek-ke *öösi* *hereč-ten-ke-me-n*
which-CLIT old days linger-3SG-DIM-ACC-3SG

hereči-ǯeen-ǯe-m
linger-DUR-FUT-1SG

Giller-giller-gu *göö-niken* *göön-ǯid-diǯi*
Giller-giller-INT.CLIT say-SIM.CONV say-PROG-ANT.CONV

erek *Ñuŋeje-ŋ-čil* *nemke-meči-l-le-n*
this N'ungeje-AL.POS-COMIT shoot-REC-INCH-NONFUT-3SG

'-*Giller-giller-gu*, but blame yourself, if you challenge me, how long can I refrain from the fight, father N'ungeje, - saying that he started shooting at N'ungeje.'

(572) *erek* *hagdi* *hagdi-gčin* *asu-m* *goru*
this old old-EQUAT how many-ACC for_a_long_time

kusi-ket-či-n *dabda-jač-ta-n*
fight-DISTR-FUT-3SG loose-ATTEN-NONFUT-3SG

'Well, the old man is an old man, how long can he resist.'

(573) *Ŋisulañ-gu* *ǯaadini*
Ngisulan'-INT.CLIT son:VOCAT

Ŋisulañ *eliwen-de*
Ngisulan' really-CONJ.CLIT

Ŋisulañ *hooni-kan*
Ngisulan' mighty-DIM

Ŋisulañ *bi-se-nni-le*
Ngisulan' be-NONFUT-2SG-CLIT

Ŋisulañ *ajaaw-ča-wa-s*
Ngisulan' like-PERF.PART-ACC-2SG

'-*Ngisulan*', sonny, you are really a valiant warrior!'

(574) *Ŋisulañ* *ǯoldan-ǯa-m*
Ngisulan' reward -FUT-1SG

Ŋisulañ *ǯaadini*
Ngisulan' son:VOCAT

Ŋisulañ *e-mne-ke-mu*
Ngisulan' not_do-PROB-DIM-1SG.POS

Ŋisulañ *tere-ǯeeñ-ne*
Ngisulan' overwhelm-DUR-NEG.CONV

Ŋisulañ	*göön-ni*
Ngisulan'	say-NONFUT.3SG

'-*Ngisulan*', I shall reward you with anything you like, cannot resist you any more.'

(575)

tačin	*göö-niken*	*erek*	*etike-nǯe*	*ŋaadi-nǯa-j*
so	say-SIM.CONV	this	old man-AUGM	bow-AUGM-REF.POS.SG

nooda-riǯii	*tegende-n*
throw-ANT.CONV	colapse-NONFUT.3SG

'Saying so, old N'ungeje threw his bow on the ground and sank down totally exhusted.'

(576)

Ö-ö	*ötel*	*iaami*	*e-če-s-ku*
Oh-EPENTH	long ago	why	not_do-PERF.PART-2SG-CLIT

göön-e
say.NEG CONV-EPENTH

'-Well, why didn't you say this earlier? - answered Helniken.'

(577)

erek	*bej-čen*	*ǯuu-la-j*	*ii-re-n*
this	man-DIM	house-LOC-REF.POS.SG	enter-NONFUT-3SG

'Helniken entered (N'ungeje's) yurta.'

(578)

hagdi	*asi*	*tege-č-te-n*
old	woman	sit_down-STAT-NONFUT-3SG

'There sits an old woman.'

(579)

hulu-ǯaka-n	*dila-ŋa-n*	*malu-la*
chase-Nloc-3SG	head-AL.POS-3SG	"place of honour"-LOC

bi-ǯ-de-n
be-PROG-NONFUT-3SG

'Head of Hilini, that Helniken has pursued, lies on 'malu' (the "place of honour" in the traditional jurta).'

(580) *erek* *ečin* *bi-weeč-tiǯi-de* *bej*
this this_way be-HABIT-ANT.CONV-CONJ.CLIT man

muču-han-da-j *ñeke-ǯe-l-le-n*
return-MOM-PURP.CONV-REF.POS.SG do-PROG-INCH-NONFUT-3SG

'Helniken stayed some time by N'ungeje as his guest. Then he started to get ready for the journey homeward.'

(581) *Ŋisulañ-gu* *ǯaadini*
Ngisulan'-INT.CLIT son:VOCAT

Ŋisulañ *Helnike-ken*
Ngisulan' Helniken-DIM

Ŋisulañ *hooni* *bej-e*
Ngisulan' mighty man-EPENTH

Ŋisulañ *bi-niken*
Ngisulan' be-SIM.CONV

Ŋisulañ *oon-a* *ečin-e* *muču-d-ǯi-nni*
Ngisulan' how-EPENTH this_way-EPENTH return-PROG-FUT-2SG

'-*Ngisulan'*, sonny, being a mighty warrior, how can you return like that?!'

(582) *Ŋisulañ* *hii-ŋene*
Ngisulan' you-CLIT

Ŋisulañ *ǯal-ǯi-da* *e-ǯi*
Ngisulan' mood-INSTR-CONJ.CLIT not_do-NEG.IMP.2SG

ǯaw-gara-r
catch-PAST.ITER-NEG.CONV

Ŋisulañ *göön-ni*
Ngisulan' say -NONFUT.3SG

artača-ǯa-l-la-n[32] *ejlini-ǯe-l-le-n*
plead-PROG-INCH-NONFUT-3SG beg-PROG-INCH-NONFUT-3SG

'-*Ngisulan*', don't be cross with me, - N'ungeje began to plead him.'

(583) *Hör-de-j* *mereke-sen-de-j*
go-PURP.CONV-REF.POS.SG return-MOM-PURP.CONV-REF.POS.SG

ñeke-ǯe-l-le-n *Helniken* *göön-ni*
do-PROG-INCH-NONFUT-3SG Helniken say-NONFUT.3SG

Iaa-nna-wu-ka *göön-ni*
what_do-NEC.PART-1SG-CLIT say-NONFUT.3SG

'-What shall I do then? - asked Helniken, getting ready for the journey.'

(584) *tawar* *hii-ken*
that one you-DIM

Ŋisulañ *maa-daŋa-l-bi* *beje-ŋe-l-bi*
Ngisulan' kill-PAST.PART-PL-REF.POS.SG man-AL.POS-PL-REF.POS.SG

bi-če-du-ten *oo-wkan-ǯid-li*
be-PERF.PART-DAT-3PL make-CAUS-PROG-IMP.2SG

'-*Ngisulan*', first revive the men you have killed.'

(585) *Es,* *bi* *ečin* *oon* *oo-wkan-ǯi-m* *göön-ni*
no I this_way how make-CAUS-FUT-1SG say-NONFUT.3SG

köke-če-l-bu *oč-ča-l -bu*
die-PERF.PART-PL-ACC finish-PERF.PART-PL-ACC

'-How on earth can I revive the dead?!'

(586) *hooni* *bej-ken*
mighty man-DIM

Ŋisulañ *bi-niken*
Ngisulan' be-SIM.CONV

---

32 < Jak. *aapmaa* 'plead'.

Ŋisulañ *tara-wa-gu*
Ngisulan' that-ACC-INT.CLIT

Ŋisulañ *oon* *turku-ǯi-nni*
Ngisulan' how not able-FUT-2SG

huj-u-ten *tumne-sn-iken* *huuku-s-li*
wound-ACC-3PL spit-MOM-CONT.CONV stroke-ATTEN-IMP.2SG

irge-niken *bi-če-dur*
sorcer-SIM.CONV be-PERF.PART-DAT:REF.POS.PL

oga-lla *göö-niken*
raise-IMP:2PL say-SIM.CONV

'-*Ngisulan*', being a mighty hero, why couldn't you? Spit on the wound, rub it, sorcering: "Arise as you were!".'

(587) *bej-čen* *eliwen-de* *ömen* *hurke-m* *tačin*
man-DIM really-CONJ.CLIT one youth-ACC so

göö-niken *tumni-sn-iken* *huku-sn -e-n*
say-SIM.CONV spit -MOM-CONT.CONV scoop-MOM-NONFUT-3SG

bi-če-di *hekerkiŋ-či-n*
be-PERF.PART-DAT:REF.POS.SG jump out -STAT-NONFUT.3SG

beje-ŋe-n *eme-ǯ-deke -n*
man-AL.POS-3SG come-PROG-COND.DS.CONV-3SG

oon *bi-si-n-da* *tači-kan*
how be-PAST-3SG-CONJ.CLIT like that-DIM

'And indeed, when Helniken spitted on wounds of one youth and rubbed it, sorcering. The youth jumped to his feet, unharmed, as he had been before when he came.'

(588) *erek* *beje-ŋe-l-bi* *beket-ke-me -n* *tačin*
this man-AL.POS-PL-REF.POS.SG all-DIM-ACC-3SG so

urgi-n *örile-m-de* *iaa-w-da*
revive-NONFUT.3SG camp-ACC-CONJ.CLIT what-ACC-CONJ.CLIT

e-s-ni *hula-r* *beket-ke-me -n*
not_do-NONFUT-3SG leave-NEG.CONV all-DIM-ACC-3SG

'So Helniken revived all population of the encampment.'

(589) *Neril-Neril* *Hilini-ken* *eluken* *hii-ken* *iaaka* *tawara*
Neril-Neril Hilini-DIM brother you-DIM what this

dila-ŋ-ka-mi *bi-če-ken-du-n*
head-AL.POS-CLIT-REF.POS.SG be-PERF.PART-DIM-DAT-3SG

oo-wka-li
become-CAUS-IMP.2SG

Neril-Neril *göön-ni*
Neril-Neril say-NONFUT.3SG

'-*Neril-Neril*, Hilini, revive the head of my brother that you cut, - said Neruk, the shaman-woman.'

(590) *erek* *Hilini* *bi-mi* *erek* *noku-ča-d-di*
this Hilini be-COND.CONV this hang-STAT-PROG-NONFUT.PART

dil-u *atal-liǯii* *eme* *tumne-sn-iken*
head-ACC take off-ANT.CONV so spit-MOM-CONT.CONV

huuku-sne-niken *Iaakkar-ja* *erek* *bej*
stroke-MOM-SIM.CONV what-ya-call-it-EPENTH this man

bej-ǯi *tuuhaŋ-či-n*
man-INSTR jump-STAT-3SG

'Hilini unfastened Giakchavul's head from the larch tree, spit on the wound, rubbed it, sourcering. The man jumped to his feet sound and well.'

(591) *erek* *Ǯajmuk* *akan-ni* *herge* *akan-ni*
this D'ajmuk brother-3SG youngest brother-3SG

'This turned out to be the youngest of D'ajmuk's brothers Giakchavul.'

(592)

erek	*Neruk-u*	*ga-d-ni*	*Neruk-u*
this	Neruk-ACC	take-NONFUT-3SG	Neruk-ACC

nulgu-niken	*amaski*	*nulge-r*
nomadize with-SIM.CONV	back	nomadize-NONFUT.3PL

'He married Neruk, and brought her with him, as they set out back to their homeland.'

(593)

hoo-ka-m	*goru*	*nulge-r*
very-DIM-ACC	for_a_long_time	nomadize-NONFUT.3PL

goru	*em-če-l*	*ureči-ten*
for_a_long_time	come-PERF.PART-PL	similar-3PL

'They have already wandered far away, apparently.'

(594)

erek	*Ñuŋeje-de*	*e-s-ni*
this	N'ungeje-CONJ.CLIT	not_do-NONFUT-3SG

eme-p-te,
leave-MED-NEG.CONV

nulge	*bi-mnin*	*nulge-r*	*gaadač*
caravan	be-CONSEC.CONV	nomadize-NONFUT.3PL	ahead

'Then Nungeje decided to follow them with a caravan, taking all their property.'

(595)

Ŋisulañ	*eregegej*
Ngisulan'	well done

Ŋisulañ	*ǯa-nil-a*
Ngisulan'	child-PL-EPENTH

Ŋisulañ	*huu-ken*	*oon-a*
Ngisulan'	you (PL)-DIM	how-EPENTH

Ŋisulañ	*nösegče-r-e*
Ngisulan'	youth-PL-EPENTH

Ŋisulañ	*beje-l-e*
Ngisulan'	man-PL-EPENTH

ereger	*nulge-du*	*bi-ǯi-s*	*buju-s-nikan-da*
always	caravan-DAT	be-FUT-2PL	go hunt-ITER-SIM.CONV-CONJ.CLIT

iaa-nikan-da	*ŋene-lle*
what_do-SIM.CONV-CONJ.CLIT	go-IMP:2PL

'-Ngisulan', my sons, you are young, set out with a caravan, nomadize together with Helniken.'

(596)

erek	*hurke-r*	*buju-niken-de*
this	youth-PL	go hunt-SIM.CONV-CONJ.CLIT

iaa-nikar-da	*nulge-r*	*gaadač*
what_do-SIM.CONV:PL-CONJ.CLIT	nomadize-NONFUT.3PL	ahead

erek	*Hilini*	*uǯ-li-tan*
this	Hilini	track-PROL-3PL

'Well, the sons set out following Hilini, living from hunting on their way.'

(597)

erek	*Giakčawul*	*bi-mi*	*Neruk-u*
this	Giakcawul	be-COND.CONV	Neruk-ACC

asi-ŋ-ga-j	*ga-d-ni*
woman-AL.POS-DES-REF.POS.SG	take-NONFUT-3SG

asi-ŋ-i	*nulgu-niken*	*hör-re-n*
woman-AL.POS-REF.POS.SG	nomadize with-SIM.CONV	go-NONFUT-3SG

'And Giakcavul married Neruk, they followed the others nomadizing.'

(598)

Hoo-ka-m	*goru*	*ŋen-ne*	*örep*
very-DIM-ACC	for_a_long_time	go-NONFUT:3PL	previous

hewej-ke-ŋ-ne-wer *em-neke-ten*
cannibal giant-DIM-AL.POS-LOC-REF.POS.PL come-COND.DS.CONV-3PL

hewej-ken *Čulpuka-nǯa* *ikeri-du-n* *nibgan-iǯii*
cannibal giant-DIM Chulpuk-AUGM bone-DAT-3SG choke-ANT.CONV

köke-če *ǯaa-l-bi* *ǯebe-ssi-ǯe-mnin*
die-PERF.PART relative-PL-REF.POS.SG eat-CONAT-PROG-CONSEC.CONV

'After traveling for a long time, they reached the place where the giant cannibal Harkilan lived once. It turned out that he has died long ago, choking with Chulpuk's bone in his throat.'

(599) *erek* *beje-l* *tačin* *nulge-r-e*
this man-PL so nomadize-NONFUT.3PL-EPENTH

bug-la-wur *is-sa*
country-LOC-REF.POS.PL reach-NONFUT.3PL

bug-la-wur *is-siǯur* *ǯa* *okaat-u*
country-LOC-REF.POS.PL reach-ANT.CONV:PL well river-ACC

bargasa-č *örin-iǯur*
opposite-INSTR make a camp-ANT.CONV.PL

bi-ǯe-l-le
be-PROG-INCH-NONFUT.3PL

'They moved forth. As they reached their homeland, they settled on both sides of the river.'

(600) *erek* *Helnike-lken* *Meŋnuni-č* *begen-ǯur*
this Helniken-PROPR Mengnuni-INSTR chief-INSTR:REF.POS.PL

bi-ǯe-l-le *okaat-u* *bargasa-či-n*
be-PROG-INCH-NONFUT.3PL river-ACC opposite (river) side-INSTR-3SG

'On one river side, Helniken became their chief, on the other side his father Mengnuni.'

(601)	*erek*	*örep*	*Metele*	*hol-liǯij*	*Meŋnuni*
	this	previous	Metele	move upstream-ANT.CONV	Mengnuni

gerbe	*oo-ča*	*oo-riǯii*	*kiŋne-č*
name	become-PERF.PART	become-ANT.CONV	ski-INSTR

eme-tle	*bi-če*
come-RES.PART	be-PERF.PART

'Metele got the new name Mengnuni, since he came to life again.'

(602)	*erek*	*noŋan-da*	*e-du*	*bi-ǯe-l-le-n*
	this	(s)he-CONJ.CLIT	this-DAT	be-PROG-INCH-NONFUT-3SG

'So they started to live there.'

(603)	*tiek*	*tierenu*	*tačin*	*bi-č-če-l*	*bi-ǯi-r*
	now	up to now	so	be-STAT-PERF.PART-PL	be-FUT-3PL

e-du	*bug-dur*
this-DAT	country-DAT:REF.POS.PL

'Perhaps, they still live there.'

2. Metele: English translation

[Once upon a time there lived Metele]. Metele had a tiny jurta. He lived from hunting hares and partridges. All his clothes were of hare-skin, the floor covering and the blanket were made of hare-skin too. His bow was made of a rib of a hare, his bow was strung with the twisted hare's sinew, his arrows were made of a hare's skin-bone. So he lived. Hunting with his bow he shot hares, hiding, and huddled up partridges. Well, so he lived for a long time.

One day somebody came downstream along the river, who was coming – he didn't know. Only the jingling of the bells was heard. He peeped out through the doorway – downstream along the river somebody was wandering, who looked like him, but had long hair and long clothes.

The woman came nearer, unpacked her reindeer, pitched a jurta on the hillside, half-conic jurta. Metele, being afraid of the reindeer of this woman hid himself. Her reindeer grazed around his little jurta, licked his frozen urine, trod on his jurta. From this day on Metele didn't go outside any more. Only when the reindeer go away, he goes outside to check the loops and traps that he had set. While inspecting them, if he saw the reindeer, he hid himself. It turned out that his loops and all are trodden down by the reindeer. It seemed as if hares and partridges dispersed, decreased in number, since the woman appeared.

Once he heard the steps – the woman approached him. Metele was scared. He didn't know what to do – either to hide himself or run away. Finally, he decided to stay.

– What will she do when she comes? – he wondered.

And that woman approached his jurta and said:

– *Deñee-gu*, Metele, and yet they call you a man! Why don't you come to visit me! I waited and waited, hoping that you would come, became bored waiting and so have come myself. The old tales relate that a man should first go to visit a woman.

At first Metele was afraid to say anything, then he said:

– I was scared that's why I didn't come to see you. I see a human being (lit. two-legged), like you for the first time.

So what could he do? He cooked a hare's pad, and treated the woman. They ate together. When they finished eating the woman pushed the dishes away and said:

– *Deñee-gu*, Metele, I've payed a visit to you, now come to see me.

– All right, I'll come, why not. – Metele said. He accompanied the woman to her jurta. He enters her jurta and sees that the jurta is very spacious and much better than his own. A very cosy jurta. Both the jurta and the clothes are warm.

Well, the woman cooked and invited Metele to the meal. The food was delicious. Well, Metele didn't come back home that evening. (He) stayed in the woman's jurta. The woman entertained him, telling different stories. So they conversed till the evening. Then the woman made up a bed for him.

– *Deñee-gu* Metele, don't go home.

So Metele began to live in that woman's jurta. So they lived for a long time. Their reindeer wandered off.

– Don't be afraid of the reindeer. – the woman taught.

Meanwhile he got used to the reindeer, learned how to graze them and so on. Once the woman said:

– *Deñee-gu*, Metele, my dear husband, our reindeer are wandering off, the pasture is far away, the reindeer are getting lost. Let us change the pasture. – she said.

But Metele didn't want to move away.

– *Gerijen-gerijen*, my dear wife, Omchek, it would be a pity to abondon my little jurta. If I move away, my five loops and five traps will be left without their owner. If you want to move away, do it alone.

The woman said:

– All right, stay (alone), stay.

She packed her things, harnessed the reindeer and moved away downstream. And Metele stayed alone. So he lived for some time. Metele set the traps and loops as he had done before. But the footprints (tracks) of hares and partridges disappeared. The days passed. It became very cold in his jurta. Although the snow covered the jurta, Metele froze inside because the reindeer had torn his tiny jurta. And he almost starves to death. And once he said to himself:

– *Gerijen-gerijen*, what a miserable life! Although my dear wife Omchek wanted me to go with her, I stayed here. I should have better followed her! Let my jurta stay here, let my loops stay here. My hare scattered, the reindeer herds of Omchek scared my partridges away, so they do not even dare to settle down. If I stay here, I starve to death for sure.

So Metele talked to himself. Well, he spent the night, waiting till dawn, and at dawn followed the tracks (traces) of his wife. So he went and went ahead. It became dark but he kept going ahead many days and nights, without any rest.

Once he saw far ahead flashes of fire. Exhausted and starving, Metele made his way towards the fire. He suffered from hunger and cold, his clothes were torn to pieces.

As he approached the jurta his wife came out and began to batter him with her crook.

– Stay in your little jurta, "How can I leave my five loops without the owner" didn't you say so, why have you then come here? Stay with the things you are so fond of. – she said.

– *Gerijen-gerijen*, my dear wife Omchek, from now on I shall do, whatever you tell me. Don't turn me out of doors! I'm so exhausted, nearly dying of hunger, I've nearly frozen to death. Don't drive me away. – he said. – Let me in.

So he begged for a long time. Then, finally, she let him in.

Meanwhile Metele's wife gave birth to a daughter. So they lived for a long time. Metele didn't hunt, spent all his time sitting in the jurta. Once his wife said to him:

– *Deñee-gu*, Metele, my dear husband, why do we live eating the meat of our tame reindeer all the time? Why don't you go hunting wild reindeer? After all there are (enough) different creatures (game) in this country. Why should we eat all the time our tame reindeer? Let's move further to new lands, there you'll be hunting.

– Let's get going, go gather our reindeer. – she said. The wife packed the clothes and their belongings and sent Metele to gather the reindeer. So he herded in the reindeer. What else could he do, if he had promised to pay heed to her words. The wife saddled an old skewbald reindeer for him. Metele riding after his wife kept falling down, he couldn't ride properly. The wife helped him to get in the saddle again, he rode a little bit and then fell down on his back again.

– *Deñee-gu*, Metele, how unskilful you are! Hold fast the bridle, how long are you going to fall down? – the wife said.

So Metele suffered all day long as they nomadized. Once they stopped, built a nomad tent, overnighted there.

"*Deñee-gu*, Metele, what if you go hunt wild reindeer till we scare them away. The traces (tracks) of wild reindeer are like the traces of tame reindeer; they look like our tame reindeer, are just bigger. When you go hunting, you'll see it yourself." When the wife said so, she caught his skewbald reindeer and saddled it for Metele. She gave him the bow and arrows and he set out. He rode for a long time until he saw wild reindeer near the upper waters of the river. He shot one of them. Then Metele began to skin it in the way he had skinned a hare. But the reindeer is much bigger: Metele tried in vain to turn it over.

So Metele is away for three days trying to skin the reindeer as a hare, turning the reindeer over, trying to remove its skin as a whole (without cutting). Finally his wife came.

– *Deñee-gu*, Metele, how unskilful you are. Where have you seen that reindeer is skinned in such a way? – she said.

She came, flayed the reindeer quickly cutting its skin. They returned to their jurta.

– Don't skin reindeer in such a way. – she taught. So Metele learned to hunt reindeer.

So they lived, from time to time nomdizing further. Once they moved again to a new place and Metele went hunting. When he was going back he saw rests of a nomad camp. When he was examining it, he heard a child crying. Looking around, he found a child covered with pine-branches in women's part of the abondoned jurta. He took that child under his arm and brought it home.

– Someone has left the child, – he explained to his wife. They looked at the child – the child turned out to be a boy.

– *Gerijen-gerijen*, my wife Omchek, I've found a child – a boy. He was covered with pine-branches and left in women's part of a abondoned jurta – he said.

– Why have you brought the devil-child from the old nomad camp? If it were a human child, it wouldn't survive, go and kill him immediately, – the wife says.

– *Gerijen-gerijen*, it's a pity for him, why should I kill him – Metele says.

He began to beat his wife. So Omchek had to suckle two children. Her daughter Chimchep grew up. When the child-boy was crying Metele scolds his wife and daughter, beats them, feeling sorry for the child.

The time passes, his daughter is growing up, but the boy doesn't grow. Meanwhile Chimchep learned to do a needlework, made her clothes herself. And the devil-foundling doesn't grow at all. All day long he sleeps, all night long he cries, doesn't let the parents sleep. Metele doesn't know what's the matter: either the child is sick or his wife feeds him badly.

One day Metele went hunting. Returning in the evening, he saw a spark flying out of the smoke-hole of his jurta. Coming nearer he hears a voice.

– *Geril-geril-geril-gu*, I'll eat my father, I'll eat my mother. Why is he dawdling like that? I can't stand that sluggishness. My mother and sister are, sure, far away by now.

– *Geril-geril-geril-gu*, when I eat my father, I'll chase them too, they cannot escape from me. – the devil says.

Metele looked into the jurta.

– My child, what's wrong with you? Where are your mother and sister? – he asks.

Looking closely Metele saw that the child became very big, his teeth grew as big as fangs, his nails became as big as harpoon's hooks, his dishevelled hair reached down to the earth. The devil-child had made a big fire, its flames reached the smoke-hole of the jurta.

– *Geril-geril-geril-gu*, my father Metele, I'm just waiting for you. I'll enjoy eating you, you, who nourished me in your bosom, I'll eat you with your bones and guts and all.

– My child, what's wrong with you? – Metele asks once more. And the devil-child saying "I'll eat you" charged at Metele. Metele started to fight with his son. And the son bites him with his teeth and tears him with claws.

– Where are your mother and your sister? – Metele asks.

– *Geril-geril-geril-gu*, I'll eat my mother, I'll eat my sister after I kill you – the devil-child answers. He chased Metele, biting and tearing him with his claws. He chased Metele around the jurta. Metele understanding that he cannot overwhelm his son, flees the river downstream. And his son pursued him, trying to catch him with his claws.

As Metele was fleeing, once he hears a voice from somewhere.

– *Čipitoru-čipitoru*, father Metele, what a nice greeting from your dear son! Why are you running away like that? When my mother and I were crying you were beating us. Now the day has come to pay for your foolishness. And you made my mother Omchek nurse the devil-child, whom you nourished at your bosom, – a voice sounds. "My brother-devil, open your mouth wide, before you'll eat the father, I throw you my mother first," – Chimchep says.

As soon as the devil opened his mouth the sound of a bowstring rang.[...]

And Metele without even looking back, keeps on running down the river. He is running and running until, exhausted to death, he began stumbling all the time on the level ground.

– What if I get caught by the devil? – he thinks and flees ahead.

As he is fleeing, he sees a pasture in front of him, a reindeer graze on both sides of the river. He's passed the pasture and wandered along the river, hiding here and there. Then he saw in front of him a nomad camp. Looking closer he found out that the camp was very big. Meanwhile Metele scared by his devil-son grew scary, keeps hiding all the time.

At some distance he saw a path to the watering-place. Metele hid in the ambush there. When it grew darker, he sees a serving woman dressed in sooty rags approaching. She scoops up with her pot water from the river and starts going back. Then Metele, hiding himself under the river bank, turns the pot over. The serving woman went back to the watering-place, scooped up the water again, but when she was climbing the bank Metele turned the pot over once again, spilling all the water.

– *Uñdalakaña-uñdalakaña*, when I was going to the watering-place before the pot never turned over like that. – she said.

For the third time she went back for water. But when she was climbing back, Metele turned over the pot once again. The serving woman collapsed on the ground (on the cliff) and burst into tears.

– *Uñdalakaña-uñdalakaña*, ages ago I used to live so well in my own country. But Kagankan, the elder, brought me to his nomad camp as a captive and made me his servant. Anyone who feels like it, can humiliate me now. Who has turned over my pot? If you are a human being, show yourself. Otherwise Kagana will beat me with his staff so hard until my head splits. What a disaster! I on my own have to cook for five dozens families and now here I've got this trouble with the pot. Come out! – she says.

So Metele jumped out from the cliff and said:

– Who are your people? I'm afraid of everybody, that's why I'm hiding here.

– *Uñdalakaña-uñdalakaña*, scoop up water into my pot and let's go to my home. – she says. So Metele takes a pot, scoops up water and follows the serving woman to her house. The serving woman was usually given some left-overs to eat (like reindeer's stomach and lungs). She feeded Metele with the rests of her meal. So Metele started to live there, hiding in her jurta. He hid there for some time, how long – nobody knows. Once when they were talking in the jurta, one of Kagana's servants heard them and run to Kagana to warn him about the stranger. As soon as Kagana heard it, he ordered to catch Metele.

– Who are you? What place have you come from? – he asks.

He took off Metele's torn clothes and dressed him as his servant, in sooty clothes made of an old covering (of the top) of the jurta. He gave him an axe and battering Metele on the head, sent him to chop wood. Metele turned out to be a strong man, pulled alone whole dried trees. And when he was not quick enough, Kagana beats him on his head with his staff.

So Metele lives there, cutting wood. Once he sees a reindeer caravan moving downstream. It's his wife coming. As soon as Metele recognized her he runs towards the pasture and hides there. And his wife, approaching the forest meadow, began to sing:

– *Deñee-gu*, father Kagankan, I'm looking for my husband who got lost. Have you seen him by chance? His traces are leading here.

Metele looked closer and saw: his daughter is leading the caravan. Behind her rides a man, then his wife, holding a cradle.

– *Deñee-gu*, father Kagankan, if my husband is by you, give me him back, you should have seen him. Metele, must have been here, his traces disappear near your pasture.

– Yes, (my) daughter, one stranger had come. – answers Kagana.

He sent his people to find Metele. And Metele keeps hiding in the forest near the pasture. He spent there three days. He must have been afraid of his wife. Well, finally he was found and brought back to the camp. Kagana presented him his own dress. When Metele put that dress on, it turned out to be too short: the sleeves hardly reach his elbows, the trouser cuffs are to his knee, the back is bare.

Meanwhile Metele's wife gave birth to a son. They called him Helniken. Metele used to stroll in the field, not far from Kagankan's nomad camp. His wife built a big jurta-tent. And Metele got a son-in-law. Well, so they live, his son is growing up, first crawling around, then begins to go. So they live.

Near the Kagana's nomad camp grow three big larches. Still there are no weapons hanging on them. And Metele doesn't ask anything: "Let it be". Meanwhile his son has grown up, started to make loops and set traps, as his father does. Once a little hare got caught in his loop. The little hare is rushing about, screeching. The boy took pity for the hare and set it free. He came to his father and said:

– Daddy, I shall not set loops any more. The little hare was crying as a baby; I've let it go. Metele began to scold him:

– How silly of you! Why set the quarry, you caught, free? You should've killed it and brought it here, – he scolds the boy. Then the boy took his (self-shooting) bow-trap and set it right on the track where his father used to stroll. And Metele hasn't the faintest idea about it. Once, as he went strolling, he got caught in the trap and cried out:

– Sonny, why on earth have you set the bow-trap right on my path, come over and help me. I've got caught.

But the boy seized a log and cracked the head of his father in two. So, Metele died, what else. When he died, a spark flashed. The boy didn't take any notice, thinking that the spark was from the log. The boy brings his father together with the bow-trap back home.

– Mammy, here is the quarry I have caught in the trap, let's eat it.

The mother says:

– Why have you killed your father, where have you seen that people eat their own fathers, how are you going to eat him?

– What are you saying, the father has taught me himself: "If anything is in the loop, don't set it free". When I've set a little hare free, he scolded me," – the boy answers.

So, what could they do, Metele has died, so they buried him.

The boy grew up. He is running around, playing all the time. Once at dusk the people gathered to dance and play games. The boy sees – not far from the camp appeared an unknown woman. The boy stays looking at the dancers at a distance, but doesn't dare to come nearer. He doesn't play together with the camp youths, because they mock him. "You've killed your own father Metele to eat, you'll become a cannibal." – so they used to tease him.

The boy pondered. "Where does this girl come from? Who is she? How come, she goes behind the hill and then suddenly disappears?" Where she enters and from where she comes out – one cannot see. The boy approaches the place where she disappears every day, hides there and starts to watch. When the young people started the dance, Helniken hid in the bushes of dwarf birch-trees, started to watch. He sees – in front of him in the bushes (as if) a door-curtain opened. And out of it comes the girl, goes to join the dancing youths. The boy let her pass and hid himself near the entrance of her jurta. When the dance was over, by midnight the girl appears again. When she came in and drew the door curtain

Helniken drew it aside. The girl drew it again and barred the door with a stick. As soon as she went to bed, Helniken drew back the double curtain again. She closed the door for the third time – he opened it again. Then the girl addressed her door like that:

– *Kujukeeke*, who has bewitched my door so that it opens all the time. It hasn't flown open in such a way before. If you are a human being, show yourself, why are you playing with the door like that.

The boy came in sight and the girl treated him. One bit the boy puts in his mouth another bit he casts into the fire (as an offer-sacrifice). He has eaten the food, then moved the dishes away. Then he spent the night there. Next morning the girl doesn't let him go. From this evening on she does not go to dance any more. Once her old mother visited that girl. She brought some food with her and treated the girl.

– *Kujukeeke*, mother, let me cook myself, you've been cooking for me long enough.

When the mother wants to go cooking, the girl doesn't let her. The mother has brought the best food, treats her daughter. When the mother comes, the girl covers the boy with a blanket, hides him. So they live for a long time. Once in the evening a rustle of wings sounds at a distance, an echoe rings:

– *Kiido-kiido-gu*, father Kagana, we've been almost frozen to death flying in cold heaven. What news can you tell us? How are you living, since we left you.

– Oh, we are getting on well, nothing special has happened. – Kagana answers.

– Make a fire! Only two of us are coming back.

– Well, what to tell you. – Kagana proceeds. – A woman, Omchek, has come here, lives nearby, at the edge of the forest meadow. She had a husband, but he died, we've buried him. She had a son, but he suddenly disappeared. – Kagana tells, while the other approach flying.

– Make a fire. – they say again.

Kagana made the fire and cast some scraps from the bottom of a woman's hand-bag into the flame to fumigate. The other ones were about to settle down, but then flew up again.

– *Kiido-kiido-gu*, father Kagana, what are you concealing, why don't you tell us the whole truth?

– I am not concealing anything. The boy got lost because of his disobedience, he must've fallen into the river and drunk there. – he says.

The other two almost reached the smoke hole of the jurta, but then flew back as if rebounded.

– *Kiido-kiido-gu*, you are still not telling us the whole truth. Sister D'ajmuk, let your husband out tomorrow. D'ajmuk hides Helniken, – they said, then settled down.

– Who are these people, who arrived? – Helniken asks his wife.

–My elder brothers returned. They have left a long time ago. – the girl answers.

– Come out tomorrow. – challenges one of the brothers.

Helniken could hardly wait till morning. His wife doesn't let him go, pitying him. "Don't go out, they want to kill you," she says.

For three days and nights she keeps him shut in, doesn't let him go out, while the brothers challenge him "Let him go". Still, on the fourth day she had to let him out.

– *Kiido-kiido-gu*, brother-in-law, Helniken, let us see what a brother-in-law I've got. We have been challenging you for three days. Let us try each others skill (who is stronger). Let's see what brother-in-law our sister D'ajmuk has found for us.

The youth (Helniken) sees that both men are strolling with the hands on the hips along the field where his father had been strolling before. As Helniken approached the brothers, and one of them says:

– *Kiido-kiido-gu*, brother-in-law Helniken, let's try our skill.

– How are we going to try it? – Helniken asks.

– *Kiido-kiido-gu*, look, on the other side where two rivers meet, there is a big larch, shoot at it.

– It's too far away, how can my arrow reach it? You, are the hosts (are at home in this land), shoot first. – Helniken says. – It's too far away, for my arrow to reach.

– *Kiido-kiido-gu*, brother Kingini, show what you are worth, take the first shot, let our brother-in-law Helniken see – one of the brothers says.

Kingini took his bow and shot at the larch: the arrow plunged into the tree-top up to the shaft.

– *Kiido-kiido-gu*, now I shall try my own skill.

– Come on. – Helniken says. – If you hit the target, I'll shoot too.

Kidani took his bow and shot: the arrow plunged into the middle of the tree up to the half.

– *Giller-giller-gu*, well done! I've never shot so far. Well, my brothers-in-law, I'll try my own skill now.

The youth ran back home, fetched his bow and shot at the larch. Straightaway his arrow split the larch from top to the bottom as a lightning.

– *Kiido-kiido-gu*, well done! Helniken, you are a real warrior! That's why the sister didn't want let you out. Now let's go (to the other bank) and take a look at our arrows. Let's take a running jump over the river.

Well, all three of them ran to the river. Helniken reached the river first, as the brother suggested, jumped over the river, the brothers followed him. When they looked at their arrows they saw that nothing was left of them – Helniken's arrow destroyed them as a lightning. The elder brother-in-law praises him:

– *Kiido-kiido-gu*, you are a real warrior, I've never seen such a good shot before. It was as a lightning.

But the younger brother became angry, taking pity of his arrow.

– *Kiŋiruki-ŋe*, Helniken, alas for my arrow, you've broken (destroyed) my arrow, – he says.

The elder brother could hardly calm him down. So they began to live together. Helniken strolls with his brothers-in-law along the meadow of his father. So they lived for a long time.

Once in the evening when they came back home after a walk and were about to go asleep, a voice sounded at a distance:

– *Hiler-hiler-gu*, warriors Kidani and Kingini, I think, you've rested enough, I've come here for your sake. Arise, father Kagana, have your people arise!

Kagana says to his people: "Arise or else we'll perish." That stranger circling five times around the camp, shot dead all the inhabitants.

– *Hiler-hiler-gu,* as if five dozens families (clans) is much enough. Whom else can I fight? D'ajmuk will be mine anyway. Omchek and Chimchep will serve me, cooking for my fifty families, going for water, we are always short of servants. And you, Chimchevul, why are you sitting like that, arise! – the voice sounded.

These people, all three of them began to fight with the stranger, only the noise of the battle is heard. They fight so for a long time, nevertheless the local men began to yield after some time.

– *Kiido-kiido-gu,* Helniken, what are you waiting for? How long, sister D'ajmuk, are you going to caress your husband, while we are doomed to death?! – he says.

The local men couldn't resist any more, they fought moaning and exhausted.

– *Kiido-kiido-gu,* Chimchevul, and I hoped that you could overwhelm him.

The battle is going on, their brother-in-law Chimchevul, is fighting straining all his forces. The youth, Helniken, wants to go out – but his wife doesn't let him go. D'ajmuk has even bound him with the belts in order to keep him inside.

– *Nikoj-gu,* brother-in-law Helniken, how long are you going to hide yourself? You are our last hope, or else we are doomed to death. – Chimchevul calls.

(Helniken sees) his brothers-in-law foam with lather (as thick as a male hare) like overdriven reindeer, they are so exhausted that one can see their lungs through their ribs. While they are fighting a droning of a whirlwind sounds. Helniken's wife looked round: downstream along the river there came a man skiing. It looks as if the skies move themselves. She sees – this man looks even better than her husband Helniken. (He is) so adroit, that his own shadow cannot follow him. She thinks: "Oh, such a handsome man, what if he perishes?" And then she finally let her husband out. As for the stranger, he is rushing ahead so quickly, as if his skies are moving by themselves. Then he starts to shoot at Hilini.

– *Kiido-kiido-gu,* Mengnuni, help us, this fight (lit. play) is a sheer torture!

The camp's warriors, all three of them crawled back to their jurta. The newcomer keeps fighting with Hilini. When Hilini shoots he parries his arrows with his skiing stick.

– *Kiŋer-gu,* Hilini, you shouldn't have come here, you lay your bones here.

D'ajmuk let Helniken out when the stranger appeared. Helniken starts to fight with Hilini. And Mengnuni takes off calmly his skies, puts them carefully aside and enters Omchek's house.

And Helniken keeps fighting with Hilini.

– *Hiler-hiler-gu,* D'ajmuk-maid has been hiding Helniken all the time, only now she let him out.

Helniken, although he is fighting for the first time, doesn't let the arrows strike him. When Hilini shoots his arrows come too late, hit the place where Helniken stood before.

– *Hiler-hiler-gu,* well done, Helniken, you are a worthy rival for me, I've never met such a rival before. No wonder that your wife D'ajmuk loves you so. But still, don't be arrogant. The others were at first fast too, faster than their own shadows.

Hilini still shoots not quick enough to hit Helniken. Now he shoots two arrows at a time, but still hits only the place where Helniken stood before. So they fight for a long time. As for Mengnuni, he doesn't care. Since his son (Helniken) has joined the fight, he stays in the house.

– *Hiler-hiler-gu*, Mengnuni, you set your hopes on your son, you don't fight, amusing yourself with your wife. How come that Metele has turned into such a warrior (lit.: from what edge of Metele could such a man jump out). Still beware!

And Helniken has already torn Hilini's clothes with his arrows, the latter cannot dodge anymore.

– *Hiler-hiler-gu*, how can my clothes look well, if the arrows tear them.

While Hilini was saying that, Helniken splintered his leg with an arrow.

– *Hiler-hiler-gu*, what does it matter, if my (fur) boot belt is torn.

While he was saying that, Helniken pierced him the forearm with his arrow.

– *Hiler-hiler-gu*, valiant Helniken, you are a real warrior, I've never met such a warrior in all the three worlds. Still beware!

As he was jumping like that on one foot, Helniken cut his other leg off with an arrow.

– *Hiler-hiler-gu*, what does it matter, if both boot-belts (suspenders) are torn. If you have no feet, you have nothing to stumble over.

Hilini being a trunk, still tries to dodge from Helniken's arrows. Helniken getting cross with him, smashed him another shoulder blade.

– *Hiler-hiler-gu,* indeed you are a mighty hero! If I were not exausted, when I met you, we could have been worthy rivals.

While Hilini's trunk is still jumping, Helniken cut finally his head off with an arrow. Hilihi's head rolled down the river. Helniken pursued it. Catching up, he kicks it to and fro like a ball, playing with it. So he chased the head for a long time.

– *Hiler-hiler-gu,* how splendid to travel light. No danger to stumble over something.

The head keeps rolling on, with Helniken hard at his heels. Helniken catching up kicks it forth.

So Helniken chased Hilini's head for a long time. Once catching up, he tossed the head up, and it fell into the river. Helniken also jumped into the river, swims chasing the head. So they drift downstream for some time.

– *Hiler-hiler-gu,* come on (hold out), many perils are waiting for us, let us try each other, see what each other are worth.

Well, as they were drifting downstream, they got caught on something and stuck fast. In the evening a giant, big as a huge tree, came down from the river bank. His claws are like harpoon hooks, teeth as big as fangs.

– Oh, delicious, I haven't caught anything like that with my fishing-tackle for a long time. I'll enjoy eating these titbits tonight, fill myself properly.

The cannibal giant unfastened his net from the weir (dam) and brought them to his house, which was built of big logs in the heart of the forest.

– Women! Cook these small fishes, I'll go set my net again.

He gave Helniken and the Hilini's head to his domestics and left.

One of the giant women set the pot cooking; the other mended the fur boots. The first one went meanwhile to gather fire wood, in order to cook the pray. The pot warmed up. Helniken is sitting inside together with Hilini's head. Now, the head said:

– *Hiler-hiler-gu*, what are you pondering over, sitting inside Harkilan's pot. If we keep sitting like that, they will cook us. They will enjoy eating us, if we do not escape.

The cannibal woman, who was watching the pot, apparently didn't hear it, kept on patching the fur boots. The fire smoked. The house being full of fumes, she rubbed her sore eyes.

– I shall watch how you escape. If you manage escaping, I'll manage as well, if not, we shall cook together here in Harkilan's pot.

– Well said. Then be on your guard. Do not miss your chance. If you overlook how shall I escape, you will remain here, – said the head and as it was jumped outside through the smoke-hole. Helniken leaped after the head in the same way, began to chase it again.

The giant-woman was still mending boots, when the cannibal-giant, having set his net, returned.

– *Keruvke*, wife Chulpuk, is the meal ready?

Going outside, he peeped into the pot and found out that it was empty.

– *Keruvke*, where are my young fishes gone? You have remained here, you must have eaten them.

– No, I haven't. – said Chulpuk. – Your sister Tosan' did the cooking, she must have eaten, pretending to go after fire wood.

– *Hujelkiñ*, when could I eat them, I was too busy mending the shoes, Tosan' did the cooking. – said Chulpuk.

When they were quarrelling like that, Tosan' returned bringing the firewood. The other attacked her without any ado.

– *Geriñču*, I haven't eaten. I just cooked them and then left immediatly for wood. My sister-in-law, Chulpuk, must have eaten them. – said Tosan'.

The two cannibal women started to fight, pulling each other by hair.

– *Keruvke*, stop fighting, I shall check both of you, come over here.

– *Geriñču*, brother Harkilan, I haven't eaten, I swear! Your wife Chulpuk stayed here, she must have eaten.

Harkilan hearing this, takes a sword and cuts Chulpuk's belly. But Chulpuk's belly is empty, why should there be anything inside.

– *Keruvke*, what a pity, you had me kill my wife, my sister Tosan'. – said Harkilan and cut his sister's belly too. But there is nothing inside either.

– *Keruvke,* all right, I shall fill myself with these two.

Harkilan cooked up the giant women and started to devour them.

As for Helniken, he kept on chasing the head as before. Catching up, he kicked it to and fro.

– *Hiler-hiler-gu*, do not be in such a hurry, soon we shall reach the place we are making our way to, it looks as if we are approaching it.

Helniken didn't care, chased him as before. In this way they approached the pasture, with a lot of reindeer grazing. Passing the pasture, Helniken saw at the far edge of the pasture, a wood-cutter dragging wood. He came dragging, almost crawling, with his huge head as big as a boulder (cliff). He dragged whole dead trees with their roots and all.

– *Hiler-hiler-gu*, my servant Ojind'a, what a miserable sight, I return suffering too, what a misfortune!

As the wood-cutter Ojind'a was dragging the tree, Helniken tread on its top. The other one drugged straining all his strength, digging his heels into the ground, but still could not move it. As for (Hilini's) head, it went ahead downstream. Ojind'a plants his feet so firmly that they sank into the ground up to his knees.

– *Tenmendeñ-Tenmendeñ*, What a nuisance! Living so, I am having trouble all the time.

He pulled the tree with all his force, still cannot move it. Annoyed, he flung the tree on the ground and was about to turn around, when Helniken cut off him the head with his sword. All at once there jumped another man out of the wood-cutter.

– *Tenmendeñ-Tenmendeñ*, where have you come from, I myself am a stranger in this land.

The wood-cutter started to fight with Helniken. Helniken didn't fight with him for a long time. After a while he shot an arrow through his breast.

– *Tenmendeñ-Tenmendeñ*, I had come here attracted by Neruk-maiden's fame. After losing (to her brothers), I had to stay here, serving as a wood-cutter. Anyhow, you'll lose too, – saying so he collapsed on the ground.

Helniken went ahead. As he was running ahead, he heard the clink of shaman's tambourine.

– *Neril-Neril*, my little brother Hilini, daring warrior, I cannot overwhelm Helniken. Don't be cross with me, don't think: "She wouldn't help me, because she fell in love with Helniken." Believe me, I cannot stand Helniken's keen gaze, his eyes are sharp as sparkles. I cannot resist him. If I could, my tambourine would have been dry. But now it is damp, wouldn't sound as it should. Hilini, don't be cross with me. – said shaman-maiden Neruk, Hilini's elder sister.

Helniken doesn't take any notice of her words: "Let her chatter ahead, whatever she wants, I shall make my way anyhow." He rushes forth.

– *Hiler-hiler-gu*, my men arise! My sister Neruk, are you actually trying to do me no harm?

As he said so, the tambourine's thunder died away. When Helniken approached, all population of the settlement, five dozen families lined up. Helniken circling around them ten times, laid all of them low.

– *Hiler-hiler-gu*, my (younger) brother, Hergenmej, come on, try your strength, what are you waiting for? If you won't go to meet the guest in a proper way, he will be disappointed. – sounded Hilini's voice from the big tent (jurta) in the middle of the encampment. Well his brother had to go out to fight Helniken.

– *Hiñöögu*, Helniken, it looks like we, youths, are of the same age. Let us try each other's skill. Below, by the foot of the mountain, there stands a huge larch, there hangs the head of your brother-in-law Giakchavul. It never happened that strangers returned alive from here.

This man, Hergenmej, keeps on shooting at Helniken. What should Helniken do? He started to shoot back. So they fought for a while, however not very long. Soon Helniken split the man with his arrow in twos, the other one collapsed.

– *Hiñöögu*, you have taken me by surprise, I was unaware of your shot, therefore I have to die like that.

As he was talking like that, another man jumped out of the jurta. The fight started anew.

– *Kevlirö*, my name is Hin'ani, come let us see who is stronger, – saying so kept on shooting.

Helniken, however, didn't fight with him long either, shot an arrow through his waist.

– *Kevlirö*, brother Hilini, no surprise that you could not endure either, had you head cut off. He has also shot me through the waist.

Saying so, he collapsed on the ground. Another man rashed out of the jurta, charged at Helniken.

– *Dekiiru-de-Deeke*, Alas for my brothers! Young unexperienced warriors, they have missed the arrow. You took them by surprise (unaware). Come on, we are not going to let the strangers return alive from here.

So Helniken fought with this new man (Himnguni) for a while, however not very long. He turned out to be just a little stronger than his brothers. Helniken split this man in twos.

– *Dekiiru-de-Deeke*, brothers, alas for us, what a misery, what a misfortune! Before I could not find a worthy rival in all the three worlds! Well done, valiant warrior! What a handsome graceful man you are! (He) appears not to be in a hurry at all. My sister Neruk, my time has come to perish. You must have fallen in love with Helniken, that's why you don't resist him (with witchcraft).

Saying so, he crept aside to die. The fourth man (Hinguni) appeared.

– *Ilgooj-kene, Ilgooj-kene*, Alas for my brothers, how they could live on, crippled, with one half of the body shot off. Previously, nobody tormented us like this. We must have been doomed to death by curses of people we have injured or killed.

So the fight began anew, they fought for a long time. After a while Helniken tore this man's clothes with his arrows to pieces. The other one couldn't dodge Helniken's arrows any more.

– *Ilgooj-kene, Ilgooj-kene*, delighted with Helniken's daring, I remembered neither to aim properly, nor to dodge, he shot my clothes to rags. Well done! How come that Omchek has given birth to such a valiant son. And my elder brother Hilini couldn't overwhelm him. So suffering in impotent rage, we perish. My father, N'ungeje although you are an old man still try to entertain our guest somehow. Well done, Helniken! He has shot all my the flesh from my bones! – saying that the loosing man, crawled home.

An old man appeared, holding his staff.

– *Ŋisulañ*, sonny, why are you starting a quarrel with my youths, bully them? What's the reason (the insult)? Beware, in my old days, I, just like you now, could not find a worthy rival.

Saying so, the old man takes his moss-grown bow and starts to shoot at Helniken.

– *Ŋisulañ*, don't boast of your strength, don't put on airs, let's try each other's skill, let me see what you are worth! Come on, suckling, I shall teach you a lesson!

The old man keeps on shooting. Being old, he is still adroit, shoots arrows all the time.

– *Giller-giller-gu*, father N'ungeje, how can I shoot at the old man.

Saying so, Helniken doesn't shoot back. He parries with his elbow N'ungeje's arrows.

– *Giller-giller-gu*, well done, it is unheard that the young should fight with the old one. How can I attack the old man? But, blame yourself, if you challenge me, how long can I refrain from the fight, father N'ungeje, – saying that he started shooting at N'ungeje. Well, the old man is an old man, how long can he resist.

– *Ŋisulañ*, sonny, you are really a valiant warrior, I shall reward you with anything you like, cannot resist you any more.

Saying so, old N'ungeje threw his bow on the ground and sank down totally exhusted.

– Well, why didn't you say this earlier? – answered Helniken.

Helniken entered N'ungeje's yurta. There sits an old woman. Head of Hilini, that Helniken has pursued, lies on the honored place 'malu'. Helniken stayed some time by N'ungeje as his guest. Then he started to get ready for the journey homeward.

– *Ŋisulañ*, sonny, being a mighty warrior, how can you return like that, don't be cross with me. – N'ungeje began to plead him.

– What shall I do then? – asked Helniken, getting ready for the journey.

– *Ŋisulañ*, first revive the men you have killed.

– How on earth can I revive the dead?!

– *Ŋisulañ*, being a mighty hero, why couldn't you? Spit on the wound, rub it, sorcering: “Arise as you were.”

And indeed, when Helniken spitted on wounds of one youth and rubbed it, sorcering, the youth jumped to his feet, unharmed, as he had been before when he came. So Helniken brought into life all population of the encampment.

– *Neril-Neril*, my brother Hilini, revive the head, that you cut. – said Neruk, the shaman-woman.

Hilini unfastened Giakchavul’s head from the larch tree, spit on the wound, rubbed it, sourcering. The man jumped to his feet sound and well. This turned out to be the youngest of D’ajmuk’s brother Giakchavul. He married Neruk, and brought her with him, as they set out back to their homeland. They have already wandered far away, as N’ungeje decided to follow them with a caravan, taking all their property.

– *Ŋisulañ*, my sons, you are young, set out with a caravan, nomadize together with Helniken.

Well, the sons set out following the caravan, living from hunting on their way. They joined Helniken and wandered ahead together. Once they reached the place where the giant cannibal Harkilan lived once. It turned out that he has died long ago, choking with Chulpuk’s bone in his throat.

They moved forth. As they reached their homeland, they settled on both sides of the river. On one river side, Helniken became their chief, on the other side his father Mengnuni. (This is Metele’s new name, since he came to life again). So they started to live there. Perhaps, they still live there.

3. Refrain words and characters in songs

Omchek, Metele's wife:
Deñee-gu

Metele:
Gerijen-gerijen

Devil's son, adopted by Metele:
Geril-geril-geril-gu

Chimchep, Metele's daughter, Chimchevul's wife:
Čipitoru-čipitoru

Kagankan's maid-servant:
Uñdalakaña-uñdalakaña

D'ajmuk, Kagankan's daughter:
Kujukeeke

Kidani, Kagankan's son:
Kiido-kiido-gu

Helniken, Metele's son:
Giller-giller-gu

Kingini, Kidani's (younger) brother:
Kiŋiruki-ŋe

Hilini, Kidani's enemy:
Hiler-hiler-gu

Chimchevul, Chimchep's husband:
Nikoj-gu

Mengnuni, revived Metele:
Kiŋer-gu

Harkilan, cannibal:
Keruvke

Chulpuk, Harkilan's wife:
Hujelkiñ

Toosan', Harkilan's sister:
Geriñču

Tenmeni, wood-cutter, Hilini's servant:
Tenmendeñ-Tenmendeñ

Neruk, shaman-woman, Hilini's sister:
Neril-Neril

Hergenmej, Hilini's (younger) brother:
Hiñöögu

Hin'anikan, Hilini's (younger) brother:
Kevlirö

Himnguni, Hilini's (younger) brother:
Dekiiru-(de)-Deeke

Hinguni, Hilini's brother:
Ilgooj-kene-Ilgooj-kene

N'ungeje, Hilini's father:
Njisulañ

4. Мэтэлэ: эвенский текст

Мэтэлэ унячакан дюлкан. Эрэк нонган кобаку, хялакив бэйчиникэн, таранги депникэн, бивэттэн. Нонган ойон бөкөччөн кобак наннадукун опча. Тэдэнни, хуллан-да кобак наннадукун опча. Эрэк бэй бими, нөкичэнни кобак эвэтлэдукун нөкиттэн. Таранган кобак хумдин томкотла илтэлкэн, кобак часамнадин нюраттан. Эрэк бэйчэн тачин бивэттэн. Тарангчанди кобак дикэнгчиддиву нэмкэриди маваттан, хялаки букчэнгчиддиву тарангди нэмкэтникэн маваттан. Ичин хокан гору бисни.

Хокан гору битчэлэн, окатангман холгич арай як-кал эмнэн, нонган эсни хар яван-да. Кинггэлэн-боралан исни букатан. Уркэй дяпкалин энгэнэкэн, холгидин, нонган урэчин бникэн, нгоном нюритэлкэн, нгоном ойолкан, хокан нодач ойолкан (аси эмнэн).

Аси эмниди, дейдэдун киргинду инэгриди, дюнгнан, калтучаккан дюв дюнгнан. Эрэк Мэтэлэ бими, эрэк аси орордин нгэлэллиди, дикэнгчивэттэн. Орарни бими, дючаман эрэли удьмиллидюр, дюван-да чапчиватта. Эрэк инэнг бими, Мэтэлэ эти нёр одни. Орар хөррэкэтэн, нёвэттэн, орар хөрчэлэтэн хуркаи, нанги итнэвэттэн. Хуркай, нанги итнэсэссими бими, ором иттиди, дикэнгкэтникэн, ичвэттэн, хуркаван-да, яван-да орар чапчичал. Эрэк кобаканган-да, хялакинган-да хингаснан урэчин, эрэк аси эмчэлэн адикуллан. Тарич тачин бидникэн, арай асинган нонгантакин гирканни исни. Эрэк дикэнгдэи-дэ некэссин, нёндаи-да некэссин, нгэлэллиди. Тарич эсни нён. «Ядин-ка эмниди», – гөнни.

Тарак аси эмниди, ириди, төрэделлэн эрэк Мэтэлэтки.

Дэнегу, Мэтэлэкэн
Дэнегу, хи-нгэн яка
Дэнегу, нярикан-а
Дэнегу, гэрбэлкэн-э.
Дэнегу, Ями эсэнни
Дэнегу, дюмидватта.
Дэнегу, Хи-кэн як-а
Дэнегу, дюмаривас
Дэнегу, алаттиди
Дэнегу, удаллиди
Дэнегу, тарпаткан-да
Дэнегу, мэнкэкэн
Дэнегу, дюмадяннам.
Дэнегу, Өтэл-титэл
Дэнегу, улгур
Дэнегу, бидгэрэрэн.
Дэнегу, Аси гэрбэлкэн
Дэнегу, дюлан-а
Дэнегу, нярикан-да
Дэнегу, дюмариван
Дэнегу, улгур бигрэн
Дэнегу, – гөнни.

Эрэк Мэтэлэ он-да гөннэй нгэлэллин, нян. «Ичин-гэл эсэм дюмиватта, киптуваттам-да, яваттам-да. Дөр бөдэлэлкэн эр элэкэс эр хину иттэм», Мэтэлэ бими. Тарак эрэк ядин, кобаканги гайсачаман өлэриди, асингди төйрэн. Дөридюр дебэддэ. Тарич дебэддиди оддиди, аликчаман хирумкэниди, төрэделлэн.

Дэнегу, Мэтэлэкэ-эн

Дэнегу, би хиндулэ

Дэнегу, дюмидяннам,

Дэнегу, нян-а хи-кэн

Дэнегу, миндулэ

Дэнегу, дюмадлила

Дэнегу, – гөнни.

«Ингэ-э, ядим-да-си, дюмадаку-та» – гөнни. Тачин гөникэн боддан эрэк асинги дюлан. Эрэк аси дюлан нгэннэкэн, эрэк дюн эмнгэн, нонган дюдун гөми, айан хо. Хо айич чакуттан, чакутин-да хо. Ойан-да, дюн-да няма. Де-э, эрэк аси бими, эрэк Мэтэлэ дептэн, өлэн. Дептэн өлэриди, улиттан. Деплэнгэн-дэ даллан хо. Эрэк Мэтэлэ бими эрэв хисэчин бими, дюлай эсни мучур. Эрэк эду биделлэн. Эрэк аси укчэнэкэн-дэ хойа бивэттэн, эчин авангчира букатин. Тачин хисэллэкэн тэгэттэн. Эрэк асинган бими Мэтэлэ харанган дейдэлин он.

Дэнегу, Мэтэлэкэ-эн

Дэнегу, хи-кэн-гу

Дэнегу, эди-дэ

Дэнегу, дюлайи

Дэнегу, хөрэденнэ

Дэнегу, – гөнни.

Эрэк Мэтэлэ тарапач асинги дюлан биделлэн. Хокам гору бисэ. Эрэк оролтан горолчилла. «Оронь-да эди нгэллэ», – гөникэн, эрэв бэйу хупкучвэттэн. Эрэк бэй *син* оролдин элэмнэн. Оронь-да эти нгэлли одни, интутти, яри одни. Тарич өмнэкэн асинган төрэделлэн

Дэнегу, Мэтэлэкэ-эн
Дэнегу, эдинкэму,
Дэнегу, оролти-да
Дэнегу, горолчилла,
Дэнегу, онгкоканти
Дэнегу, эмнгэллэ,
Дэнегу, оролти-да
Дэнегу, бэрибнэллэ,
Дэнегу, мут-нгэн як-а
Дэнегу, нулгэдгэрэ өрикичур
Дэнегу, хөнтэругэр,
Дэнегу, – гөнни.

Тачин гөнчэлэн эрэк Мэтэлэ бими, баллан.

Гэрийэн-гэрийэн,
Асийан Өмчэккэн
Гэрийэн-гэрийэн,
би-кэнэ она
Гэрийэн-гэрийэн,
унячандуки хөрэдендим
Гэрийэн-гэрийэн,
Унячами муланам
Гэрийэн-гэрийэн,

Туннгана нангкаму
Гэрийэн-гэрийэн,
Туннгана хуркаву
Гэрийэн-гэрийэн,
би-кэкэ-гу хөррэку
Гэрийэн-гэрийэн,
ача хуннгилач
Гэрийэн-гэрийэн,
эмэбдендин
Гэрийэн-гэрийэн,
Нулгэмми-кэн хи-гу
Гэрийэн-гэрийэн,
мэнкэн нулгэтсоли
Гэрийэн-гэрийэн, – гөнни.

Эрэк аси: «Эмэбли, эмэбли-дэ», – гөнни. Эрэк орми, яйи интуриди абдуи чакриди, асинган окатанги эйэки нулгэн. Эрэк Мэтэлэ өмэккэкэн эду эмэптэн. Эрэк хокам гору бисни. Эрэк Мэтэлэ хуркай, нанги одникан, хуркай-да тулучэссин, нанги-да тулучэссин. Кобаканган-да удян ачча оча, хялакинган-да ачча. Эрэк ади-да инэнгив бисни. Дюн бими ингэнин-дэ хо оча. Тарич иманнач яч-та имассиваттан, тачин-та ингэнмэттэн. Эрэк орар эйду гудэкчэл. Эрэк Мэтэлэ тарпач-та нёмун-да, көкэннэн одимдас. Тарич өмнэкэнь де төрэделлэн.

Гэрийэн-гэрийэн,
эчикэкэн оглами
Гэрийэн-гэрийэн,
Өмчэк асидук

Гэрийэн-гэрийэн,
бодуттиклан эмэбденнив, – гөнни
Гэрийэн-гэрийэн,
он-кан бидин-э
Гэрийэн-гэрийэн,
унячан бими
Гэрийэн-гэрийэн,
Унячан-да бичсөдэн-э
Гэрийэн-гэрийэн,
Туннгана нанга бими
Гэрийэн-гэрийэн,
Туннгана нанга бичсөдэн-э
Гэрийэн-гэрийэн,
Туннгана хуркаву бими
Гэрийэн-гэрийэн,
Туннгана хурка-да бичсөдэн-э
Гэрийэн-гэрийэн,
Кобакангу-да хиннгасанча-кан
Гэрийэн-гэрийэн,
Өмчэк асикан энгэйэнде
Гэрийэн-гэрийэн,
Хялакикам-да экнэнтэн
Гэрийэн-гэрийэн,
домалла хиннгасамканчал
Гэрийэн-гэрийэн,
Эчин бими бэй-дэ
Гэрийэн-гэрийэн,
эмнэву ора урэчин

Гэрийэн-гэрийэн,

Нөмэнь-дэ көкэннэву, – гөнни. Гоөникэн мэн доли торэддэн, эрэк Мэтэлэ. Эрэк, де, нгэрилэвчин, эрэв хисэчим тэгэчимнин ангаттан, нгэрилэддикэм окатанги эйэки асинги хоттун, хөттэн. Нгэнэденнэн хокан гору нгэннэн. Нгэнчэкэн нгэннэн. Тарпач-та хатараллан, ади-да инэнгив, долбанинги – инэнгинги нгэннэн. Өмнэкэн тачин нгэнэддэкэн, дюлдэлэн тог хутапкиттан. Тала нгэнэденнэн эрэк Мэтэлэ. Нёмэри-дэ урэчин, хэттэн. Дебэмэн-дэ хо, ингэнен-дэ хо, ойон бутунни гудэку. Тала дюла нгэннэлэн, асинган бими, дэпки тийунди тогтан. «Унячанди эмэпли. «Туннган хуркаву, туннган нангу мула-а!» – гөнис. «Яв гэлнэнни? Муландангди биддэкэс яка?!» – гөникэн. Эрэк бардалин эмукэнни.

Гэрийэн-гэрийэн,

Асийан Өмчэккэн,

Гэрийэн-гэрийэн,

Эдукун дюлэски якам-да гөнэкэс

Гэрийэн-гэрийэн,

этэм-э-лэ хенгкэлэ тиккэнчиденнэ

Гэрийэн-гэрийэн,

Эди мину илбадянна

Гэрийэн-гэрийэн,

Отигдади эмэддэм

Гэрийэн-гэрийэн,

Демду-дэ көкэннэву одяннан

Гэрийэн-гэрийэн,

ингэньсиду-дэ хинңгэриди

көкэмнэву одяннан

Гэрийэн-гэрийэн, – гөнни. «Эди илбэрэ» – гөнни – «бивкэли», гөникэн. Эйлинивриди, эйлинивриди-де, иврэн эрэк аси. Эрэк Мэтэлэ асаткан хутэлкэн оча. Эчин хокам гору бисни. Эрэк Мэтэлэ эти-дэ буйуссэ яр-да дюди бидвэттэ. Өмнэкэн асикан төрэделлэн:

Дэнегу, Мэтэлэкэ-эн
Дэнегу, эдинкэму
Дэнегу, эрэ она
Дэнегу, мут-нгэни
Дэнегу, ормар-нюн-да
Дэнегу, дэбникэн
Дэнегу, бидендип
Дэнегу, хи-нгэн як-а
Дэнегу, бэйнгэв-дэ
Дэнегу, гэлэткэрэли,
Дэнегу, буйускэрэли.
Дэнегу, Төр ойлин
Дэнегу, гяки бэйнгэ
Дэнегу, илэ нгэндин?
Дэнегу, Он орагдав
Дэнегу, дебэддип
Дэнегу, – гөнни
Дэнегу, Хи-кэн як-а
Дэнегу, текэ-лэ
Дэнегу, эдук нулгэридюр
Дэнегу, нэйи төрду
Дэнегу, өриннидюр
Дэнегу, буйуснгэнни

Дэнегу, тек-нэне

Дэнегу, нулгэйгэрэ

Дэнегу, мут-нгэн як-а

Дэнегу, – гөнни. «Эде, нулгэгэллэ. Орарба интули», – гөнни. – «Орарба дявли» – гөнни эрэк аси ойи хакадяллан, абдуи, эрэк Мэтэлэи орорби интунавканни. Ором интун. Ями айдин өр, гөндидеки «Хенгкэлэ төрэм эдэй тиккөн». Орми дявран, ян. Эрэк Мэтэлэ учаккан каравамкар аткичам бөн. Эрэк Мэтэлэ асинги амардадун де нулгэдэй инэнгиндякам конгдас тикэтнэн, эрэк учакту бадуссими туркутми. Асинган учакван дявриди, увканиди, бадуссиракан, дигэнтэки хэткэвэттэн, онки-да тиквэттэн. Эрэк Мэтэлэ асинги амардадунде нулгэдэй инэнгиндякам конгдас тикэтнэн. Эрэк учакту бадуссими туркутми, асинган учакван дявриди, увканиди бадуссиракан дигэнтэки хэткэвэттэн, онки-да тиквэттэн.

Дэнегу, Мэтэлэкэн,

Дэнегу, олбаньканси

Дэнегу, оваттан

Дэнегу, нёги

Дэнегу, айич

Дэнегу, дявутлила.

Дэнегу, якмантакан

Дэнегу, тикэтнэнни

Дэнегу, гөникэн. Эрэк де Мэтэлэньде инэнгив конгдас хилникэн, де нулгэн. Де өринидюр, де эрэк бэйил дюгавур-ягавур дюнгнидюр, дя, аннгара.

Дэнегу, Мэтэлэкэн,

Дэнегу, хи-нгэнэ
Дэнегу, буйум-дэ
Дэнегу, буйудли-лэ
Дэнегу, орон
Дэнегу, эдлэн
Дэнегу, хиннгасамкан.
Дэнегу, Оронни
Дэнегу, урэчкэнни
Дэнегу, удялкан.
Дэнегу, Мут оронти
Дэнегу, урэмэкэн
Дэнегу, буйун-дэ-гу
Дэнегу, гэрбэлкэн
Дэнегу, бигрэрэн.
Дэнегу, Орондукун
Дэнегу, эгдедмэкэн,
Дэнегу, буйусэлми
Дэнегу, ичэденни

Дэнегу, Мэтэлэкэн, – гөнни. Эрэк тачин гөнчэлэн, Мэтэлэ учакандяй карав учакван, таранги асинган дявран, асинган намнан эмгумэн. Нюрган-яган нөкитэн-яган эрэк асинган мэндукин бөрэн. Эрит дёданьди хөррэ. Эчин хокан гору бадуриди, гя окат дэрэхгидэдун буйурбэ иттэн. Тарангдуки өмэн буйум тиккөнни, нэмкэриди. Эрэк Мэтэлэ бими эрэнги хигиделлэн. Мэтэлэ кобаккачин төкэхэндэй некрэкэн, *аны* кобактук эгден одни. Хэмкэттиди-туркуриди хигэделлэн. Мэтэлэ илан долбанилкам инэнгив конгдас бэриптэн. Эрэк хакач хигэссидвэттэн, хумэлдинукэникэн. Тачин биддэкэн, эрэк асинган эмнэн.

Дэнегу, Мэтэлэкэн,

Дэнегу, эдинькэму

Дэнегу, олбаньканся

Дэнегу, ирэк өси

Дэнегу, буйума

Дэнегу, тачимара

Дэнегу, хигрикэмэн

Дэнегу, хариса, – гөнни. Тарак тачин гөникэн синган амаргич эмниди эрэк буйунгчэмэн хинмайач хигэснэн, дюлавур мэрэкрэн. «Хи ок-та тачимар эди хигрэр» – гөнни. «Буйум эди тачимар хигивэттэ». Эрэк Мэтэлэ тачимар эрэгэр буйусникэн бивэчиддэн. Буйум-яв мари одни, таттан. Эрэк нулгэнникэн нулгэнникэн бидвэттэ. Өмнэкэн нулгэриди өриниди нян-да буйун. Эрэк Мэтэлэ буйуриди эмэргэддэкэн дюкчами одни. Ок-кал өтэрэп дюкчами урэчин. Эрэв дюкчамилба энгэнденэкэн, бивэчиддэкэн, илэ-гэл кунга хонганни исни. Эрэнгчэми гэлэттиди бакран, өмэн дюкчан чонгалан хэрдэдун хэгтэч дасапча. Эрэв кунгав гариди [дюлан дя хөрун] өгниди хинниди. «Як-та эрэк кунгав эмэнчэ», – гөникэн, иттэкэн, таранган нярикаккан кунга.

Гэрийэн-гэрийэн,

Асийан Өмчэккэн

Гэрийэн-гэрийэн,

Би-кэнэ як-а

Гэрийэн-гэрийэн,

няри хуткэвэр

Гэрийэн-гэрийэн,

бакадяннам

Гэрийэн-гэрийэн,

дюкчамиду эмэнчэлэн

Гэрийэн-гэрийэн,

чонгкалкандур

Гэрийэн-гэрийэн,

хэгтэкэндюр дасадяньчал

Гэрийэн-гэрийэн, – гөнни. «Дюкчами арингкаван хи ягай эмунни? Ери кунга индин кунга-да бичэ бими. Ядай эмунни, тек-мэдэ мали», – гөнни.

Гэрийэн-гэрийэн,

Гудейэ-гу

Гэрийэн-гэрийэн,

Ягай мадяндим?

Гэрийэн-гэрийэн, гөникэн. Эрэк нян эрэк асинги хяттамаллан-да нян-да. Эрэк-де эрэк Өмчэк бими дёр кунгав өкутникэн-де бисни. Чимчэп-тэ эгделлэн. Эрэк кунганги хонгнин айи дялби дёрикэмэтэн нэйивэттэн. Эньмэн-дэ-яван-да, Чимчэпи-да хяттаваттан, эрэк хути, няри хути, мулами. Эрэк кунгал исур, тарпач-та эгдер ор. Асачкан, хунадин-да, эгден. Эрэк-кэнэ дюкчами арингкана *аны* эти исур бивэттэн. Чимчэп эгделлэн, хэрэчэнггэй-ягай хэрэдвэттэн. Эрэк эвикэчидемнин ирэнггэи-таранггай очваттан, мэн ойгай хинганни. Эрэк дюкчами-нган арингкан бими эти исур, эрэк омолгон, бакадякан хутэн. Долбаниндякам конгдас хонгматтан, инэнги конгдас хуклэвэттэн. Эрэк эньми-дэ эти хуклэвкэн, амми-да эти хуклэвкэн долба хонгандий. Эрэк Мэтэлэ хадун «Хуту бутэннэн-дэ», – гөвэттэн, хадун асинги-да гөвэттэн «Айич эсэнни улитта -як-та», – гөникэн.

Тарич өмнэкэн-де буйун. Буйуриди, эмэргэддэкэн, хисэчин эмэргэддэкэн, дюн халкамчакандун тоган нэргин нёддэн. Тала арай төрэн иддэн, эмнэкэн.

Гэрил-гэрил-гэрил-гу,

амийав-да дебдим-э

Гэрил-гэрил-гэрил-гу,

энийэв-дэ дебдим-э

Гэрил-гэрил-гэрил-гу,

як-та-гал удайканни

Гэрил-гэрил-гэрил-гу,

амийа Мэтэлэньде,

Гэрил-гэрил-гэрил-гу,

бэркэчэндедукий

Гэрил-гэрил-гэрил-гу,

якман эти эмнэ

Гэрил-гэрил-гэрил-гу,

як-та-го удайканни

Гэрил-гэрил-гэрил-гу,

энийэ-дэ горолчакан-кэ этэн-гу бисэ-лэ

Гэрил-гэрил-гэрил-гу,

экийэ-дэ Чимчэпчэн горолчакан-кэ этэн-гу бисэ

Гэрил-гэрил-гэрил-гу,

– гөникэн төрэнни исни дю долан.

Гэрил-гэрил-гэрил-гу,

амийакам дептиди, аймакандя хөчэддим

Гэрил-гэрил-гэрил-гу,

илэ төрлэ нгэндис

Гэрил-гэрил-гэрил-гу, – гөнни. Эрэк Мэтэлэ бими уркэи анган, уркэлий энгэнни. «Дя, як оданни?! Энинси-дэ илэ нгэннитэн, экэнси-дэ илэ нгэннитэн?», – гөникэн хуттукий улгэмэмэссиллэн. Эрэк хутэн итэн эгден кунялдагчин оча, остан эгден элгэлдэгчин оча. Нюритэньден төрли исси, навлангайа тэгэчиддэн, тоги бими, халкамчакандy дуручэ.

Гэрил-гэрил-гэрил-гу,
амаран Мэтэлэкэн
Гэрил-гэрил-гэрил-гу,
хинкэм-кэ-эсэм алачиддам
Гэрил-гэрил-гэрил-гу,
ханнгайи дулакандун иргэчэдекус
Гэрил-гэрил-гэрил-гу,
икэрикэмэс
Гэрил-гэрил-гэрил-гу,
хөктэй мукчукандун
Гэрил-гэрил-гэрил-гу,
голидяндям

Гэрил-гэрил-гэрил-гу, – гөнни. «Дя-а, як оданни?» – хуттэкий гөссин. Хутэн бими тачин гөмнин, дэпки тугулчин, «дебдим», – гөникэн. Эрэк Мэтэлэ бими эрэк омолгачил хулбэрэллэн, хутумэчиллэн. Омолган бими, гадач иччидэ остади-да осиникан нгэннэн. (Мэтэлэ) «Эрэк энэнси-дэ, экэнси-дэ илэ хөрритэн?»

Гэрил-гэрил-гэрил-гу,
экийэв-дэ дебдем
Гэрил-гэрил-гэрил-гу,

энийэв-дэ дебдем

Гэрил-гэрил-гэрил-гу,

хинэндев-кэнэ мудактаку

Гэрил-гэрил-гэрил-гу, гөникэн, эрэк Мэтэлэв мудникан-да, яникан-да хулутэллэн. Дюв эрэли нёматтан. Нёматтиди эрэк кусикэчиссириди-дэ *ани* хутти дабдан. Эрэк окатанги эйэки нённи гадач эрэк Мэтэлэ бими. Эрэк омолгодмар бими осиникан хөттэн хэпкэссиникэн. Тачин хокам гору хөлумэттэн. Тачин хөлумэчиддэкэн илэ-дэ илэ төрэн исни, бэйди-дэ эсни уталла.

Чипитору-чипитору,

амаран Мэтэлэкэн

Чипитору-чипитору,

гудел(л)икэс омолгос хинкэмэ онякчакан

Чипитору-чипитору,

хинкэмэ онякчакан айича бакалдан

Чипитору-чипитору,

ядай нёнгчидянни

Чипитору-чипитору,

хонгнакан муту-гу хяттагранни

Чипитору-чипитору,

амтали акариди

Чипитору-чипитору,

дюкчамикан арингкаван

Чипитору-чипитору,

ханнгайи дулакандун иргэрис

Чипитору-чипитору,

энинэкэн Өмчэккэм өкучукэнгнэнни, гөникэн төрэн

исни. «Элукэн, дюкчамикан арингкан, арингкасан, хи-кэнэ амнгайи турадянни, амийави эдлэсэ дебэддэ, энийэкэм нодаддаку, амнганьдян турадли-ла», – гөнни. Эрэк амнгаи турран, эрэк дюкчами арингка(н), Мэтэлэ омолгон. Амнгал турринюнни өмэтту, эрэк, як-кал, ивдэн кингкэнукэн исни. Эрэк Мэтэлэ эрэв-дэ эсни эсэн, эсни-дэ көйэттэ, окатанги эйэки гадач нённи. Эрэк тутчакан туттэн. Эрэк туттэн-дэ, *сэнен* ачча оча. Букатин нгисулэтнэвэттэн-дэ-яваттан-да нгун нгундун. «Эрэк арингка*нюн*, арингкангунюн, эдэн бокна», – гөникэн нёнгчин.

Тачин нгэнэддэкэн, дюлдэлэн онгкачакан одни. Эрэв онгкав елтэнни. Окату бардалдулин онгкар орар. Эрэк бэй нгэннэн окат хөлилин дикэйкэтникэн нгэннэн. Нгэнчэлэн, өрилчэкэн өрингчин. Көйэттэкэн, хокан хойа. Эрэк Мэтэлэ бими, эрэк омолгоди нгэлэлчэдий, бэйэч бэкэччин нгэлли одни. Эчин дикэнгчиникэн эмнэн. Эрэк тарич дюгармакан одни. Тарак дюгармали мөв мөлингкэтэн. Эрэк эду тигэттэн, тэгэттэн. Хисэлэддэкэн өмэн асикан эмнэн. Ачураньтакан тэтуттэн. Екэ яллан оча ойон бэкэчэн. Эрэк екэчэнди мөв хукусниди, төтэддэкэн, эрэк Мэтэлэ бими эмкэрэнги өйчихэндиддэкэн, екэчэмэн одюс танни. Екэчэнни өнгкэлбэн. Екэчэн өнгкэлбэчэлэн, нян-да мөв хукуснан, мучуриди. Эрэк нян-да ойчин. Эрэк Мэтэлэ нян-да танни екэчэмэн. Мөнгчэмэн эйду өнгкэвкэнни.

Уньдалаканя-уньдалаканя,
эрэ-гу отла эр-кэнэ дюгурмали
Уньдалаканя-уньдалаканя,
мөнггэй-дэ-гу мөлидгэрэрэм

Уньдалаканя-уньдалаканя,

эчин ок-та-гу, эникэнэ-гу

Уньдалаканя-уньдалаканя,

эсни-кэнэ-гу хорнидгарара

Уньдалаканя-уньдалаканя, – гөнни. Тачин гөникэн илистан мөнггэй мөллэн. Эрэк мөлчэлэн, таранги-да төтухэндиддэкэн, өнгкэн. Эрэк утакан тарпачкан-да эмкэрэнги хэйэдун тэгэньдэриди хонгандяллан.

Уньдалаканя-уньдалаканя,

өтэл-титэл бувйади бингсикэми

Уньдалаканя-уньдалаканя,

би-дэ-кэнэ бэйэмдэс-кэнэ бидгэрэрэм

Уньдалаканя-уньдалаканя,

Каганчакан

Уньдалаканя-уньдалаканя,

өрилйэкэми утаканган эмучэдукун

Уньдалаканя-уньдалаканя,

як-та бэкэчин мөйэденьмэттэн

Уньдалаканя-уньдалаканя,

екэчэму якан-я-гу өнгкэчэденнэн

Уньдалаканя-уньдалаканя,

бэйкэн-гу бими илладлила-гу. Каганкана

Уньдалаканя-уньдалаканя,

чорамиди эмниди

Уньдалаканя-уньдалаканя,

мяткаму-да-гу калтаканна одяннан

Уньдалаканя-уньдалаканя,

як-та-гала хилусканни

Уньдалаканя-уньдалаканя,
туннган дянну өрилэньдэкэм
Уньдалаканя-уньдалаканя,
өмэккэкэн уличидвэттэм
Уньдалаканя-уньдалаканя,
элэ як-агу эмниди каргискама илутадяннан
Уньдалаканя-уньдалаканя,

– гөнни. Эрэк Мэтэлэ таракам-мак хэкэркингчин кубдэкэнгдукий. Эрэк Мэтэлэ гөнни. «Элэ як урэчин бэйил бисэ. Эр бэйилди нгэлми дикэнгчиддэм»

Уньдалаканя-уньдалаканя,
тавара-гу екэчэндуву мөнггэвэр хукусниди
Уньдалаканя-уньдалаканя,
би-кэн дюлавур хөрэденьгэрэ
Уньдалаканя-уньдалаканя,

– гөнни. Эрэк Мэтэлэ бими эрэк утакан екэчэмэн гариди, таду мөнггэй мөллиди, эрэк утакан дюлан нгэннэн. Эрэк аси бими *гуди хэргэтчин* деплэнгэттэн, *эвтэ ангаткандин* деплэнгэттэн. Эрэк бэйил эмэндэнгуттэн ирэв-тарав дебгэрэчэл. Эрэк Мэтэлэ таду дикэнгчин. Тачин хокам гору дикэнгчин. Ади инэнгив бидэнгэн эсни хавра. Тачин дикэнгчиддэкэн, укчэнмэчиддивутэн долдариди, өмэн бэлтэлкэ амандулай Каганала туттиди, мэтун. Кагана бими, тарав долдариди, эрэк Мэтэлэв хэпкэниди,(хэпкэнни эрэк Мэтэлэв). «Иргич эмнис, ядук эмэнни?» – гөникэн. Эрэк Мэтэлэ ойван тар-да гудэку ойван нукриди, нян ачурань-такан тэтун. Тобангаган бөн. Де, эрэк Мэтэлэ дилван тогтаникан, мов моливчин. Эрэк Мэтэлэ энги бэй бичэ урэчин, нинкату кубэчич эмуникэн, мов молидвэттэн. Таранги туркуттэкэн бими, эрэк Кагана эмникэн, эрэв Мэтэлэв чорамичанди дилван тогтиваттан.

Тачин биддэкэтэн, Мэтэлэ могай ирассидяннакан, окатангман холгич нулгэ ичун. Асинган эмэденни ичун. Эрэк Мэтэлэ тарав иттиди онгкала нённи, дикнэн. Эрэк аси бими авландула хемнин, тѳрэникэн эмнэн.

Дэнегу, амаран

Дэнегу, Каганачан

Дэнегу, би-нгэн яка

Дэнегу, бэрнэкэми

Дэнегу, гэлэтэддэм, хи-кэн ярис

Дэнегу, ичэддис?

Дэнегу, удяканни

Дэнегу, эрйэкэклэт

Дэнегу, эмэденнин

Дэнегу,

Гѳникэн. Эрэк Мэтэлэ кѳйэттэкэн, хунадян нёгран, хунадян амардалан ѳмэн бэй бадунни ичун. Тарак амардадун асинган бадуддан, бэбэникэн эмэддэн.

Дэнегу, амаран

Дэнегу, Каганакан

Дэнегу, эмчэ бисэкэн

Дэнегу, бѳргэдли-лэ

Дэнегу, иччэс-дэ-ку бигрэдин,

– гѳнни.

Дэнегу, Мэтэлэкэн

Дэнегу, эмчэ бидин

Дэнегу, эркэн хи-кэн

Дэнегу, онгкалас-а

Дэнегу, иссиди

Дэнегу, удяканни бэриптэн.

«Ингэ-э, ачэй, өмэн бэй эмнэн, тарак эмэ бичэ бидин», – гөникэн эрэк этикэн бими өрилми бэкэткэмэн гэлэтукэнни. Мэтэлэ бими дикнэн, нённи онгкала. Эрэк Мэтэлэ илан инэнгилкэн долбаниву конгдас дикэнгчин, бугин онгкадун. Асингди нгэлэлчэ-дэ бичэ бидин. Де, тачин гэлэтэвчириди, дя, бакчалатан, бакридюр эмур. Эрэк Кагана Мэтэлэду ойган мэн ойи бөрэн. Эрэк Мэтэлэ Кагана ойван тэттэкэн бими, өсэн ечэндулин одни. Истанни буйанни бими хэннгэндулин одни. Эрэк Кагана кучукэн бичэ бидин, нирин-да ян-да ичун.

Тар-да бисэкэн, эрэк Мэтэлэ няри хутэлкэн оча. Таранган гэрбэн Хэлникэн. Эрэк Мэтэлэ бими эрэк кунтэклэ галанивачаддан. Өрилэн мудандун өринни. асинган эмниди тэридекэн дюв дюнгнан. Кутэтэлкэн оча. Эрэк горкам бисни, тачин бидвэттэн. Эрэк Мэтэлэ бими эду өрилэнду нян нонган бэгэн одни. Эрэк як-та бэй бисни эсни хавра. Эрэгэр тачин бивэчвэттэн.Хутчэнни тарпач-та миркэвэчэллэн, гиркаватти одни. Тачин гору бисэ. Эрэк илан нерми бисни. Илан нермилэ як-та ачча. Нонган эсни-дэ улгэмивэттэн, «Бидсонюн-дэ». Тачин биддиди, биддиди, хутчэнни хуркав-яв хуркатти одни, нангу-да яв-да амнгачими тулвэттэн. Тарич өмнэкэн хуркалан бими кобакиккан хорча. Эрэк кобакингчанни бими мэкукми чярнганникачакан мэкукрэн. Тарангчами иллаллиди кунгайакан тинни кобакангчами.

Амандулан эмниди гөнни. «Ама, би этэм-элэ хуркатта» – гөнни. «Кобакангканти кунгагчин хонгнан», – гөнни. «Тугөми тинэм». «Эрэк кунга як тайалан, хуркала хорчав ядай тинэнни? Мариди эмурэкэс яка!», – гөникэн, эрэк хути нэгиттэн, эрэк кунгайакачан эмнэкэн. Тачин нэйивриди, бэркэм он-да, бэркэм туллэн амми галанивачангкадун, эрэк кунга бими. Эрэк (Мэтэлэ) яв ядин, эрэк эсни хар Мэтэлэ, яв одяккон. Өмнэкэн бадикар галаниватнариди, Мэтэлэ бими, хути бэркэндулэн хорран. Эрэк бэркэнндулэ хорриди, *тэгэндэ*риди, кунидяллан. «Дя, хи ями бэй гирканcкадун бэркэм туллис?» – гөнни. «Би эрэк бэркэндулэ хоррам, айнали!» Эрэк кунгайакан дюдук голангкав нангтиснан-да, эрэк амми дилван кампас голангкач еттэн. Аманни ядин – көкэйэттэн. Як-кал як хутануканни эсни *кисанна*. (Голангка(й) тоган хутануканидин гэрбэттэн). Эрэк амми бими бэркэлкэкэнь ирран дюлай. «Эне-э, эрэк би амяв дебдэвэр хуркариди эмурэм хорчалан», – гөнни. – «Эрэк амми ядаи манни. Ирэк өси бэй амми дептивэн иттис, амми ичин дебэннэс?». «Ями амэ мэнди гөнин». «Як-та хорракан, эди тингнэр», – гөнин. Би кобак хорчав тинчалаву мину нэйирин», – гөнни. Эрэк ядир, эрэв бэйунгур көкэчэлэн одчалан, имара.

Эрэк кунгайакан эгден одни. Тарпатта тутэнэллэн. Тутэнникэн, бидвэттэн, эвикэтникэн. Өмнэкэн эвикэчиддэн, эрэк өрилэн, хисэчин хисэллэкэн, нөргэнэлвэттэ, эвикэчилвэттэ. Гякич эвидвэттэ. Кунгайакан көйэттэкэн, арай өрилэн мудандулан ок-та эдэнгэн иттэ аси, эмниди, ичувэттэн. Эрэк көйэттэн, өрилэндулэ эникэн эмнэ бугинак.

Өрилэндулэ эсни холуватта. Элэ эмэссирэкэн, бэлтэлкэн бими кунгайакан дэлби иркангнаватта. «Амми Мэтэлэв дебдэй некрис, бэй этигэн одай некэнни, дебдэй марис» – гөникэн. *Нар* тарич инэньмэттэ. Тарич өмнэкэньде, тарич эрэк мянни кунгайакан. «Эрэк ядук эмгэрэчэ бидин, таварак як бичэ бидин», – гөникэн. «Ядук. Эрэк төрэ амкачан хэрдэлэн нгэнниди бэрибвэттэн.» Илэ-дэ нгэннивэн эсни ичвэттэ, тадук нёддэкэн-дэ эсни ичвэттэ. Эрэк де бэрибэнгкэлэн далилан эрэгэр хисэнтэн далиллан, көйэттэн. Өмнэкэн хисэчин, бэлтэлкэл нөргэнэлчэлэтэн, Хэлникэн бими, аймакань көйэттиди-де, нивэт хаттун букчэнгчирэкэн, эрэк дюлдэлэн нивэтэнгэн уркэтнгэчин мэнкэн ангаптан. Ангариди асичакан нөрэн. Букатин эрэк кунгайакан көйэттэн. Эрэк өрилэндулэ нөргэнэддилдулэ хөрчэлэн, эрэк кунгайакан бими, дялупки ирэн. Дялупки ириди, эду дикэнгчин. Эрэк нөргэннивэр одчалатан, долбани дулаканни елтэнчэлэн, эрэк аси ирэн. Эрэк аси ичэлэн бими, эрэк Хэлникэн бими, дикэнгчириди, уркэй дасчалан, уркэвэн анган, дэссихэнчэлэн. Эрэк гивундин уркэтми нян-да дассан. Дассиди, дэссисникэндун, нян-да уркэтмэн ангаран. Кунгайакан эду дикэнгчиникэн ади-да дюпти уркэтэлкэн тарангчиман ангаваттан. Эрэк аси тарпаткан-да иливран дассан. Нян-да анган. Тарпач-та эрэк аси төрэделлэн уркэткий.

Куйукэкэ, эрэкэ-гу
Куйукэкэ, уркэтэни
Куйукэкэ, якам нунгутми
Куйукэкэ, ангабнадянни

Куйукэкэ, эрэв отлакан
Куйукэкэ, эсэнни-дэ
Куйукэкэ, ангабнаграра
Куйукэкэ, эрэки яка
Куйукэкэ, ангалдядяннан
Куйукэкэ, бэйкэн біми-гу
Куйукэкэ, нөденсөли-гу,
Куйукэкэ, иденсөли-гу
Куйукэкэ, уркэч ява
Куйукэкэ, эвикэчэнни?

Куйукэкэ, – гөнни. Эрэк кунгайакан дэски ирэн. Эрэк тачин гөнчэлэн, эрэк аси кунгангчами дебдэн өлэттэн. Эрэк кунгайакан өмэн дигнэкэм амнгалай хинэснэн, өмэн дигнэкэм тогла улэн. Аликван хирумкэнни. Эрэк бэйчэн эду дюмачидяллан. Эрэк аси бими эрэв кунгайакам эти нөвкэн одни. Дөридюр хисэчин эвинэклэ-дэ эсни нөвэттэ. Өмнэкэн эрэк энинни атикан эмнэн. Эненни атикан дебдэн эмуриди уличэссин.

Куйукэкэ, энерэн
Куйукэкэ, би-кэн як-а
Куйукэкэ, мэнкэн-дэ-гу
Куйукэкэ, деплэнггэй-гу
Куйукэкэ, иритиддэку
Куйукэкэ, якман ху-кэн
Куйукэкэ, иритэдендис

Куйукэкэ, – гөнни. Эрэк эньми ириттэй некэссирэкэн, эсни иритукэн. Эрэк энинни деплэ айдиван эмуникэн, эрэк уличвэттэн хунадди. Эньми эмнэкэн, кунгангчами хулладі тининикэн дасваттан, дяйваттан. Тачин бисни. Хокам гору бис.

Тачин хокам гору бичэлэтэн, өмнэкэн хисэчин биддэкэтэн, илэ-дэ илэ дэтлэ кисаланни исни. Илэ-дэ-илэ улдан.

Кидо-кидо-гу, амаран Каганачан

Кидо-кидо-гу, ингэнэттэ хиннгэрэп нянангкамар хиликэндун

Кидо-кидо-гу, отиньде-дэ көкэрэп

Кидо-кидо-гу, Няна як-а укчэнэкэлкэр биденис-а?

Кидо-кидо-гу, хөрчэдуку онакчакан аич биденис?

Кидо-кидо-гу, – гөнни.

«Ингэ-дэ айич биддэп», – (Кагана) гөнни. «Як-та укчэнэк ачча» – гөникэн. Кагана дюн додукун баргучанни исни. «Тогйаками дурудли-лэ».

Кидо-кидо-гу, амаран Каганачан

Кидо-кидо-гу, дөкэр бими мэриндиддэп

Кидо-кидо-гу, – гөнни.

(Кагана) «Эрэк як бидин?» – гөнни – «Өмчэк гэрбэ аси өриниди биддэн нимэчэч, тавар авлан мудандулан» – гөникэн эрэк Кагана. «Этикэн бисин. Этикэн көкэрин. Тарав имаритан. Омалгалкан бисин, омолгон бэриптэн ун бидемнин», – гөникэн Кагана. Эрэк эмэдемнин, «Тогу дурули» гөникэн, бэй бими гөнни. Тог авсай тимнэриди, эрэк Кагана тоги дурун урэчин, авсай тимнэдин имтэн урэчин. Эрэк бэйил хэссэки тикэргидемнин, өгэски нячалантан исни.

Кидо-кидо-гу, амаран Каганачан

Кидо-кидо-гу, якам-гала дяйучанни?

Кидо-кидо-гу, – гөнни.

«Эс, яв-да эсэм дяйутта», – гөнни. «Тар бэриптин кунга, көрни ходукун мөлэ-дэ яла-да тикчэ бидин. Тикчэ-ккэ этэн бисэ», – гөнни. Эрэк тачин гөникэн, эрэк бэйкэр бими дӧрэкэн амаски тосангчир халкамчалавур исадямнин.

Кидо-кидо-гу, Тар-да-вала бисэкэнэ

Кидо-кидо-гу, хи-нгэнэ

Кидо-кидо-гу, бэкэткэмэни айич эсэнни укчэнэддэ

Кидо-кидо-гу, гөникэн.

Кидо-кидо-гу, Элукэнэ Дяймуккаран

Кидо-кидо-гу, бэйэнгкэми тиминнакан нӧгэтнгэнни, гөникэн,

Кидо-кидо-гу, Дяймуккан-гу дяйучаддан

Кидо-кидо-гу, Хэлникэкэм

Кидо-кидо-гу, гөникэн эрэк аманни.

Тачин гөндиддиди-дэ, тикэргэнни исни. (Хэлникэн) «Де, як бэйилни эмнэ?» – гөникэн эрэк асингдукий улгэмнэн. – «Би акнилбу эмэргэрэ», – гөнни. «Хөрдэнгэтэн гораллан» – гөнни эрэк аси. «Тиминак нӧгнгэнди», – гөнни.

Эрэк бэйчэн тиминак ориван аран алаттан. Асинган эти нӧвкэн, кайиттан. «Хину мадавур некрэ, эди нӧрэ», – гөникэн. Эрэк илан долбанив кайиттан, эти нӧвкэн. Эрэк акнилни эринессивэттэ, «Нӧвли», – гөникэн. Эсни аси төрут эти нӧвкэн. Де, тарич илан долбанив кайиттиди деөмнэкэн нӧвкэнни.

Кидо-кидо-гу, кутэтйэн Хэлникэкэн

Кидо-кидо-гу, хину би-кэн як урэчин кутэтэлкэн-гу

бисэм-э

Кидо-кидо-гу, гөникэн, хэмкэндэй иллаллачам эринеддэм

Кидо-кидо-гу, – гөнни.

«Хоникамас хонимкандай нөкэму Дяймуккана як урэчвэн кутэткэку некчиддэн», – гөникэн – «Хэмкэттэй эринеддив», – гөнни. Эрэк бэйчэн бэйингэлни нонган аманни галанивачангкалин кунтэкли галанивачадда, этэктур дявридюр дёкэр бими. Эрэк Хэлникэн тала нгэннэн. Тала нгэнчэлэн, – гөнни.

Кидо-кидо-гу, Хэлникэкэн кутэткэн

Кидо-кидо-гу, хоникамар хэмкэткэрэ

Кидо-кидо-гу, – гөнни.

«Ичин хэмкэчиннэт, яч хэмкэчиннэт?» – гөнни.

Кидо-кидо-гу, тар баргила, налдикан кунтэклэн ичэсли-лэ

Кидо-кидо-гу, эгден нермикэн илаттан

Кидо-кидо-гу, таркама нэмкэдли-лэ

Кидо-кидо-гу, – гөнни.

«Э-э, гор-а», – гөнни. «Он тала исукандим?! Бугалкан бэй, хуйэ нёгалла». Тачин гөникэн, эрэк Хэлникэн бими гөнни. «Тарак горон хо!» – гөнни. – «Би эмнэву исукан».

Кидо-кидо-гу, элукэн Кингиникэн он-ди-чакан бигрэнни

Кидо-кидо-гу, хи-кэнэ нёгадли-ла

Кидо-кидо-гу, кутэткэмэр Хэлникэкэн ичиддэн,

гөнни. Эрэк тачин гөнчэлэн, эрэк Кингини бими, нгади гаридий, эрэк нерминьдев нэмкэн. Нерминьдев нэмкэн, нерминьде хурэлин ингэтэн хорран, нюран.

Кидо-кидо-гу, няна би-кэн хэмкэндэку

Кидо-кидо-гу, – гөнни.

Хэлникэн: «Гэ, хэмкэли», – гөнни. «Хи навканакас, нян би хэмкэндингэву», – гөнни. Эрэк Кидани бими *эмэ*, нгади гаридий нэмкэн. Нюран бими дулакаклий ириди, нерми дулакаклан хорран.

Гиллер-гиллер-гу, эрэгэгэй

Гиллер-гиллер-гу, би-кэни ок-та горла эчукэн нөклэденнэ

Гиллер-гиллер-гу, далила нөкиткэрэрэм

Гиллер-гиллер-гу, тарвачамур горла эчу-кэн нөкичэддэ

Гиллер-гиллер-гу, кэлиннэйэ-лэ хэмкэньдиддэку

Гиллер-гиллер-гу, ядин-да-си

Гиллер-гиллер-гу, гөникэн.

Эрэк кунгайакан дюлай туттиди, нөкий гаридий, эмнэн. Эрэк нөкий гаридий, эмнидий, де, эрэк нермингэндевэтэн нөклэн. Эрэк нерминдекэм хурэдукун хаттун мудан хяркичагчин нгэнукэнни өмнэкэйэ.

Кидо-кидо-гу, эрэгэгэй Хэлникэкэн

Кидо-кидо-гу, айдит ай бэй бисэнни

Кидо-кидо-гу, би хунадю тивоми-дэ дяйучатча

Кидо-кидо-гу, – гөнни.

Гэ-няна-гу нөкикэрбур

Кидо-кидо-гу, окатангур бардайалан тухандяп тутэмникэн

Кидо-кидо-гу, – гөнни.

Тачин гөниди, эрэк илнидюр даран иллидюр тутэллэ. Эрэк Хэлникэн дюлэгэч нгэннэн. Эрэк гөнчэгчинни окатангур бардадукун бардалан эрэк Хэлникэн тухангчин *арай*. Эрэк дялни амардадун туханькатта. Эрэк нөкилдулэ эмнидюр, ичэссирэкэтэн, эрэк данилни нөкилни ачча бикэнни. Хяркачагчин нгэнчэ. Эрэк хагди дан эркэделлэн.

Кидо-кидо-гу, Хэлникэн эливэн-дэ хони бэйкэн бидемнэсэ

Кидо-кидо-гу, ирэк өси эчи-кэнэ нэмкэдэнгмэн (эсэм хар)

Кидо-кидо-гу, Хяркатлагчин нгэнукэнни, нэмкэденнис

Кидо-кидо-гу, – гөнни.

Гядмар бими, нөдмэр бими хираллан, эрэк Кингини, нюри мулаллиди.

Кингируки-нгэ, Хэлникэн

Кингируки-нгэ, мулакэ-э-да ингэткэму хайудяннис

Кингируки-нгэ, гөникэн эрэк. Эрэк аканни-де дялби дя аран одуканни.

Эрэк бэйчэн тачин некэддидюр-оддидюр биддэ. Эрэк Хэлникэн аманни галанивачангка кунтэкэнгнин данилчал галанивачадваттан. Тачин эрэгэр хокан гору биддэ. Тачин бидидюр, өмнэкэн хисэчин, тачин гиркавачиддидюр, хисэчин эмнидюр, хуклэхэнчэлэтэн, долбайакан төрэн иллэн нян-да.

Хилер-хилер-гу, Матала Киданийа Кингэнийэ

Хилер-хилер-гу, бикэн яка, элэкэн-дэ хөччэсэни бидини-гу

гөникэн дачадяннам

Хилер-хилер-гу, Гэлилэй өгин олла

Хилер-хилер-гу, амара Каганакан өрилкэми огин овкали, – гөнни. Гөникэн, төрэн исни. Эрэк берусэлэ «Өгин олла, көкэрэп», – гөникэн, эрэк Кагана өрилми бэлэтэлкэлби өгин овканни. Эрэк бэй бими эрэв өрилэм туннгаракан токараснан

Хилер-хилер-гу, туннган дяннукан өрилэн асун бидин

няна ялкан бисэпэ. Дяймук аси миннги-т-к-этэн одяннала

Хилер-хилер-гу, – гөнни.

Өмчэккэн, Чимчапкэнэ мяна дянну өрилкэму дебдэтэн ириттис-э. Мөнгэтэн мөлидис-э, утакан-да камаг бигрэн

Хилер-хилер-гу, Чимчэвулкэн хи-дэ яддай бидинни, өгин оли

Хилер-хилер-гу, гөникэн, төрэн исни. Эрэк бэйэл илнидюр туханькатта. Эрэк кусиделлэ, кусидентэн ивэттэн. *Син* горкам кусикэттидюр бугалкар бэйил дабдара.

Кидо-кидо-гу, кутэтйэн Хэлникэкэн хи-ка ява алаччинни?

Элукэни Дяймуккана бэйэнгкэми ягдав-такан билгудянни?

Кидо-кидо-гу, Дёсачакан одангканни

Кидо-кидо-гу, гөникэн, төрэн исни.

Эрэк дабдачал бэйил асум гору кусидюр?! Дабдаримдасал, отинтан исни.

Кидо-кидо-гу, Чимчэвулкэн

Кидо-кидо-гу, тек-элэ

Кидо-кидо-гу, хину-дэ элсучэн-э гэрбэттиву, гөникэн, кусикэчидентэн ивэттэн. Эрэк авасадмар-да Чимчэвул отидянни исимдэс бивэттэн. Эрэк кунгайакан нөдэй ичин-дэ төлэски, нөдэй некэссими туркун. асинган *кайич*ваттан. Өсөмикэн урултинди-дэ, яди-да уйчивэттэн эрэв Хэлникэм, эрэк аси, эрэк Дяймук.

Никой-гу, бэнэрйэн

Никой-гу, Хэлникэкэн

Никой-гу, ягдав-такан

Никой-гу, дикэнгчинни?

Никой-гу, хину-нюн-дэ иниттэп

Никой-гу, эртэкэн-дэ

Никой-гу, бидэнгкэнти

Никой-гу, эне-дэ

Никой-гу, дёсачакан

Никой-гу, одангканни

Никой-гу, гөникэн, эрэк, унгэн, Хэлникэми-дэ эринэнни исни. Аавасадмар тарпач-та, тарпач-та эрэк бэйил бими, мирдутэн эгден кобак көрбэтэн дин чоглика чоглинаснан, эвэтлэтэн дяпкалин эвтэтэн ичун. Нгисулэтнэникэн, кусисиддэ. Тачин кусиддэкэтэн як-кал курэлэн исни, өсөмикэн мэнкэн кинггэргиттимдэс-тэ яримдас-та. Эрэк аси энгэнэкэн, арай окатангман холгичакан бэйчэкэн эмнэн кингнэч. Өсөми кингнэн мэнкэн бутумэттэн. Эрэк аси көйэттэкэн, Хэлникэдукун букатин нодадмар бэй. Мэнкэн хинянди хэткун. Эрэк аси бими гөнни. «Ө-ө, нодак-е бэй көкэмэллэн», гөникэн, эрэв кайичадяки бэйэнги нёврэн. Эрэк холгич эмэ бэй бими, киннгнэн мэнкэн бутумэттэн, эрэгэр. Эрэк бэйэнгэтэн бими, эмэ бэйэнгэтэн бими, бэйу / Хилини/ нэмкэчэллэн.

Кидо-кидо-гу, Мэнгнуникэн

Кидо-кидо-гу, маннуйатли

Кидо-кидо-гу, отигдадюр

Кидо-кидо-гу, эвиденнэп

Кидо-кидо-гу, гөникэн. Эрэк бугалкар бэйил илнидю дюлавур миркэснэ. Эрэк эмэ бэй бими букатин эрэк Хилининюн нэмкэтмэчэллэн. Өсөмикэн хэбгэрэн игэлкэн бивэттэн, бэйэнде нэмкэрэкэн, хэбгэрди тогвэттэн.

Кингэр-гу, Хилиникэн-и

Кингэр-гу, илэ гу төрлэ

Кингэр-гу, икэрикэми

Кингэр-гу, гөлидэй эмэденнис

Кингэр-гу, гөникэн.

Эрэк аси бими Хэлникэми нөгрин, эрэк бэй эмчэлэн. Эрэк Хэлникэн нөриди, нэмкэмэчиделлэкэн, Мэнгнуни бими кингнэйи-йайи нукриди, алла-дин нэриди, эрэк Өмчэк дюлан ирэн.

Эрэк бэй бими Хэлникэнюн кусиделлэ.

Хилер-хилер-гу, Дяймук аси

Хилер-хилер-гу, Хэлникэм дяйучаддиди, тиндиденни

Хилер-хилер-гу, гөникэн, эрэк кусикэчиделлэн Хэлникэнюн. Хэлникэн-дэ элэкэс кусикэчэлэдди гөми, эннэ навра. Эрэк Хилини бидекэгдэвэн нэмкэвэттэ.

Хилер-хилер-гу, эрэгэгэй

Хилер-хилер-гу, Хэлникэкэн

Хилер-хилер-гу, айдит айа гасани ичулэдди урэткэнни

Хилер-хилер-гу, эр отла эрвэчкэмэн бэйу эчу бакалдар

Хилер-хилер-гу, тар-да бисэкэн энгнийэ эди ховлаграра, нонакан бэйэ бэкэчин хингэчикэн хинякандюр бидгэрэрэ

Хилер-хилер-гу, эрэгэгэй

Хилер-хилер-гу, Дяймук аси тивөми Хэлникэнду билгудянча

Хилер-хилер-гу, гөникэн. Эрэк Хэлникэм өмникэн-дэ эти навкан, эрэк билэкэгдэвэн нэмкэвэттэн. Ичичикэн-дэ дюптич нэмкэвэттэн, эрэк Хэлникэн билэкэгдэн бивэттэн. Хокам гору кусикэттэ. Мэнгнуни-дэ эсни кисанна. Омолгай кусиделчэлэн, дюлай ирин. Тачин:

Хилер-хилер-гу, Мэнгнуникэн омолгайи иничэллиди, аймаканьдя асингди билгудянни. Мэтэлдук ирэнгдукун кирандукун эрвэчкэнни бэйкэн балдарин

Хилер-хилер-гу, маннули-ла

Хилер-хилер-гу, гөникэн.

эрэк Хэлникэн тарпачкан-да эрэв Хилини ойван чөрэкэллэн. Бэйэнгэн адгунга-да туркучиллэн урэчин. *Хилер-хилер-гу,* якман-да этэн адда ади нюру киснадякан оййакаму

Хилер-хилер-гу, – гөнни.

Тачин гөндиддив, гад гайсанги чэлгэс нэмкэн.

Хилер-хилер-гу, гада тири хэгдэрридин ядин-да-си өсэдендим, гөникэн. Ун-дэ тачин гөникэн, туханкачиддив, эрэк бэйчэн гад хуракинги чэлгэс нэмкэн.

Хилер-хилер-гу, эрэгэгэй Хэлникэкэн

Хилер-хилер-гу, эливэн-дэ /хоникан/ бимнэ-гэ-сэ, илан төрду гаснгайи эчу бакадянна

Хилер-хилер-гу, эрэгэгэй маннудли-ла

Хилер-хилер-гу, эрич-кэ ядим өсэдим

Хилер-хилер-гу, гөникэн

таркилаки туханкачиддан, гад бөдэлди. Тачин тусанаддив гад бөдэлэнги чэлгэс нэмкэн, өмэн өмчэн эмэпчэ.

Хилер-хилер-гу, тэри тири хэгдэррикэндин ядин-да-си өсэдим

Хилер-хилер-гу, гэлилэ, *ката* этэм хивсэтнэр ач хөнкилэч тусанабган оча бидин

Хилер-хилер-гу, гөникэн. Эрэк энгэнегдэ биникэн

бэйэнгэн таракат хэйукрэн. Эрэк Хэлникэн бими абаланниди, нян-да гад исакинги эдес нэмкэн.

Эрэгэгэй

Хилер-хилер-гу, Хэлникэкэн

Хилер-хилер-гу, эрэгэр айич айа бисэнни-лэ

Хилер-хилер-гу, эникэкэн хэчиденнэ, бакалдача бими - кэни, эливэн-дэ айкан гасан бичэ бимчэс

Хилер-хилер-гу, гөникэн.

Эрэк энгэнегдэ ориди туханькачидяллан. Тачин-да тусанаддив Хэлникэн бими диланги помпос нэмкэн. диланган окатангман эйэки чөндунэснэн. Эрэк Хэлникэн диланги хөттэн. Диланги бими эрэгэр хэкиникэн эртэки-дэ хэкисвэттэн, тарртаки-да хэкисвэттэн. дилангди эвиникэн тутэллэн гадач. Хокам гору нгэннэн.

Хилер-хилер-гу, эйэмдиди одяннам

Хилер-хилер-гу, иликэнэ бөдэлди хорнидяндям

Хилер-хилер-гу, гөникэн.

эрэк бэйэнгэн иду-да эсни хоруватта, диланган гадач чөндуннэн, эрэк бокниди диланги хэкисвэттэн горйалан.

Гиллер-гиллер-гу, эрк дияндя хэбденнэкэнни

Гиллер-гиллер-гу, одяннан. Эрмэлкэнде эвикэтникэн

Гиллер-гиллер-гу, төрэнгйэкэми хомидяндак(у),

Гиллер-гиллер-гу, гөникэн.

Эрэк диланги хэкиникэн, нгэнэддэн. Хокан гору нгэнниди, эрэк бэй өмнэкэн диланги өгэски титаканни. дилангдякан өгэски нгэнниди окатла хөррэн. Окаттаки тикрэн, окат мөлэн тикрэн. Эрэк Хэлникэн бими диланги амардадун туттэн, окатла тухангчин. Эрэк диланги дилангчал өмэтту окатла эйэснэн, гадач окату эйэки. Хокан гору эйэнни.

Хилер-хилер-гу, Хэлникэкэн

Хилер-хилер-гу, маннудли-ла

Хилер-хилер-гу, эчикэн нгэнэддэкэт

Хилер-хилер-гу, каргис хойа биден-элэ, Хоникамас хэмкэчиддэк(у)

Хилер-хилер-гу, гөникэн.

Ун эйэндидемнин яду-гал хорра. Эду хордидянна. хисэчин арай дегидитан тэнгкэдук эгден тэнгкэ дин бэй херэн. Остан эгден элгэлдэгчин, итэн эгден кунялдагчин. «Ө-ө, алагда, эрэк укилэву як-та эдэнгэн хорра гораллан. Эрэв хисэчим тирэнгкэвур каняраннал очал бисэп» Эрэк хэвэйкэнде эрэв кэнгэрэлкэкэнь укидукуй гариди, бэйэнгэлби хурун. Тэнгкэ дулакандулан эгден утэмкэр илаттан. Тала эмурэн. «Асал-а, хэйкэчэнгчэмур ириллэ» гөнни. «би нян-да тулнэдэку» гөникэн. Эрэк дилу, нян эрэв бэйу, Хэлникэм, бөриди, кэнгэрэньдей тулнэн.

Эрэк кянгундял бими эду иритэделлэн, гя унтаньдяй такукасиддан, гя бими могай тавнан, эрэк хэйкэчэнгэлби иридэй. Эрэк хэвэйкэн кэнгэри тулнэн. Эрэк екэтэн хөкэлэддэн. Эрэк бэй бими (Хэлникэн), екэчэнди тэгэттэн, гяйи көйэтникэн, диланги көйэтникэн. Диланган бими гяткий төрэделлэн, дил дилан биникэн.

Хилер-хилер-гу, Хэлникэкэн

Хилер-хилер-гу, якандя мэргэнди Харкилакан екэндедун тэгэчэнни

Хилер-хилер-гу, эчин кубэчич ириридюр дебэдендир

Хилер-хилер-гу, Харкилакан эрэв хисэчим тирэнгкэйи каняраддин

Хилер-хилер-гу, гөникэн

«Эдук эсэкэт нёна» – гөнни. Эрэк кянгундя бими, тарав-да этимдэс долдар. Унтай ханганасиддан. Дюй хансакан, ясали хикникэн. «Хи-кэнэ, ичин нённас? Би хину-нюн этурэм» гөнни. «Хи нёнакас, нёндим, эсэкэс-тэ, хиннюн эду ирдим».

Эрэгэгэй,

Хилер-хилер-гу, тачимар няна гөндидми-кэн аймаканьдя көйэчидли, делудикэс

Хилер-хилер-гу, эди-мэкэн делурэ-лэ

Хилер-хилер-гу, – гөнни. «Айич көйэтли, делуминюн, эмэбдинни эду» Тачин гөндидемнин, эрэк дилан диланганьдян халкамчали тохангчин. Эрэк бэй-дэ диланги амардадун тухангчин. Эрэк-де хөтмэттитэн. Эрэк кянгундя бими, унтай ханганассидяннакан, хэвэйкэн эмнэн, кэнгэрэй туллиди.

Кэрувкэ, асийан

Кэрувкэ, Чулпуккан

Кэрувкэ, илэ-йэкэ-т

Кэрувкэ, яран иррэн?

Кэрувкэ,

төлгиди эмниди екэй ичиссирэкэн, як-та ачча екэ долан.

Хэйкэчэнгкэрти:

Кэрувкэ, илэ нгэннитэн

Кэрувкэ, янгнисана

Кэрувкэ, ху-кэн як-а

Кэрувкэ, эду бидникэн

Кэрувкэ, дебэсэнчэл

Кэрувкэ, бисэс-э

Кэрувкэ, гөникэн.

«Э-э, би эчу дептэ», – гөнни тавар Тосань иритэдемнин, дебэснидюр, нёчэ бидин, могай тавнасан биникэн.

Хуелкинь, ок-а дебэддим-а

Хуелкинь, эр унтай

Хуелкинь, такусаддам

Хуелкинь, Тосанькана

Хуелкинь, талавара

Хуелкинь, екэчэми

Хуелкинь, ярутаддин

Хуелкинь, гөнни.

Гөникэн, эрэк тачин гөмэчиддэкэтэн, эрэк Тосань ин, мой нгалникан. Эрэк *аны* Тосанюр ойлан тикрэ.

Гэриньчу, би эчу

Гэриньчу, дебэддэ

Гэриньчу, өлэриди

Гэриньчу, хөрэснив

Гэриньчу, өикэн

Гэриньчу, Чулпуккан

Гэриньчу, мэнкэн-кэтэн

Гэриньчу, депчэ бис-э

Гэриньчу, гөникэн.

Эрэк дёр кянгундял ани тарич мэр доли хутумэчиллэ нюриттукур.

Кэрувкэ, эделлэ-лэ

Кэрувкэ, кусикэттэ

Кэрувкэ, гэ хункэмэ

Кэрувкэ, ичиддэку

Кэрувкэ, эвэски-кэ

Кэрувкэ, эмэллэ-лэ

Кэрувкэ, гөнни.

Гэриньчу, акаран

Гэриньчу, Харкилан

Гэриньчу, би эчу

Гэриньчу, дебэддэ

Гэриньчу, эчу, эчу

Гэриньчу, дебэддэ

Гэриньчу, Чулпук өйи

Гэриньчу, эмэптин

Гэриньчу, нонган-ккэ этэн

Гэриньчу, депчэ бис-э

Гэриньчу, гөникэн.

Харкилан бими эрэк хиннгапандяй гариди, Чулпук урувэн хөкиснэн. Чулпуклэн ядук бидин, яв-да эчэ дептэ, урлэ-н як-та ачча.

Кэрувкэ, мулакйада

Кэрувкэ, атикаму

Кэрувкэ, мавкананни

Кэрувкэ, элукэн Тосанькан

Кэрувкэ, гөникэн, нөткий ян, нөй урвэн хөкин, Нөн урлэн ачча

Кэрувкэ, эрэгэгэй

Кэрувкэ, эрэнгэлби

Кэрувкэ, тирэнгкэй

Кэрувкэ, каняраддим

Кэрувкэ, гөникэн,

эрэк Харкиланьдя кянгуньдянгалби бэймэлутэн өлэтникэн, дебэделлэн. Эрэк нонган дебэддэн.

Эрэк Хэлникэн бими, диланги хулуникэн, гадач хөррэн. Эр ичин нгэннин-дэ, тачин нгэньмэттэн, хэкэникэн-дэяникан-да.

Хилер-хилер-гу, эди-гилэ мэнуденнэ, исанналавур ок-тавула бисэкэн, исадяндяп

Хилер-хилер-гу, текэ яка далбаладдил урэчкэнти

Хилер-хилер-гу, гөникэн.

Эрэк Хэлникэн тарав эсни долдаватта, *син бир* хэкэникэн, хулувэттэн. Тачин хулумэчиддэкэтэн, онгачакан одни. хокан хойа орон онгкача. Эрэк онгка долин нгэннэн гадач. онгка долин нгэнэдникэн, онгка мудандулан часки, онгкав елтэнчэлэтэн, ойиндямкар мов хутусиденннэн. Эгден тэнмэк дин дилалкан миркэденнэн. Нинкатангган тэкэлкэкэнь ялкакань ираддан.

Хилер-хилер-гу, ойиндякан болиньдякан ондичакан бигрэнни, отигдадюр эмэденнэм

Хилер-хилер-гу, эртэкэнтэ бидэнгкэнти

Хилер-хилер-гу, гөникэн.

Эрэк бэй монги ирникан, хутусиддив (хякитангандян), (Хэлникэн) нинкатанган хурэдун төрэн. Эрэк нонган-да бими, бинарассими, туркун. Эрэк диланган гадач эйэки хөррэн. Эрэк ойиндякан нян-да бинарран, нидэррэн өсөмикэн хэннгэкли. Эрэк:

Тэнмэндэнь-Тэнмэндэнь, як-та-гала хинарканни одяннан

Тэнмэндэнь-Тэнмэндэнь, бэйкэн эчин оракан

Тэнмэндэнь-Тэнмэндэнь, як бэкэчин киргис оваттан

Тэнмэндэнь-Тэнмэндэнь, гөникэн, бинарран, туркун. Эрэк туркуриди, тарпатта монганьдяй улэмнин, эсэндиддив. Эрэк бэйчэн бими, амаргич ойиндя дилван хиннгапанди калтас хонаснан. ойиндя чайдадукун бэй бэйди тухангчин.

Тэнмэндэнь-Тэнмэндэнь, эркэн няна иргичикэнди эмэлэнни

Тэнмэндэнь-Тэнмэндэнь, би-дэ-вул эмэкэн бэй бисэм-э

Тэнмэндэнь-Тэнмэндэнь, гөникэн, эрэк бэйэнгэн кусикэчэллэн. Эрэк ойиндянюн нгунэкэм кусикэттэн, эсни тачикан гору кусир. Эрэк энгэньмэн помпас нэмкэн.

Тэнмэндэнь-Тэнмэндэнь, Нэрук аси игйэлэн эмниди монгандавур молидддам, дабдариди

Тэнмэндэнь-Тэнмэндэнь, хи-до-гу бими-кэн

Тэнмэндэнь-Тэнмэндэнь, яка-гу-дэ дэгэрэкчэн тэрэдинни

Тэнмэндэнь-Тэнмэндэнь, гөмнин, бэйэнгэнден тикрэн.

Эрэк бэй елтэс хөррэн. Тачин тутэллэн дюлэски. Тачин тутэддэкэн, илэ-гэл илэ унтун дирэлэнни исни.

Нэрил-Нэрил, элукэнэ Хилиникэн

Нэрил-Нэрил, эрэгэй би-нгэн яка эмнэкэму тэрэденнэ

Нэрил-Нэрил, дялди-да эди дявадда-ла

Нэрил-Нэрил, Хэлникэкэм эйэлдиди

Нэрил-Нэрил, эсэнни айчидянна

Нэрил-Нэрил, гөникэн,

Нэрил-Нэрил, эдилэ көмэлэддэ

Нэрил-Нэрил, дэпкикэнэ ичиснэкэн

Нэрил-Нэрил, дэпкикэкэн ичэснскэн, дяйатнарам

Нэрил-Нэрил, ясалканни тогканни эмэркэнни

Нэрил-Нэрил, өсөмикэн хуйалкиннан.

Нэрил-Нэрил, эрэгэгэй

Нэрил-Нэрил, эмнэкэму тэрэденнэ

Нэрил-Нэрил, мут-нгэн як-а тэрэннэлэ бисэкэтэ

Нэрил-Нэрил, унтундекэн илуритлий илугрэрэн-гу текэгу

Нэрил-Нэрил, унтундети дэрбуденчэ

Нэрил-Нэрил, Хилиникэкэн тардаман бисэкэн

Нэрил-Нэрил, дялди-да эди дявгарар

Нэрил-Нэрил, гөникэн, төрэн исни.

Эрэк бэйчэн эсни киханна. «Төрэдли-гул, яли-гул, исаннай исчам», гөнигчин дюлэски-ттэ туттэн.

Хилер-хилер-гу, берусэлэ өгин олла

Хилер-хилер-гу, эрэгэгэй Нэрук экикэн

Хилер-хилер-гу, эрэк янни

Хилер-хилер-гу, энилэчэн эсэнни-гу дэпкэнэ-лэ

Хилер-хилер-гу, – гөнни.

Тачин гөнинюнни унтунгэн игэн бэриптэн. Эрэк бэй нгэннэкэн букатин, дэпки мян дянну өрилэн илаттан, бэкэчинден дэпки нэмкэлэмнин, эрэк бэйчэн эрэв өрилэндев мяракайа токараснан.

Хилер-хилер-гу, элукэн Хэргэмэйкэн маннули-ла

Хилер-хилер-гу, якама алачанни?

Хилер-хилер-гу, эсэкэс няна матамадда көмэлдин

Хилер-хилер-гу, гөникэн, хулудекэн бэй төрэнни исни. Эгден кэркэтэ дю илаттан өрилэн дулакандулан. Тала дюла төрэнни исни. Эрэк ядин, эрэк бэй кусикэчэллэн.

Хинөгу, бэйкэнэ

Хинөгу, Хэлникэкэн

Хинөгу, урэчилэ

Хинөгу, иламаткар

Хинөгу, бисэпэ.

Хинөгу, авагчан-кэ

Хинөгу, хонила биден.

Хинөгу, Хоникамар

Хинөгу, хэмкэлдэгэр.

Хинөгу, Тавагара нгяйдалан

Хинөгу, нермилэ

Хинөгу, тавара

Хинөгу, асингканси

Хинөгу, аканни

Хинөгу, Гякчавалкан

Хинөгу, дилканни

Хинөгу, нокучаддан

Хинөгу, Элэ эмчэ

Хинөгу, бэйкэнэ

Хинөгу, өси өсидун

Хинөгу, эсэп

Хинөгу, мучуграр

Хинөгу, гөникэн.

Эрэк бэйчэн (Хэргэнмэй) нэмкэллий харан эрэв бэйу. Эрэк бэй Хэлникэн-дэ ядин, нэмкэлэвчэ бэй, нэмкэмэчиллэн. Эрэк кусикэттиди, эсни тачикан гору кусиддэ, асун-да кусидэнги-дэ эсни хара. Эрэк бэйэнги гасимиван нинnган, тадук тикрэн.

Хинөгу, хөкчэснэнни

Хинӧгу, энгуттиди

Хинӧгу, эркэнэ

Хинӧгу, эчикэн

Хинӧгу, одяннам

Хинӧгу, гѳнни.

Тачин гѳникэн, яддакан, нян-да ѳмэн бэй тухангчин, дюдук. Нян-да нэмкэмэчиделлэн.

Кэвлирѳ, бикэнэ

Кэвлирѳ, Хиняникан

Кэвлирѳ, гэрбэму

Кэвлирѳ, бигрэрэн.

Кэвлирѳ, Хэлникэн

Кэвлирѳ, маннули-ла

Хинӧгу, авагчан-кэ

Хинӧгу, хонила биден.

Кэвлирѳ, -гу текэлэ

Кэвлирѳ, гѳникэн эрэк нэмкэмэчиллий хан. Эрэк бэйчэн, Хинянив бими эсни гору нэмкэттэ, энгэненги чикас нэмкэн.

Кэвлирѳ, акаран

Кэвлирѳ, Хилиникэн

Кэвлирѳ, бэднэчэ-дэ

Кэвлирѳ, -гу бисэнни

Кэвлирѳ, диландяйи

Кэвлирѳ, чикиврис.

Кэвлирѳ, Минкэм яка

Кэвлирѳ, этэккэму чикакран

Кэвлирѳ, гѳникэн.

Эрэк бэйчэн тикчэлэн, нян-да додукун ѳмэн бэй нӧрэн.

Нян-да нэмкэмэчэллэн.

Дэкиру-дэ-Дэкэ, мулакйада, нөнгикэрбу мудаланни.

Дэкиру-дэ-Дэкэ, Тавара

Дэкиру-дэ-Дэкэ, ач хавкалалбу, элэкэс иламатал

Дэкиру-дэ-Дэкэ, бими-кэн энгучиддэ.

Дэкиру-дэ-Дэкэ, Маннудли-ла.

Дэкиру-дэ-Дэкэ, Элэ эмчэв бэйкэми эсэп-мэйэ амаски мучувгарар – гөникэн, нэмкэмэчиллэн.

Эрэк тачин нэмкэмэчиддиди, эрэв-дэ бэйу эсни гору нэмкэрэ. Нөнгчилдуки-нюн аран ходмакан урэчин. Эрэк бэйэнги нян-да гасимиван нэмкэн.

Дэкиру-дэ-Дэкэ, акнийала

Дэкиру-дэ-Дэкэ, эртэкэнтэ бидэнгкэнти,

гөнни

Дэкиру-дэ-Дэкэ, Хэлникэкэн

Дэкиру-дэ-Дэкэ, дулан төрду

Дэкиру-дэ-Дэкэ, гаснгайи

Дэкиру-дэ-Дэкэ, эмнэкэнни

Дэкиру-дэ-Дэкэ, бакадянна

Дэкиру-дэ-Дэкэ, эрэгэгэй

Дэкиру-дэ-Дэкэ, нодлаканни

Дэкиру-дэ-Дэкэ, боркатканни

Дэкиру-дэ-Дэкэ, өллэчкэнси

Дэкиру-дэ-Дэкэ, өсөмикэн этимдэскэн минятнар

Дэкиру-дэ-Дэкэ, эркэнэ

Дэкиру-дэ-Дэкэ, Нэрук эки

Дэкиру-дэ-Дэкэ, эртэкэнтэ

Дэкиру-дэ-Дэкэ, көкэрэп

Дэкиру-дэ-Дэкэ, Хэлникэм эйэллиди

Дэкиру-дэ-Дэкэ, эсэнникэн-дэ дэпкиденнэ

Дэкиру-дэ-Дэкэ, гөникэн.

Тачин гөникэн, эрэк ач гасимилач миркэвчиссиделлэн. Тарпачкан-да дигитан бэйэнгэтэн нөрэн.

Илгой-кэнэ Илгой-кэнэ, эрэгэгэй

Илгой-кэнэ Илгой-кэнэ, мулакйада нөнгикэрбу аччалтанни текэ она бэйил огран

Илгой-кэнэ Илгой-кэнэ, тачикамар гасимитан нэмкэвчэ

Илгой-кэнэ Илгой-кэнэ, мулакйада нөнгикэрбу

Илгой-кэнэ Илгой-кэнэ, хилгидянни. Эр отлакан

Илгой-кэнэ Илгой-кэнэ, эр муту эчикэни эстэн хилгэдгэрэр

Илгой-кэнэ Илгой-кэнэ, Хойав бэйу хонгимкиндур хадипкадун хадилаврап

Илгой-кэнэ Илгой-кэнэ, гөникэн, эрэк бэйчэн кусикэчиделлэн.

Эрэк хокан гору кусикэттэн. Эрэк бэйэнги ойван тарпачкан-да чөрэкэллэн, эрэк Хэлникэн бими. Эрэк бэй адгунга-да туркучэллэн.

Илгой-кэнэ Илгой-кэнэ, эрэгэгэй Хэлникэкэн ноддукуна имкачандий

Илгой-кэнэ Илгой-кэнэ, нэмкэннэй омнгаридий, илатми,

Илгой-кэнэ Илгой-кэнэ, эчикэн эникэкэн адагадда, ойками чөрэкэнгчин нэмкэвэттэн.

Илгой-кэнэ Илгой-кэнэ, Эрэгэгэй Хэлникэкэн

Илгой-кэнэ Илгой-кэнэ, Өмчэк аси иргидэ-гу кирандукун эрвэчкэнни нода бэйкэн балдаданган, эрвэчкэнни хони бэйкэн балдадяннин.

Илгой-кэнэ Илгой-кэнэ, эрэгэгэй акийакан Хилиникан бэднэчэкэн бисэнни

Илгой-кэнэ Илгой-кэнэ, эне-дэ-мэн, тикуня-да

Илгой-кэнэ Илгой-кэнэ, отигдадюр эвиденнэп

Илгой-кэнэ Илгой-кэнэ, амарани Нунгэйэкэн

Илгой-кэнэ Илгой-кэнэ, эртэкэнтэ бидэнгкэнти

Илгой-кэнэ Илгой-кэнэ, хагди бэйэ яканав

Илгой-кэнэ Илгой-кэнэ, ичин-нэр-дэ авангчили

Илгой-кэнэ Илгой-кэнэ, эрэгэгэй хисак-такан уллэкэму ачча окан нэмкэденнэн

Илгой-кэнэ Илгой-кэнэ, гөникэн,

эрэк бэй дабдариди, нгисулэтнэникэн дюткий миркаснан. Чорами дявутникан этикэн нөрэн, эрэк Нюнгэйэ.

Нгисулань, дядини

Нгисулань, Хэлникэн

Нгисулань, хи-нгэн яка

Нгисулань, нөсэгчэр

Нгисулань, бэйэл

Нгисулань, хусэличэтэн

Нгисулань, ян-да хяннус бидин

Нгисулань, маннули

Нгисулань, Би-дэ-кэнэ

Нгисулань, өтэл-титэл

Нгисулань, нөсэгчэнди

Нгисулань, хингэчин-дэ

Нгисулань, гаснгай эчу

Нгисулань, бакадда-ла

Нгисулань, гɵникэн, этикэн нёддэн. Тар-да биникэн *окарап*, навта хечэ нгадиндяй гаридий, нэмкэделлэн.

Нгисулань, энгнийэ эди

Нгисулань, ойлиграра

Нгисулань, ойлиграра

Нгисулань, дядини

Нгисулань, би-нгэнэ

Нгисулань, хоникамас

Нгисулань, хэмкэчиддэм,

Нгисулань, он-ди бэйкэн

Нгисулань, биденнис

Нгисулань, он-ди бэйкэн

Нгисулань, биденнис

Нгисулань, Тек эсикун

Нгисулань, диксамнакан

Нгисулань, маннули

Нгисулань, эдук-тэ дюлэски

Нгисулань, хойава

Нгисулань, бакалдадянни

Нгисулань, хойава

Нгисулань, бакалдутчинни

Нгисулань, гɵникэн, нэмкэчэллэн эрэк этикэн. Эрэк этикэнгэн хэнгэт, эрэгэр бэйнюн нэмкэмэчиллэн.

Гиллер-гиллер-гу, она-ди-гу нэмкэдендям

Гиллер-гиллер-гу, амаран Нюнгэйкэкэн

Гиллер-гиллер-гу, маннуйатли

Гиллер-гиллер-гу, гɵникэн эрэк Хэлникэн бими, эникэн нэмкэр, этикэн Нюнгэйэ нгадиван нюраман ечэньдин алчидяллан.

Эдерэдей

Гиллер-гиллер-гу, ирэккэ өси

Гиллер-гиллер-гу, хагдикана дэпкэндэнгмэни долдаддиди

Гиллер-гиллер-гу, маннули-ла, он-да-кана дэпкэндидендим. Тар-да бисэкэн дялди эмикэн дявадянна.

Гиллер-гиллер-гу, хи-нгэн яка нгачаддакас, он-да-кана

Гиллер-гиллер-гу, илачандям, ирэк-кэ өси хэрэттэнкэмэн хэрэчидендем

Гиллер-гиллер-гу, гөникэн, гөндиддиди, эрэк Нюнгэйэнгчэл нэмкэмэчиллэн.

Эрэк хагди хагдигчин асум гору кусикэтчин, дабдайаттан.

Нгисулань-гу Дядини

Нгисулань, эливэн-дэ

Нгисулань, хоникан

Нгисулань, бисэнни-лэ

Нгисулань, айавчавас

Нгисулань, дёлдандям

Нгисулань, Дядини

Нгисулань, эмнэкэму

Нгисулань, тэрэденнэ

Нгисулань, гөнни.

Тачин гөникэн, эрэк этикэнде нгадиндяй нодариди, тэгэндэн. «Ө-ө, өтэл ями эчэс-ку гөнэ?»

Эрэк бэйчэн дюлай ирэн. Хагди аси тэгэттэн. Хулудякан диланган малула биддэн. Эрэк эчин бивэттиди-дэ, бэй мучухандай некэделлэн.

Нгисулань-гу Дядиня

Нгисулань, Хэлникэкэн

Нгисулань, хони бэйэ

Нгисулань, биникэн

Нгисулань, она эчинэ мучуддинни

Нгисулань, Хи-нгэнэ

Нгисулань, дялди-да эди дявгарар

Нгисулань, гөнни, *артачадяллан.* Хөрдэй, мэрэкэсэндэй некэделлэн, (Хэлникэн) гөнни. «Яннаву-ка?» – гөнни.

– Тавар хи-кэн,

Нгисулань, мадангалби бэйэнгэлби бичэдутэн овкандидли.

– «Эс, би эчин он овкандим» – гөнни, «көкэчэлбу, одчалбу?»

Хони бэйкэн

Нгисулань, биникэн

Нгисулань, тарава-гу

Нгисулань, он туркудинни?

Хуйутэн тумнэсникэн, хукусли, хиргэникэн «Бичэдур огалла!» – гөникэн. Бэйчэн эливэн-дэ, өмэн хуркэм, тачин гөникэн, тумнисникэн, хукуснэн. бичэдий хэкэркингчин бэйэнгэн, эмэддэкэн он бисин-да, тачикан. Эрэк бэйэнгэлби бэкэткэмэн тачин урчин, өрилэм-дэ, яв-да эсни хулар бэкэчкэмэн.

Нэрил-Нэрил, Хилиникэн, элукэн, хи-кэн яка тавара дилангками бичэкэндун овкали

Нэрил-Нэрил, гөнни. Эрэк Хилини бими, эрэк нокучадди дилу аталлиди, *эмэ* тумнэсникэн, хукуснэникэн, Яккарйа, эрэк бэй бэйди тухангчин. Эрэк – Дяймук аканни, хэргэ аканни. Эрэк Нэруку гадни. Нэруку нулгуникэн, амаски нулгэр. Хокам гору нулгэр, гору эмчэл урэчитэн. Эрэк Нюнгэйэ-дэ эсни эмэптэ. Нулгэ бимнин нулгэр. гадач.

Нгисулань, эрэгэгэй

Нгисулань, дянил-а

Нгисулань, ху-кэн она

Нгисулань, нөсэгчэрэ

Нгисулань, бэйэлэ

«Эрэгэр нулгэду бидис, буйусникан-да-яникан-да, нгэнэллэ.» Эрэк хуркэр буйуникэн-дэ яникар-да нулгэр гадач. Эрэк Хилини удлитан. Эрэк Гякчавул бими Нэруку асинггай гадни, асинги нулгуникэн хөррэн. Хокам гору нгэннэ. Өрэп хэвэйкэнгнэвэр эмнэкэтэн, хэвэйкэн Чулпукандя икэридун нибганиди, көкэчэ, дялби дебэссидемнин.

Эрэк бэйэл тачин нулгэрэ, буглавур исса. Буглавур иссидюр-дя, окату баргасач өринидюр биделлэ. Эрэк Хэлникэлкэн Мэнгнунич бэгэндюр биделлэ окату баргасачин. Эрэк өрэп Мэтэлэ холлидий, Мэнгнуни гэрбэ оча, ориди кингнэч эмэтлэ бичэ. Эрэк нонган-да эду биделлэн. Тек терэну тачин биччэл бидир эду бугдур.

5. Мэтэлэ: русский перевод

У Мэтэлэ маленькая юрта. Он жил тем, что промышлял зайцев и куропаток. Вся одежда у него сделана из заячьих шкурок, подстилка и одеяло – тоже из заячьего меха. Лук у него из ребра зайца, тетива лука из заячьих сухожилий скручена, стрелы сделаны из берцовых костей зайца. Вот так он и жил. Стреляя из лука, убивал зайцев прячущихся и притаившихся куропаток. Так долго живёт.

Прошло много времени, и вот однажды идёт кто-то вниз по течению реки, кто идёт – неизвестно. Только перезвон колокольчиков слышится. Выглянул через дверное отверстие (юрты): вниз по течению вдоль реки кочует кто-то, вроде на него похожий, но с длинными волосами и в длинной одежде.

Женщина, приблизившись, развъючила своих оленей, разбила юрту на склоне горы, полуконусную юрту. А Мэтэлэ, испугавшись оленей той женщины, прячется. Её олени вокруг его юрточки пасутся, лижут (замерзшую) мочевину, прямо на юрту наступают. С этого дня Мэтэлэ совсем перестал выходить на улицу. Только когда олени уходят, выходит на улицу, идёт проверять поставленные петли и капканы. Когда их проверяет, если видит оленей, то прячется. Смотрит – все петли-капканы олени затоптали.

Зайцы и куропатки, вроде, разбежались, уменьшились в числе с тех пор, как женщина появилась.

И вот однажды слышит он шаги – женщина к нему идёт. Мэтэлэ испугался: то ли спрятаться ему, то ли убежать (не знает, что делать). В конце концов, не стал убегать. «Что-то будет делать, когда придёт?» – подумал (сказал).

А та женщина, подойдя, вошла в юрту и заговорила:

«Дэне-гу, Мэтэлэ, а ещё мужчина называется. Почему в гости не идёшь? Я ждала-ждала, когда ты в гости придёшь, не вытерпела, и вот сама в гости иду. В давние времена, говорят, что к женщине в дом мужчина (первый) в гости идёт, предания были».

Мэтэлэ сначала и сказать что-либо боится, затем (говорит):

«Как-то не собрался в гости, оробел. Человека (букв. двуногого), вот тебя, впервые вижу».

Ну, что будет делать, сварил заячью ногу, женщину угощает. Поели вдвоём. Когда поели, женщина отодвинула посуду и говорит:

«Дэне-гу, Мэтэлэ, я у тебя побывала в гостях, теперь ты ко мне приходи в гости».

«Ладно, что делать, приду», – говорит Мэтэлэ. Проводил женщину домой.

Заходит в её юрту, (видит): юрта очень просторная, гораздо лучше, чем его юрта. И юрта, и одежда вся теплые.

Ну, эта женщина еду варит, Мэтэлэ угощает. Еда у неё очень вкусная. Ну, Мэтэлэ в этот вечер домой не вернулся. Стал там жить.

Женщина развлекает его рассказами. Так до вечера

сидят. А женщина стелит ему постель (рядом) у стенки юрты.

«Дэне-гу, Мэтэлэ, домой не иди», мол.

Так Мэтэлэ зажил в юрте той женщины. Долго так жили. Их олени далеко разбрелись. «Оленей не бойся», – женщина учит. Вот он привык к оленям, перестал их бояться, научился пасти оленей. И вот однажды женщина говорит:

«Дэне-гу, Мэтэлэ, муженёк, наши олени разбредаются, пастбище далеко стало, олени теряются, сменим-ка мы стойбище», – говорит. А Мэтэлэ не хочет (уезжать).

«Гэрийэн, женушка Омчэк. Как я от своей юртишки уйду, жалко домик. Пять петель, пять капканов, если уеду, без хозяина останутся. Если хочешь перекочевывать, перекочевывый сама (одна)!»

Жена (говорит): «Ну оставайся, оставайся!». Имущество своё собрала, оленей навьючила и откочевала вниз по течению реки. И вот Мэтэлэ один остался. Долго так один живёт. Мэтэлэ ставит, как прежде, капканы и петли. Но следы зайцев и куропаток исчезли. И вот сколько-то дней так прошло. В доме очень холодно стало. Хотя и снегом завалило юрту, всё равно мёрзнет: олени юртишку изорвали. Вот Мэтэлэ от голода чуть не умирать стал. И вот однажды говорит (себе):

«Гэрийэн, вот дожил. Жена Омчэк хотя уводила ведь, а я остался. Пойду-ка я по её следу. Юртишка пусть остаётся, пять петель-капканов пусть остаются. Зайцы мои разбежались, стада Омчэк всех моих куропаток распугали, так что даже не садятся. Если здесь останусь, наверное, так и умру с голоду».

Так говорит себе Мэтэлэ. Ну, ждёт рассвета, переночевал и, когда встал, сразу на рассвете пошёл по следам жены.

Вот идёт-да-идёт. Уже темнеет, всё равно несколько дней и ночей без передышки идёт.

Вот однажды идёт, видит: впереди огонь сверкнул. Туда направился Мэтэлэ, истощённый и обессиливший. И голодно и холодно, одежда вся порвалась.

К той юрте подошёл, а жена его, выйдя навстречу, стала посохом колотить. «Оставайся в своей юртишке. «Пять петель-капканов жалко!» говорил. Чего сюда пришёл? Оставайся с тем, что жалел», – говорит. Потом всё-таки пустила в юрту.

«*Гэрийэн-гэрийэн,* женушка Омчэк, впредь, что ни скажешь, всё исполню. Не прогоняй меня, измучился я, с голоду помираю, от холода чуть не замёрз. Не гони», – говорит. «Пусти в юрту».

Долго он умолял-упрашивал, потом жена пустила. У Мэтэлэ родилась дочь. Так долго живут. Этот Мэтэлэ не охотится, всё в юрте сидит. Вот однажды жена ему говорит:

«Дэне-гу, Мэтэлэ, муженёк, что это мы живём, всё время питаясь мясом домашних оленей. Почему бы тебе не пойти на охоту на дикого оленя. Ведь на земле всякой твари предостаточно. Что всё домашними оленями питаться. Давай-ка откочуем на новую территорию, туда переселимся, там охотиться будешь».

«Откочуем, оленей пригони», – говорит.

Жена одежду, имущество собирает, а Мэтэлэ послала за оленями. Вот пригнал он оленей. Что поделаешь, сам же говорил: «Поперёк слова не скажу». Жена дала ему старого пегого оленя в качестве верхового оленя. Едет Мэтэлэ за женой следом и то и дело с оленя падает, не умеет ездить верхом. Жена ему помогает сесть в седло, немного проедет и снова навзничь падает.

«Дэне-гу, Мэтэлэ, какой ты неловкий, за уздечку хорошенько держись, до каких пор падать будешь?», – говорит жена.

Так Мэтэлэ весь день напролёт мучается – кочует. Вот перекочевали, разбили стоянку, заночевали там.

«Дэне-гу, Мэтэлэ, иди-ка на диких оленей охотиться, пока мы их не распугали. Следы у диких оленей, как у домашних, и сами они на наших оленей похожи, только покрупнее. Пойдёшь на охоту, сам увидишь».

Сказав так, жена ловит ему пегого верхового оленя, седлает. Дала ему свой лук и стрелы, с ними отправился. Долго ехал, пока в верховьях реки диких оленей увидел. В одного оленя выстрелил, свалил. Начал Мэтэлэ его свежевать, как зайца свежуют. Однако олень гораздо больше: Мэтэлэ, как ни старается, не в силах его перевернуть.

Вот уже трое суток Мэтэлэ отсутствует. Всё пытается, как с зайца, шкуру целиком снять, переворачивая. Вот приехала жена.

«Дэне-гу, Мэтэлэ, какой же ты неумелый, где это ты видел, чтобы так оленя свежевали?», – говорит.

Приехала, оленя быстро (шкуру разрезав) освежевала, домой вернулись. «Оленей так не свежуй», – говорит.

И вот Мэтэлэ стал на оленей охотиться, научился. Так и

живут они, время от времени перекочёвывая. Вот однажды перекочевали на новое место, и Мэтэлэ отправляется на охоту. Когда уже собрался возвращаться, видит: старое стойбище. Когда стойбище осматривает, раздался детский плач. Поискал и нашёл ребёнка, прикрытого еловыми (хвойными) ветками, на женской половине покинутой юрты. Этого ребёнка взял, сунул себе за пазуху, домой понёс. «Кто-то ребёнка оставил», – говорит. Посмотрели, ребёнок – мальчик.

«*Гэрийэн-гэрийэн,* жена Омчэк, я нашёл ребёнка-мальчика, оставленного в старом стойбище, на женской половине, ветками прикрытого», мол.

«Зачем принёс ребёнка-чёрта со старой стоянки. Какой ребёнок бы выжил, если бы обычным ребёнком был, сейчас же убей», – говорит жена.

«*Гэрийэн-гэрийэн,* жалко, зачем убивать буду», – говорит Мэтэлэ. Стал свою жену колотить. Пришлось Омчэк двух детей кормить. (Дочка) Чимчэп подросла. Когда ребёнок плачет, своих домашних Мэтэлэ ругает, да колотит, жалея ребёнка. Время идёт, его дочка подрастает, а ребёнок – чёрт всё не растёт. Чимчэп уже выросла, кроме игр рукодельем стала заниматься, одежду себе шьёт. А чёрт-найдёныш так и не растёт. Днём он спит, а всю ночь напролёт плачет, родителям спать не даёт. Мэтэлэ не знает, что и думать: то ли болеет ребёнок, то ли жена плохо нянчит.

Вот однажды отправился Мэтэлэ на охоту. Возвращается с охоты вечером, видит – из домового отверстия юрты искра вылетела. Подходит, а из дома голос доносится:

«*Гэрил-гэрил-гэрил-гу*, отца съем, мать съем, что он всё медлит – не возвращается. Нет мочи терпеть из-за его медлительности. Мать с сестрой уже далеко, наверное, ушли», – голос слышится.

«*Гэрил-гэрил-гэрил-гу*, вот съем отца, за ними погонюсь, куда от меня денутся», – говорит чёрт.

Мэтэлэ заглянул в юрту. «Дитё, что с тобой? Где твоя мать с сестрой?», – расспрашивает. А у ребёнка зубы выросли, как клыки, почти размером с крючья остроги стали. Волосы растрёпанные, до земли, огонь развёл такой, что до дымового отверстия достаёт.

«*Гэрил-гэрил-гэрил-гу*, папаша Мэтэлэ, тебя-то я и поджидаю, тебя, меня выпестовавшего, вместе с костями и внутренностями отведаю (съем)».

«Дитя, что с тобой?», – Мэтэлэ спрашивает. А чёрт, со словами «съем тебя» бросился на Мэтэлэ. Мэтэлэ стал с сыном бороться, сражаться. А сын зубами и когтями рвёт Мэтэлэ.

«Мать с сестрой куда подевались?» – (Мэтэлэ) спрашивает.

«*Гэрил-гэрил-гэрил-гу*, матушку съем и сестрёнку съем, и тебя прикончу» – отвечает чёрт, гоняется за Мэтэлэ, грызёт его зубами, рвёт когтями.

Вокруг дома гоняется за Мэтэлэ. Мэтэлэ, видя, что уступает сыну, проигрывает, побежал вдоль реки вниз по течению. А сын сзади гонится, так и хочет когтями схватить. Долго Мэтэлэ убегает от погони, как-то раз откуда-то голос раздался.

«*Чипитору-чипитору*, батюшка Мэтэлэ, хорошо же тебя

любимый сынок встречает! Чего убегаешь? Когда мы (с матерью) плакали, нас колотил. Теперь расплачивайся за свою глупость. И этого, на груди пригретого тобою, чёрта, ещё маму Омчэк заставлял кормить (грудью)», – голос раздался.

«Братец-чёрт, открой рот пошире, прежде чем отца съешь, сброшу тебе матушку, разинь рот», – (Чимчэп) говорит. Чёрт только рот разинул, и в этот момент звон тетивы раздался.

А Мэтэлэ даже не оглядывается, так и бежит себе вдоль реки, бежит да бежит, пока сил совсем не стало. То и дело спотыкается на ровном месте. «Как бы чёрт не догнал», – думая, всё дальше бежит.

Вот бежит он, впереди пастбище виднеется, по обоим берегам (реки) олени пасутся. Пастбище миновал, по берегу реки, прячась, бредёт. Вот идёт, впереди стойбище, присмотрелся – очень большое. А Мэтэлэ, напуганный сыном-чёртом, стал всех бояться. Пугливым стал, прячась идёт. Вот впереди показалась тропа, по которой по воду ходят. Там притаился – сидит. Когда стало темнеть, женщина-служанка идёт, в лохмотья одетая, одежда вся в саже запачкана. Зачерпнула в котёл воды, пошла, а Мэтэлэ, затаившись под обрывом, котёл потянул – перевернул. Снова служанка вернулась, набрала воды. Когда стала подниматься, Мэтэлэ котёл снова опрокинул, вода вся расплескалась.

«*Уньдалаканя-уньдалаканя*, прежде когда по этой тропе за водой ходила, (котелок) никогда не зацеплялся, не опрокидывался», – говорит. В третий раз за водой пошла. Наверх когда карабкается, (Мэтэлэ) снова разлил.

Эта служанка на землю так и рухнула как подкошенная, зарыдала.

«*Уньдалаканя-уньдалаканя*, давным давно в своей стране и я как человек жила. С тех пор как Каганкан-старейшина в своё стойбище привёл и в служанках держит, всякий кому не лень издевается. Кто котелок мой опрокинул, если человек ты, выходи. А то Кагана своим посохом станет колотить, так что голову того и гляди расколет. Что за мучение! На пять десятков семей одной приходится стряпать, а тут ещё что за напасть появилась», – говорит.

Ну, Мэтэлэ из-под обрыва выскочил, говорит: «Что вы за люди будете? Это я от страха перед людьми здесь прячусь».

«*Уньдалаканя-уньдалаканя*, в котелок воды набери и пойдём ко мне домой», – говорит.

Вот Мэтэлэ взял у служанки котелок, набрал воды и идёт к ней домой. Эта служанка объедками (желудком и лёгкими оленя) питалась. Вот остатками еды Мэтэлэ покормила. Вот Мэтэлэ там прячась живёт. Долго там прячется, сколько времени – неизвестно.

И вот когда они однажды в юрте разговаривали, услышал их один из людей (слуг) Кагана, побежал предупредить Кагана. А Кагана, как это услышал, приказал Мэтэлэ схватить. «Что это за человек, откуда пришёл?», – спрашивает. Порванную одежду с Мэтэлэ снял, одел его как слугу в одежду из старой верхней покрышки (юрты), сажей запачканную. Дал ему топор, и, колотя Мэтэлэ по голове, посылает дрова рубить. А Мэтэлэ, вроде сильный мужчина, в одиночку сухие деревья притаскивает, когда за дровами ходит. А если не справляется, то его Кагана посохом по голове колотит.

И вот когда живёт там Мэтэлэ, по дрова ходит, однажды (видит): вниз по течению караван оленей движется. Видно, что едет его жена. Как это Мэтэлэ увидел, побежал к пастбищу, там спрятался. А жена, как только выехала на поляну, запела:

«Дэне-гу, отче Каганкан, ищу пропавшего, ты его не видал ли? Его следы прямо сюда ведут».

Мэтэлэ присмотрелся, первой едет его дочь, за ней едет какой-то мужчина, потом жена его едет, люльку держит.

«Дэне-гу, отче Каганкан, если к тебе приехал, то верни, видел его, наверное. Мэтэлэ, верно, сюда пришёл, возле пастбища следы его теряются».

«Да, дочка, один человек приходил, путник», – отвечает Кагана, послал всех своих людей искать Мэтэлэ. А Мэтэлэ всё прячется, в лесу возле пастбища, трое суток там прячется. Жены испугался, что ли. Ну вот, наконец, нашли его, привели. Тогда Кагана Мэтэлэ свою одежду дал. Когда Мэтэлэ одежду надел – коротка: спину видать, рукава кухлянки ему по локоть, обшлага штанов по колени.

Так или иначе, у Мэтэлэ родился сын. Назвали Хэлникэн. И вот Мэтэлэ по полю прогуливается. Стойбище рядом разбили. Жена его большую юрту-шатёр поставила. И зять (по имени Чимчэвул) у Мэтэлэ появился. Так долго живут. Мэтэлэ стал предводителем, старейшиной своего стойбища.

Сколько людей у него – неизвестно.

Вот живут они, сынок его подрастает, ползал, потом ходить начал. Так живут они.

Возле стойбища (Кагана) растут три большие лиственницы. На них ничего (никакого оружия) не висит. А Мэтэлэ ни о чём и не спрашивает: «Будь как будет».

Вот его сын подрос, петли мастерить стал, как отец, капканы ставит. Вот однажды попался к нему в петлю зайчонок. Этот зайчонок бьется в капкане, верещит. Пожалел его мальчик и отпустил. Приходит к отцу, говорит: «Папа, не буду больше петли ставить. Зайчонок как ребёнок плачет, потому отпустил». Мэтэлэ стал его ругать. «Какой ты дурной, зачем попавшее в петлю отпускаешь? Надо было убить (добычу) и принести».

Мальчика отругал. А тот тогда взял и поставил самострел прямо там, где обычно отец прогуливается. А Мэтэлэ о том не знает, не ведает.

Вот однажды пошёл прогуливаться, попал в самострел, завопил:

«Сынок, зачем на дороге самострел поставил, иди выручай, я в него попал».

А мальчик дома полено схватил и стукнул отца по голове, так что расколол.

Что делать, умер Мэтэлэ. Когда умер, искра вспыхнула. Мальчик не обратил внимания (думает, что искра от полена). Приносит отца вместе с самострелом домой. «Мама, вот добычу, в петлю попавшую, принёс, есть будем».

Мать говорит: «Зачем отца убил, где это видано, чтобы

отца есть, как есть будешь?»

«Как так, отец сам говорил: «Если что попадётся, не отпускай!». Меня, когда отпустил зайчишку, ещё ругал», – отвечает мальчик.

Ну что поделаешь, не стало Мэтэлэ, его похоронили.

Вот мальчик вырос. Стал бегать везде, играть. Всё играет. Вот однажды, когда стало смеркаться, жители затеяли игры и танцы. Мальчик смотрит – неподалёку от стойбища незнакомая девушка появилась. Мальчик наблюдает, но к стойбищу близко не подходит. К жителям не присоединяется, потому что те его дразнят. «Отца своего съесть хотел, людоедом станешь». Все насмехаются.

Вот мальчик задумался: «Откуда эта девушка всё приходит, кто такая. (Как это) за холм заходит и исчезает». Куда заходит и откуда выходит – не видно. Вот приблизился он к тому месту, где она каждый день исчезает, сел, наблюдает. Вот однажды, когда молодёжь завела хоровод, Хэлникэн притаился в зарослях карликовой берёзы, наблюдает. (Смотрит) впереди в кустарнике как будто дверной полог сам открывается. Оттуда выходит девушка, направляется к танцующей молодёжи. А мальчик мимо неё прошёл, там внутри притаился. Когда танцы-хороводы закончились, полночь наступила, входит девушка. Когда она зашла и дверную занавеску закрыла, Хэлникэн тайком её снова раскрыл. Та снова заперла палкой, только спать легла, Хэлникэн снова дверную занавеску открыл. В третий раз закрыла, снова открыл. Тогда девушка обратилась к своей двери:

«*Куйукэкэ*, эта дверь чем заколдована, что всё время открывается. Прежде так не распахивалась. Если человек ты, покажись, заходи, зачем дверью забавляешься?!»

Мальчик вышел, женщина его кормит. А мальчик один кусочек в рот отправляет, другой в огонь (в жертву) кидает. Поел, отодвинул посуду. Там заночевал. Девушка его не отпускает. И вечером (они) на танцы не ходят.

Однажды к той девушке старуха-мать пришла. Принесла с собой еду, угощает.

«*Куйукэкэ*, мама, давай я сама варить буду, до каких пор тебе готовить».

Когда мать хочет идти еду готовить, та её не пускает. Мать лучшую еду принесла, дочь угощает. Когда мать приходит, девушка мальчишку одеялом прикрывает, прячет. Так долго живут.

Однажды вечером вдалеке послышался шум крыльев, так что эхо раздаётся.

«*Кидо-кидо-гу*, отец Кагана, совсем замёрзли пока летели в небесной выси, в муках умираем. Что нового расскажешь? Хорошо ли жили, с тех пор как мы ушли?»

«Хорошо живём, ничего нового», – отвечает Кагана.

«Разведи огонь, вдвоём возвращаемся», – говорят (сыновья Кагана – Кидани и Кингини).

«Ну что рассказать», – говорит Кагана. «Женщина Омчэк прикочевала, поблизости живёт, на краю поляны. Был у неё муж, помер, похоронили его. Был сын, куда-то исчез вдруг», – рассказывает Кагана, пока те подлетают.

«Разведи огонь», – снова говорят.

Кагана огонь развёл, туда со дна женской сумки крошки-мусор кинул, для воскурения.

Вот те уже собрались сесть, снова взлетели.

«*Кидо-кидо-гу*, отец Кагана, что скрываешь, всего не рассказываешь?»

«Ничего не скрываю. Потерялся мальчишка, из-за своего баловства, наверное, в реку упал – утонул», – говорит, а те двое только было подлетели к дымовому отверстию юрты, снова отпрянули.

«*Кидо-кидо-гу*, всё равно ты всё не рассказываешь. Сестрица Дяймук, выводи своего мужа назавтра. Дяймук Хэлникэна прячет», – говорят, сели.

«Что за люди пришли?», – Хэлникэн у жены спрашивает.

«Это мои старшие братья вернулись. Давно уехали», – отвечает девушка.

«Завтра же выходи», – говорит (старший брат Кидани).

Юноша (Хэлникэн) утра еле дождался. Жена не выпускает, жалеет. «Не выходи, они хотят тебя убить», – говорит. Три дня взаперти держит, не выпускает, хотя братья зовут да зовут, «выводи, выпускай», мол, на четвёртый день всё-таки выпустила.

«*Кидо-кидо-гу*, зять Хэлникэн, что за зятем я обзавёлся? Чтобы проверить, три дня пришлось вызывать. Померимся-ка силой. Проверим, что за зятя нам сестрица Дяймук нашла».

Юноша смотрит, эти мужчины вдвоём прохаживаются подбоченившись по полю, где его отец прогуливался. Хэлникэн туда направился, подошёл, а тот (Кидани) говорит:

«*Кидо-кидо-гу*, зять Хэлникэн, давай силой мериться».

«Как будем мериться?» – Хэлникэн спрашивает.

«*Кидо-кидо-гу*, смотри, на той стороне, в месте слияния двух рек, растёт большая лиственница, в неё стреляй».

«Далеко – о, как попаду? Вы – местные люди, стреляйте первыми!», – говорит Хэлникэн. – Очень уж далеко, не достану стрелой».

«*Кидо-кидо-гу*, братец Кингини, покажи свою удаль, стреляй первым, пусть зять Хэлникэн посмотрит», – говорит Кидани.

Кингини взял свой лук, выстрелил в лиственницу: стрела его вошла по древко в вершину лиственницы.

«*Кидо-кидо-гу*, сейчас себя испытаю».

«Давай, – говорит Хэлникэн. – Если попадёшь, я стрелять буду».

Кидани снял свой лук, выстрелил, стрела наполовину в середину дерева вошла.

«*Гиллер-гиллер-гу*, здорово! Я так далеко никогда не стрелял, вблизь только стрелял. Ну, шурья, испытаю-ка я себя».

Этот юноша домой побежал, принёс свой лук, выстрелил в лиственницу. Сразу как молнией лиственницу сверху донизу расколол.

«*Кидо-кидо-гу*, молодец Хэлникэн, и впрямь ты добрый молодец, поэтому сестрица и не хотела тебя выпускать. Теперь отправимся-ка, посмотрим на свои стрелы, на другую сторону реки с разбегу прыгнем».

Ну побежали они втроём к реке. Хэлникэн первый

прибежал, как Кидани и предлагал, перепрыгнул на другой берег, за ним братья перепрыгнули. Когда посмотрели на свои стрелы, увидели: от стрел братьев ничего не осталось – как молнией стрела Хэлникэна уничтожила их. Старший шурин Кидани стал его хвалить:

«*Кидо-кидо-гу*, действительно удалец ты, никогда раньше не видел, чтобы так стреляли. Как молния выстрелил».

А младший брат Кингини разгневался, жалко стало, что стрелу загубил.

«Кингируки-нгэ, Хэлникэн, как жалко, древко стрелы мне сломал» – говорит Кингини.

Старший брат его насилу успокоил.

Ну вот, зажили они вместе. Хэлникэн прогуливается вместе с шурьями по поляне своего отца. Долго так живут. Вот однажды вечером, когда пришли с прогулки, спать ложатся, издалека голос раздаётся:

«*Хилер-хилер-гу*, богатыри Кидани с Кингини, я вот подумал, наверное, достаточно вы отдохнули, за вами приехал. А ну поднимайтесь, отец Кагана, поднимай своих людей (обороняться)!»

Кагана говорит. своим людям: «Поднимайтесь, погибаем». Этот пришлый человек пять раз облетел вокруг стойбища, стрелами всех жителей скосил.

«*Хилер-хилер-гу*, пять десятков семей разве много, с кем тут ещё сразиться, Дяймук всё равно моя будет, Омчэк с Чимчэп служанками для моих пятидесяти семейств стряпать будут, за водой ходить, служанок всегда не хватает. Чимчэвул, чего сидишь, поднимайся», – голос раздался.

Эти люди (Кидани, Кингини и Чимчэвул) втроём с пришельцем сражаются, только шум боя слышен. Долго так сражаются, только всё равно местные люди стали проигрывать.

«*Кидо-кидо-гу*, Хэлникэн, а ты чего ждёшь? Сестрица Дяймук, сколько ещё мужа своего ласкать будешь? Погибель наша настаёт», – говорит.

Вот местные люди сколько смогут дальше сражаться, проигрывают, со стенанием бьются, изнемогают.

«*Кидо-кидо-гу*, Чимчэвул, я-то считал, что ты справишься».

Бой продолжается, зять их, Чимчэвул, тоже из последних сил сражается. А юноша Хэлникэн всё хочет выйти – жена не пускает. Дяймук даже ремнями его связала, чтобы не вышел.

«*Никой-гу*, шурин Хэлникэн, до каких пор прятаться будешь, на тебя только и надежда. Смерть-гибель пришла», – зовёт (Чимчэвул).

(Смотрит Хэлникэн) у его зятя Чимчэвула (как у загнанного оленя) пена пенится размером с самца зайца, так истощен, что меж рёбер лёгкие проглядывают. Вот пока бьются, послышался гул вихря. Женщина (жена Хэлникэна) оглянулась – вниз по течению вдоль реки мужчина на лыжах идёт. Кажется, что лыжи сами катятся. Смотрит, мужчина вроде бы ещё красивее, чем Хэлникэн. Такой ловкий, что и тень за ним не успевает. Она думает « О-оо, такой красивый мужчина, как бы не погиб» – и выпустила , наконец, своего мужа. А приезжий человек мчится, лыжи сами, вроде, скользят. Вот, стал стрелять в Хилини.

«*Кидо-кидо-гу*, Мэнгнуни, помоги, в муках сражаемся (букв. играем)».

Местные богатыри, втроём, полумёртвые поползли к себе в юрту. А прибывший мужчина всё с Хилини сражается: когда тот стреляет, стрелы его лыжной палкой отбивает.

«*Кингэр-гу*, Хилини, зря сюда приехал, кости твои здесь лягут».

А жена Хэлникэна выпустила, с тех пор как появился незнакомец. Хэлникэн вышел, начал с Хилини сражаться. А Мэнгнуни лыжи снял, аккуратно уложил и вошёл в дом к Омчэк.

А Хэлникэн всё с Хилини сражается.

«*Хилер-хилер-гу*, Дяймук дева, всё Хэлникэна прятала, теперь только выпускает».

А Хэлникэн, хоть и впервые сражается, не даёт в себя (стрелой) попасть. Хилини, когда стреляет, промахивается, в то место, где тот прежде стоял, попадает.

«*Хилер-хилер-гу*, ай-да удалец, Хэлникэн, действительно, вроде достойный меня соперник, раньше такого не встречал. Всё равно особо не задавайся, поначалу и другие были резвые, быстрее своей тени. Молодец, недаром тебя жена Дяймук ласкает».

Хилини никак не может попасть в Хэлникэна, с опозданием стреляет. Двумя стрелами сразу стреляет, всё равно промахивается, туда, где тот прежде стоял, попадает. Долго так сражаются. А Мэнгнуни на них и внимания не обращает. С тех пор, как сын его (Хэлникэн) вышел сражаться, в доме сидит.

«*Хилер-хилер-гу*, Мэнгнуни, на сына надеешься, не сражаешься, с женой тешишься. Как только Мэтэлэ в такого человека мог превратиться?! Ну, держись!»

А Хэлникэн одежду Хилини стрелами всю порвал, тот уже не успевает увёртываться.

«*Хилер-хилер-гу*, одежонке как не прохудиться, если стрелы её задевают».

Пока Хилини это говорил, Хэлникэн ему ногу стрелой раздробил.

«*Хилер-хилер-гу*, что за беда, если одна подвязка для унтов порвалась».

Пока говорит, Хэлникэн снова стрелой предплечье рассёк.

«*Хилер-хилер-гу*, удалец Хэлникэн, действительно, богатырь ты, в трёх мирах такого не встречал. Ну, держись!»

Пока Хилини прыгает, Хэлникэн ему вторую ногу стрелой отсёк.

«*Хилер-хилер-гу*, подвязки обе порвались, не беда, без ног даже удобнее, нечем спотыкаться».

Хилини, хотя одно туловище осталось, всё равно от стрел увёртывается. Ну, Хэлникэн рассердился и вторую лопатку ему раздробил.

«*Хилер-хилер-гу*, Хэлникэн, и впрямь большой удалец, если бы я, когда тебя повстречал, не был усталым, был бы достойным соперником».

И вот Хилини, у которого ни рук ни ног не осталось, Хэлникэн и голову стрелой снёс. Голова покатилась вниз вдоль реки. А Хэлникэн гонится за ней. Когда догоняет, туда-сюда пинает, так забавляется. Долго так её преследует.

«*Хилер-хилер-гу*, налегке путешествую, хорошо, что ноги ни за что не цепляются».

Голова так и катится, Хэлникэн гонится за ней, пинает (говорит):

«*Гиллер-гиллер-гу*, что за забава! Головой забавляясь, вокруг света обойду».

Долго так гонится, однажды догнал, подбросил голову вверх, та в реку упала.

Плывёт по реке, Хэлникэн тоже в воду бросился, плывёт за головой вниз по течению реки. Долго так плывут.

«*Хилер-хилер-гу*, Хэлникэн, держись, дальше нас опасности подстерегают, померимся силой».

И вот пока плывут, где-то зацепились, застряли. Вечером с берега спускается великан Харкилан, размером с дерево. Когти у него как крючья остроги, зубы как клыки. «О-о, вкусно! Давненько мне в вершу ничего не попадалось. Сегодня вечером полакомлюсь».

Вот великан-людоед снял сеть-вершу с запруды, понёс их к себе в избу в чаще леса. Приносит: «Женщины! Варите мальков, я пошёл вершу опять ставить». Отдал Хэлникэна и голову своим домашним, а сам ушёл.

Эти великанши-людоедки стали готовить, одна унты чинит, другая дрова для костра собирать пошла, чтобы сварить добычу. Вот котёл разогрелся. А Хэлникэн в нём сидит, на голову поглядывая. А та ему говорит:

«*Хилер-хилер-гу*, Хэлникэн, с какими мыслями

здесь сидишь? Нас так сварят и съедят. Харкилан нами полакомится, если не удерём».

Людоедка, которая за котлом смотрит, вроде, это не слышит, унты зашивает. Костёр чадит, глаза разъедает, она глаза трёт.

«Сам-то как удерёшь, я посмотрю. Если сможешь убежать, и я за тобой, если нет – оба здесь сваримся».

«*Хилер-хилер-гу*, молодец, если так говоришь, то смотри как следует, не прозевай (как убегать буду), а то здесь так и останешься».

Сказал так, и хоть и голова, выскочил на улицу через дымовое отверстие. Хэлникэн за головой так же выпрыгнул, снова (за ней) гонится.

Вот великанша унты чинит, людоед поставил вершу, вернулся.

«*Кэрувкэ*, жена Чулпук, ну что, сварились или нет?»

Вышел на улицу, в котёл заглянул, а там ничего нет.

«*Кэрувкэ*, мальки куда подевались, вы сами здесь оставались, сами и съели, наверное».

«Не, я не ела, – говорит Чулпук. – Это Тосань здесь пока готовила, наверное, съела, а сама сделала вид, что ходила за дровами».

«Хуелкинь, когда бы я съела, тут унты чинила, Тосань за котлом присматривала», – говорит Чулпук.

Вот пока так разговаривают, возвращается Тосань с дровами. Те на неё набросились.

«*Гэриньчу*, я не ела, как сварила, так и ушла, невестка Чулпук сама, верно, съела», – говорит Тосань.

Вот две великанши стали драться, таскают друг друга за волосы.

«*Кэрувкэ*, прекратите драку, обеих проверю, идите-ка сюда».

«*Гэриньчу*, братец Харкилан, не ела я, клянусь, не ела. Невестка Чулпук оставалась, она и съела».

Харкилан берёт саблю и распорол Чулпук живот. Откуда внутри что будет, в животе ничего нет.

«*Кэрувкэ*, жаль, жену убить заставила, сестрица Тосань», – взял и сестре живот вспорол, и у сестры в животе ничего нет.

«*Кэрувкэ*, молодцы, ну ладно, этими перекушу», – говорит Харкилан, великанш сварил и стал есть.

А Хэлникэн всё за головой гонится. Как шёл, так и идёт: голову, когда догонит, пинает.

«*Хилер-хилер-гу*, не больно торопись, скоро уже дойдём, куда путь держим, теперь уже, вроде, недалеко».

А Хэлникэн его не слушает, всё гонится. Вот пришли они к пастбищу, очень много оленей пасётся. Пересекли пастбище, Хэлникэн смотрит – впереди дровосек-Ойиндя дрова тащит. Голова у него огромная, с утёс величиной. Тащит сухое дерево вместе с корнями.

«*Хилер-хилер-гу*, Ойиндя-слуга, вот жил не тужил, с мучением возвращаюсь».

Вот дровосек дерево тащит, а Хэлникэн незаметно на верхушку и наступил. Тот тащит, упирается, сдвинуть не может. А голова Хилини дальше вниз по течению катится. Дровосек так сильно упирается, что провалился по колени в землю.

«Тэнмэндэнь-тэнмэндэнь, что за жизнь такая, что за напасть», – упирается, но сдвинуть не может. С досады бросил дерево, только обернулся, а Хэлникэн ему саблей голову напрочь срубил. А из дровосека выпрыгнул другой человек.

«Тэнмэндэнь-тэнмэндэнь, откуда такой пришёл, и я пришлый человек!»

Стал дровосек с Хэлникэном сражаться. Хэлникэн однако с ним недолго сражался, грудь насквозь прострелил.

«Тэнмэндэнь-тэнмэндэнь, услышав о славе Нэрук-девы, пришёл (свататься), а вот пришлось дровосеком стать, как проиграл. Да и тебе с ними не управиться», – сказал и упал замертво.

А Хэлникэн дальше помчался. Вот бежит, послышался грохот бубна.

«*Нэрил-Нэрил*, братец Хилини, удалец, не могу одолеть, не серчай (зла не держи), не говори: «Влюбилась в Хэлникэна, потому не спасла», не разочаровывайся (во мне), не могу взгляда Хэлникэна выдержать, отворачиваюсь, до того взгляд у него пронзительный, огнём так и сверкает. Молодец, не одолеть, если бы бубен бы сухой был, а теперь и мой шаманский бубен намок, не звенит. Хилини, зла на меня не держи», – говорит Нэрук (сестра Хилини).

А Хэлникэн и внимания не обращает. «Пусть болтает, всё равно дойду» – вперёд мчится.

«*Хилер-хилер-гу*, жители, поднимайтесь (на защиту), сестрица Нэрук, действительно мне не противится?»

Как сказал это Хилини, грохот бубна затих. Хэлникэн идёт, смотрит – против него всё население стойбища выстроилось. Хэлникэн десять раз выстрелил, всех жителей стойбища скосил.

«*Хилер-хилер-гу*, братец Хэргэнмэй, ну держись, выходи биться, чего ждёшь? Если не пойдёшь встречать гостя (т.е. биться), тот будет разочарован», – голос преследуемого человека (Хилини) раздаётся из большой шатровой юрты, стоящей посередине стойбища. Ну что делать, тот человек, Хэргэнмэй, вышел сражаться.

«Хинёгу, Хэлникэн, вроде бы, мы с тобой сверстники, посмотрим, кто из нас сильнее будет, давай силой мериться. Внизу у подножия горы лиственница высится. На ней голова твоего шурина Гякчавула. Из пришедших сюда людей уже давно никто живым не возвращался».

Этот человек, Хэргэнмэй, знай себе стреляет. А Хэлникэн что будет делать, если в него стреляют, стал сражаться с ним. Сколько сражались – неизвестно, только не особо долго сражались. Того человека Хэлникэн пополам стрелой рассёк, тот рухнул.

«Хинёгу, застал меня стрелой врасплох, потому так умираю» – говорит, а в это время ещё один мужчина из юрты выскочил, снова стали сражаться.

«Кэвлиро, моё имя Хиняни, держись Хэлникэн, посмотрим, кто сильнее», – говорит, и знай стреляет. А Хэлникэн и с Хиняни долго не сражался. Скоро прострелил ему поясницу насквозь.

«Кэвлиро, брат Хилини, неспроста, видно, ты уступил,

дал себе голову срубить, смотри, и мне он поясницу прострелил».

Сказал так и упал Хиняни. Ещё один мужчина выскакивает, снова сражаются.

«*Дэкиру-дэ-Дэкэ*, как жаль, братьев моих прикончил, неопытных, юнных, пропустили (стрелу), ну держись, мы незнакомцев отсюда живыми не отпускаем».

Сражаются, с этим человеком, но недолго. Чуть посильнее своих братьев оказался. Того человека пополам рассёк.

«*Дэкиру-дэ-Дэкэ*, братья, вот не было беды, Хэлникэн, прежде в трёх землях я себе равного не встречал. Удалец ты, какой он статный, бравый, вроде бы сражаясь даже не торопится. Сестрица Нэрук, вот погибель настала. Наверное, влюбилась в Хэлникэна, потому и не сопротивляется, не использует свои колдовские чары».

Так сказал, отполз в сторону. Четвёртый человек вышел.

«Илгой-кэнэ, Илгой-кэнэ, ого-го, жалко братьев, погубил, как жить будут, когда половина искалечена, жалко братьев замученных. Прежде нас так никто не мучил. Наверное, кровь многих людей пала на нашу голову. Прокляты мы, заколдованы».

Стали сражаться, долго сражаются, но и этому человеку Хэлникэн одежду всю изорвал, тот уже не может увёртываться.

«Илгой-кэнэ, Илгой-кэнэ, дивясь на удаль Хэлникэна, как следует и прицелиться забываю, увернуться не могу, одежду мою в лохмотья превратил. Молодец! Как это у Омчэк такой удалой сын родился?! И старший брат Хилини не устоял. Вот в бессильном гневе, мучаясь, играем-сражаемся. Отец Нюнгэйэ, смотри, до чего дожили, хоть и старик, постарайся гостя как-нибудь развлечь! Ого – стреляет так, что стрелы рвут мышцы, но костей не ломают», – говорит побеждённый (богатырь), пополз израненный домой. Из дома вышел старик опираясь на посох.

«*Нгисулань*, сынок, чего это ты и молодёжь задираешь, драку затеял, что за обида такая? Ну держись, в давние времена я, как и ты, соперника не имел», – так говоря, берет свой лук, мхом поросший, стал стрелять в Хэлникэна.

«*Нгисулань*, не очень-то задавайся, сынок, померимся-ка силами, посмотрим, что ты за человек. Ну, сосунок, держись, сейчас многое тебе придётся испытать».

Этот старик всё стреляет. Хотя и стар, а ещё бодрый, стреляет да стреляет.

«*Гиллер-гиллер-гу*, как стрелять буду, отец Нюнгэйэ, держись»

Хэлникэн в ответ не стреляет, от стрел Нюнгэйэ локтем заслоняется.

«*Гиллер-гиллер-гу*, молодец, где это видано, чтобы со стариком сражаться. Как сражаться буду, ну да ладно, пеняй на себя, если вызываешь на поединок, до каких пор буду стоять сложа руки», – говорит Хэлникэн, стал стрелять в Нюнгэйэ. А тот старик, он и есть старик, сколько сражаться сможет?

«*Нгисулань*, сынок, действительно, удалой ты молодец, всё, что ни пожелаешь, отдам – вознагражу, не могу противиться».

Говорит старик Нюнгэйэ, лук свой бросил, сел на землю.

«Ну, чего же раньше не сказал», – говорит Хэлникэн.

Зашёл в дом к Нюнгэйэ. Там старуха сидит. Голова Хилини, за которой он гнался, на почётном месте лежит. Ну, погостил Хэлникэн у них, домой стал собираться.

«*Нгисулань*, сынок, Хэлникэн, раз ты такой богатырь, чего так возвращаешься, смилуйся!», – стал умолять его старик.

«А что нужно делать?» – спрашивает Хэлникэн, собрался уже уезжать.

«*Нгисулань*, убитых тобою людей оживи, как были».

«Как оживлю, если не стало их, умерли?»

«*Нгисулань*, сильным человеком будучи, как не сможешь? На рану плюнь, погладь, произнеся заклинание «Как были, встаньте!».

И впрямь, Хэлникэн плюнул на раны одного юноши, погладил-поворожил, и тот вскочил живой как ни в чём не бывало. Так всех убитых людей оживил, всё население стойбища.

«*Нэрил-Нэрил*, братец Хилини, оживи ту отрубленную голову», – говорит Нэрук-шаманка.

Хилини снял отрубленную голову Гякчавула, плюнул, погладил, тот вскочил как ни в чём не бывало. Это, оказывается, брат Дяймук, младший из её братьев.

Гякчавул взял Нэрук в жёны, откочевали обратно (на родину Хэлникэна). Далеко уже откочевали. Тут и Нюнгэйэ решил за ними откочевать со всем имуществом.

«*Нгисулань*, сыновья, вы молодые, отправляйтесь-ка с

караваном, с ними кочуйте!»

Вот сыновья откочевали вслед за Хэлникэном, по пути охотой промышляют. Долго так вместе кочуют. Пришли в то место, где жил людоед Харкилан, а тот, оказывается, давно как умер, подавившись костью Чулпук.

Вот приехали в свои края, остановились стойбищем по обоим берегам реки. Вождями у них стали на одном берегу Хэлникэн, на другом его отец Мэнгнюни (то стало новое имя Мэтэлэ, воскресшего, вернувшегося на лыжах). Так зажили там. Может, до сих пор там живут.

References

Benzing, J. 1955. *Lamutische Grammatik.* Wiesbaden: Steiner.

Burykin, A. A. 2004. *Jazyk maločislennogo naroda v ego pis'mennoj forme (na materiale èvenskogo jazyka).* Sankt-Peterburg: Peterburgskoje Vostokovedenije.

Cincius, V. I. 1947. *Očerk grammatiki èvenskogo (lamutskogo) jazyka.* Leningrad: Učpedgiz.

Doerfer, G. 1978. Classification problems of Tungus. In G. Doorfer and M. Weiers (eds.). *Tungusica 1.* Wiesbaden: Harrawitz

Kazama, S. 2003. *Ewen Texts and Grammar* (Publications on Tungusic languages and cultures 23). Suita: Osaka Gakuin University.

Kazama, S. 2009. *Ewen texts 2* (A) (Publications on Tungusic languages and cultures 45/A). Tokyo: Tokyo University of Foreign Studies.

Kim, Juwon. 2011. *A Grammar of Ewen.* Seoul: SNU Press.

Lebedev, V. D. 1978. *Jazyk èvenov Jakutii.* Leningrad: Nauka.

Lebedev, V. D. 1982. *Oxotskij dialekt èvenskogo jazyka.* Leningrad: Nauka.

Lebedeva, Zh. K. & Lebedev, V. D. 1986. *Epos oxotskix èvenov.* V zapis'ax N.P. Tkačika. Jakutsk.

Malchukov, A. L. 1995. *Even.* (Languages of the World/Materials, Vol. 12). Munich: Lincom Europa.

Malchukov, A. L. 2008. *Sintaksis èvenskogo jazyka: strukturnye, semantičeskie, kommunikativnye aspekty.* St. Petersburg: Nauka.

Matić, D. & Lavrillier, A. (eds.). 2013. *Even Nimkans by Dar'ja Osenina. Dar'ja Osenina ewedi nimkar. Evenskie nimkany Dar'ji Oseninoj.* Fürstenberg: Kulturstiftung Sibirien.

Menges, K. H. & Ryčkov, K. M. 1993. *Drei Schamanengesänge der Ewenki-Tungusen Nord-Sibiriens*: aufgezeichnet von Konstantin Mixajlovič Ryčkov in den Jahren 1905/1909/ hrsg., übers. und mit einem grammatisch-etymologischen Kommentar vers. von Karl H. Menges. Abhandlungen der Nordrhein-Westfälischen Akademie der Wissenschaften, 89.

Myreeva, A. N. 1980. O zapevax v evenkijskix skazanijax. In: E.I. Korkina et al. (eds.). *Voprosy jazyka i folklore narodnostej severa*. Jakutsk: Jakutskoe Knižone izdatel'stvo, 93-102.

Myreeva, A. N. & Trofimov, N. G. 1990. *Èvenkijskie geroičeskie skazanija*. Novosibirsk: Nauka.

Novikova, K. A. 1958. *Èvenskij foklor*. Magadan: Magadanskoe Knižone izdatel'stvo.

Novikova, K. A. 1960. *Očerki dialektov èvenskogo jazyka*. vol. 1. Leningrad: Nauka.

Novikova, K. A. 1980. *Očerki dialektov èvenskogo jazyka*. vol. 2. Leningrad: Nauka.

Robbek, V. A. 1989. *Jazyk evenov Berjozovki*. Leningrad: Nauka.

Vasilevich, G. M. 1966. *Istoričeskij fol'klor èvenkov. Skazanija i predanija*. Leningrad: Nauka.

Metele

An Ewen Epic Tale by Darja Mixajlovna Osenina

Metele meets Ömchek. A lone hunter Metele meets Ömchek, his future wife. She teaches him how to herd reindeer and other nomadic skills. Ömchek bears a daughter.

Metele adopts a devil child. Metele finds a devil-child in the abandoned camp and adopts him. After a while the child turns into the evil spirit and chases Metele. Metele narrowly escapes saved by his daughter.

Metele at Kagankan's camp. The fleeing Metele finds refuge at Kagankan's camp. Kagankan makes him his servant and treats him badly. Once a caravan arrives at Kaganakan's camp, led by Ömchek, who turns out to be Kagankan's daughter. Metele reunites with his wife. His wife bears him a second child, a son to be named Helniken.

Metele gets killed by his son Helniken. Helniken inadvertently kills his father Metele, after Metele teaches him not to let loose anything caught in the trap, and ultimately gets caught in the bow-trap himself.

Helniken meets D'ajmuk. As Helniken grows up, he falls in love with a girl, D'ajmuk, who turned out to be Kagankan's daughter. They start living together.

Helniken is challenged by his brothers-in-law. Kagankan's sons return from their travels. They find out about Helniken's liaison with D'ajmuk and challenge Helniken. Helniken competes with his brothers-in-law and wins the shooting competition.

Helniken fights with Hilini. Another challenger Hilini comes to woo for D'ajmuk. D'ajmuk's brothers cannot resist him and are saved from the imminent death by a stranger, a warrior Mengnuni, who turns out to be the revived Metele, and by his son Helniken. Helniken finally overwhelms Hilini and cuts his head. Hilini's head, still alive, flees and Helniken chases it.

Helniken's encounter with the cannibal-giant Harkilan. As Helniken is chasing Hilini's head, they both got caught in the giant Harkilan's trap. Harkilan tells his wife and sister to cook them for meal. They however escape; the suspicious Harkilan kills his wife and sister.

Helniken at Hilini's camp. Helniken arrives at Hilini's camp, fights his brothers and kills them one by one. Even their sister's Neruk shamanistic forces fail to stop him. Finally, Helniken is challenged by their father, N'ungeje, but after initially refusing to fight an old man ultimately overwhelms him as well.

Helniken triumphantly returns home. Helniken reconciles with N'ungeje, revives his sons, marries his daughter Neruk. After some time Helniken returns with his wife and his new relatives' home, there they all live happily. He also reunites with his father Metele, revived as a warrior Mengnuni.

Keywords: Ewen, Altaic languages, Tungusic folklore, epic tales, endangered language, language documentation